GOVERNMENT PROCEDURES AND OPERATIONS

BENEFITS AND COSTS OF FEDERAL REGULATIONS AND UNFUNDED MANDATES

GOVERNMENT PROCEDURES AND OPERATIONS

Additional books in this series can be found on Nova's website under the Series tab.

Additional E-books in this series can be found on Nova's website under the E-book tab.

CONGRESSIONAL POLICIES, PRACTICES AND PROCEDURES

Additional books in this series can be found on Nova's website under the Series tab.

Additional E-books in this series can be found on Nova's website under the E-book tab.

GOVERNMENT PROCEDURES AND OPERATIONS

BENEFITS AND COSTS OF FEDERAL REGULATIONS AND UNFUNDED MANDATES

TRAVIS F. WATSON
AND
LEROY GIBSON
EDITORS

Nova Science Publishers, Inc.
New York

Copyright © 2012 by Nova Science Publishers, Inc.

All rights reserved. No part of this book may be reproduced, stored in a retrieval system or transmitted in any form or by any means: electronic, electrostatic, magnetic, tape, mechanical photocopying, recording or otherwise without the written permission of the Publisher.

For permission to use material from this book please contact us:
Telephone 631-231-7269; Fax 631-231-8175
Web Site: http://www.novapublishers.com

NOTICE TO THE READER

The Publisher has taken reasonable care in the preparation of this book, but makes no expressed or implied warranty of any kind and assumes no responsibility for any errors or omissions. No liability is assumed for incidental or consequential damages in connection with or arising out of information contained in this book. The Publisher shall not be liable for any special, consequential, or exemplary damages resulting, in whole or in part, from the readers' use of, or reliance upon, this material. Any parts of this book based on government reports are so indicated and copyright is claimed for those parts to the extent applicable to compilations of such works.

Independent verification should be sought for any data, advice or recommendations contained in this book. In addition, no responsibility is assumed by the publisher for any injury and/or damage to persons or property arising from any methods, products, instructions, ideas or otherwise contained in this publication.

This publication is designed to provide accurate and authoritative information with regard to the subject matter covered herein. It is sold with the clear understanding that the Publisher is not engaged in rendering legal or any other professional services. If legal or any other expert assistance is required, the services of a competent person should be sought. FROM A DECLARATION OF PARTICIPANTS JOINTLY ADOPTED BY A COMMITTEE OF THE AMERICAN BAR ASSOCIATION AND A COMMITTEE OF PUBLISHERS.

Additional color graphics may be available in the e-book version of this book.

Library of Congress Cataloging-in-Publication Data

Benefits and costs of federal regulations and unfunded mandates / editors, Travis F. Watson and Leroy Gibson.
    p. cm.
  Includes index.
  ISBN 978-1-61942-293-3 (hardcover)
 1. Unfunded mandates--United States. 2. Delegated legislation--United States. 3. Delegated legislation--United States--Costs. 4. Intergovernmental fiscal relations--United States. I. Watson, Travis F. II. Gibson, Leroy.
  HJ275.5.B46 2011
  336.73--dc23
                            2011045804

Published by Nova Science Publishers, Inc. ✝ *New York*

Contents

Preface vii

Chapter 1   2011 Report to Congress on the Benefits and Costs of Federal Regulations and Unfunded Mandates on State, Local, and Tribal Entities
Office of Management and Budget   1

Chapter 2   Joe Aldy Peer Review of Draft Report on Benefits and Costs   143

Chapter 3   Review of Draft 2011 Report to Congress on the Benefits and Costs of Federal Regulations and Unfunded Mandates on State, Local, and Tribal Entities
Christine Jolls   147

Chapter 4   Michael Greenstone Peer Review of Draft Report on Benefit   151

Chapter 5   Richard Williams Public Comment on Draft Report on Benefit   157

Chapter 6   Draft 2011 Report to Congress on the Benefits and Costs of Federal Regulations
Daniel V. Yager   165

Index   185

PREFACE

This book presents an overview of the Draft 2011 Report to Congress on the Benefits and Costs of Federal Regulations and Unfunded Mandates on State, Local, and Tribal Entities and the benefits and costs of the U.S. Government's regulatory program. The decomposition of benefits and costs of regulations by agencies, and in some cases by major categories of benefits, are instructive. The 10-year look back is valuable to illustrate the longer-term trends in benefits and costs of government regulations and recommendations for reform.

Chapter 1 - In accordance with the Regulatory-Right-to-Know Act, the Office of Management and Budget (OMB) prepared this draft Report to Congress on the Benefits and Costs of Federal Regulations (Report). This is the fourteenth annual Report since OMB began issuing this Report in 1997. The Report summarizes estimates by Federal regulatory agencies of the quantified and monetized benefits and costs of major Federal regulations reviewed by OMB over the last ten years.

Chapter 2 - The *Draft 2011 Report to Congress on the Benefits and Costs of Federal Regulations and Unfunded Mandates on State, Local, and Tribal Entities* presents in a transparent, concise, and understandable manner the benefits and costs of the U.S. Government's regulatory program. In the context of the recent heated but not always illuminating public discussion of the economic impacts of Federal regulations, this report will serve as a thoughtful resource. The decomposition of benefits and costs of regulations by agencies, and in some cases by major categories of benefits, are instructive. The 10-year look back is valuable to illustrate the longer-term trends in benefits and costs of government regulations. The recommendations for reform will improve the implementation and consideration of economic analysis in the design of government rules. The Office of Management and Budget should be commended for a job well done in synthesizing and summarizing the economic benefits and costs of government regulations. In the following I present a few major comments on the report and then some detailed comments on the text.

Chapter 3 – Christine Jolls has reviewed the draft report. Her main substantive recommendation is the addition of reference to agency *experimentation* to examine the effects of regulation. Studies of such experimentation would usefully complement the retrospective analysis emphasized by the draft report (and, in some cases, would reduce the need for such retrospective analysis).

Chapter 4 – Michael Greenstone is writing in response a request for a review of the Draft 2011 Report to Congress on the Benefits and Costs of Federal Regulations and Unfunded Mandates on State, Local, and Tribal Entities. His overall assessment is that this is an excellent report. It is a model of clarity and it is evident that OIRA is unafraid to tackle the important issues that feed into designing regulations that provide maximum benefits to American citizens at a minimum cost. It also draws upon the latest academic research in a way that is very productive for formulating policy, not just for making debating points. All of this is evident in many of the innovative regulatory policies that the Obama Administration has introduced.

Chapter 5 - OMB has produced a thorough and useful report based on the instructions in the Regulatory-Right-to Know-Act. Requiring agencies to produce both more (particularly in the case of independent agencies) and better quality analysis is the right direction for OIRA. However, OIRA should be cautious about over claiming success, particularly based on our analysis of the quality of regulatory impact analyses to date. Of course, OIRA must rely on the agencies for this analysis. The focus on retrospective review, in particular, how best to accomplish retrospective review, is a welcome one. Finally, the authors urge caution when embracing behavioral economics in analyzing the benefits of market interventions. In particular, the authors note that the happiness research may not ever develop into useful metrics and, given its current state, is not ready for prime time use in RIA's.

Chapter 6 - The authors are writing in response to the notice and request for comments issued by the Office of Management and Budget (OMB) regarding its Draft 2011 Report to Congress on the Benefits and Costs of Federal Regulations. Last year, in reply to OMB's request in its 2010 Draft Report for suggestions about regulatory changes that might increase employment, innovation, and competitiveness Draft Report for 2010, HR Policy Association submitted a proposal for reform of regulations and regulatory processes related to the Fair Labor Standards Act (FLSA). The Association's comments were endorsed by 11 leading U.S. employers. The OMB, in its 2010 Final Report, vowed to "consider the recommended reforms." As a courtesy, on September 23, 2010, the Association forwarded its OMB comments regarding the FLSA to you for your department's review.

In: Benefits and Costs of Federal Regulations ...
Editors: Travis F. Watson and Leroy Gibson

ISBN: 978-1- 61942-293-3
© 2012 Nova Science Publishers, Inc.

Chapter 1

2011 REPORT TO CONGRESS ON THE BENEFITS AND COSTS OF FEDERAL REGULATIONS AND UNFUNDED MANDATES ON STATE, LOCAL, AND TRIBAL ENTITIES[*]

Office of Management and Budget

EXECUTIVE SUMMARY

In accordance with the Regulatory-Right-to-Know Act,[1] the Office of Management and Budget (OMB) prepared this draft Report to Congress on the Benefits and Costs of Federal Regulations (Report). This is the fourteenth annual Report since OMB began issuing this Report in 1997. The Report summarizes estimates by Federal regulatory agencies of the quantified and monetized benefits and costs of major Federal regulations reviewed by OMB over the last ten years (see page 8, below, for the criteria for identifying "major" regulations for this report).

The principal findings are as follows.

- The estimated annual benefits of major Federal regulations reviewed by OMB from October 1, 2000, to September 30, 2010, for which agencies estimated and monetized both benefits and costs, are in the aggregate between $132 billion and $655 billion, while the estimated annual costs are in the aggregate between $44 billion and $62 billion. These ranges reflect uncertainty in the benefits and costs of each rule at the time that it was evaluated.
- Some rules are estimated to produce far higher net benefits than others. Moreover, there is substantial variation across agencies in the total net benefits produced by rules. For example, the air pollution rules from the Environmental Protection Agency (EPA) produced 62 to 84 percent of the benefits and 46 to 53 percent of the costs.[2]

---

[*] This is an edited, reformatted and augmented version of a publication by the Office of Management and Budget, dated 2011.

Most rules have net benefits, but several rules have net costs, typically as a result of statutory requirements.

- During fiscal year 2010, executive agencies promulgated 66 major rules.
  - For 18 rules, the issuing agencies quantified and monetized both benefits and costs. Those 18 rules were estimated to result in a total of $18.8 billion to $86.1 billion in annual benefits and $6.5 billion to $12.5 billion in annual costs.
  - For two rules, the issuing agency (the Department of the Interior) quantified and monetized only benefits. Both of these rules involved migratory bird hunting. For these two rules, the agency estimated total one-year benefits of $500 million to $600 million.
  - For eight rules, the issuing agencies quantified and monetized only costs. For these rules, the agencies estimated total annual costs of $200 million to $300 million.
  - For 32 rules, the issuing agencies quantified and monetized only the budgetary transfer amounts.
  - For six rules, the issuing agencies were able to quantify and monetize neither benefits nor costs.
- The independent regulatory agencies, whose regulations are not subject to OMB review under Executive Order 12866, issued 17 major final rules. With the exception of the Nuclear Regulatory Commission's fee recovery rule, all of these rules were issued to regulate the financial sector. The Government Accountability Office (GAO) reported that none of the 17 rules assessed both anticipated benefits and costs. The Federal Reserve System did not assess benefits and costs for its rules. The joint rule between the Federal Reserve System and the Federal Trade Commission assessed only costs. The Securities and Exchange Commission monetized costs for six of its nine rules.

It is important to emphasize that the figures here have significant limitations. When agencies subject to Executive Orders 13563 and 12866 have not quantified or monetized the benefits or costs of regulations, or have not quantified or monetized important variables, it is because of an absence of relevant information. Many rules have benefits or costs that cannot be quantified or monetized in light of existing information, and the aggregate estimates presented here do not capture those non-monetized benefits and costs. In fulfilling their statutory mandates, agencies must often act in the face of substantial uncertainty about the likely consequences. In some cases, quantification of various effects is highly speculative. For example, it may not be possible to quantify the benefits of certain disclosure requirements, simply because the impact of some such requirements cannot be specified in advance. In other cases, monetization of particular categories of benefits (such as ecological benefits and homeland security benefits) can present significant challenges. As Executive Order 13563 recognizes, some rules produce benefits (such as reductions in discrimination on the basis of disability or prevention of rape) that cannot be easily or adequately captured in monetary equivalents.

In addition, and significantly, prospective estimates may contain erroneous assumptions, producing inaccurate predictions; retrospective analysis, recently required by Executive Order

13563, can be an important way of increasing accuracy. While the estimates in this Report provide valuable information about the effects of regulations, they should not be taken to be either precise or complete. The increasing interest in retrospective analysis, inside and outside of government, should produce improvements on this count, above all by ensuring careful evaluation of the actual effects of rules. This process should improve understanding not only of those effects, but also of the accuracy of prospective analyses, in a way that can be brought to bear on such analyses when they are written.

OMB emphasizes that careful consideration of costs and benefits is best understood as a way of ensuring that regulations will improve social welfare, above all by informing design and development of various options so as to identify opportunities for both minimizing the costs of achieving social goals (cost-effectiveness) and maximizing net social benefits (efficiency). OMB and agencies continue to take steps to improve both quantification and monetization. Consistent with this effort and in compliance with the Regulatory Right-to-Know Act, this Report also offers a number of recommendations for reform.

There are two unifying themes. The first is the importance of ensuring that regulation (including protection of public health, welfare, safety, and our environment) is undertaken in a way that promotes the goals of economic growth, innovation, competitiveness, and job creation. By promoting these goals, agencies will be in a better position to avoid excessive regulation, to eliminate unnecessary burdens, and to choose appropriate responses. The second unifying theme is the importance of ensuring that regulation is evidence-based and data-driven, and hence based on the best available work in both science and social science (with full respect for scientific integrity).

To that end, the Report briefly outlines recent steps and best practices that are consistent with OMB's recent recommendations for flexible, empirically informed approaches; increased openness about costs and benefits; and the use of disclosure as a regulatory tool. For the future, the Report recommends, among other things, that:

1. consistent with Executive Order 13563, regulatory decisions and priority-setting should be made in a way that is attentive to the importance of promoting economic growth, innovation, job creation, and competitiveness.
2. consistent with Executive Order 13563, agencies should promote retrospective analysis of existing significant rules, with careful exploration of their actual effects and, when appropriate, consideration of steps to streamline, modify, expand, or repeal them.
3. agencies should accompany all economically significant regulations with (1) a tabular presentation, placed prominently and offering a clear statement of qualitative and quantitative benefits and costs of the proposed or planned action, together with (2) a presentation of uncertainties and (3) similar information for reasonable alternatives to the proposed or planned action.
4. agencies should carefully explore how best to treat nonquantifiable variables and should continue to use "breakeven analysis" when quantification is not possible, with such analysis defined as the specification of how high the unquantified or unmonetized benefits would have to be in order for the benefits to justify the costs.
5. consistent with OMB Circular A-4, agencies should consider the use of cost-effectiveness analysis for regulations intended to reduce mortality risks, and should specifically consider the development of estimates for the "net cost per life saved."

6. consistent with Executive Order 13563, and in particular the emphasis on "the open exchange of information and perspectives among State, local, and tribal officials, experts in relevant disciplines, affected stakeholders in the private sector, and the public as a whole," agencies should bring rulemaking into the twenty-first century by promoting public participation and transparency through the use of Regulations.gov and other technological means.
7. in order to promote trade and exports, and thus to increase job creation, agencies should promote regulatory cooperation initiatives with key trading partners.

To promote the goals of Executive Order 13563, the draft of this Report invited public suggestions on how best to promote retrospective analysis of rules that may be outmoded, ineffective, insufficient, or excessively burdensome, with a view toward modifying, streamlining, expanding, or repealing them in accordance with what has been learned. OMB continues to be interested in such suggestions, with the ultimate goal of promoting an improved regulatory culture in which significant rules are periodically evaluated and where appropriate, modified, simplified, expanded, or repealed.

A possible approach to the potential difficulty of advance assessment of costs and benefits involves rigorous experimentation with respect to the likely effects of regulation; such experimentation, including randomized controlled trials, can complement and inform prospective analysis, and perhaps reduce the need for retrospective analysis. To the extent feasible and consistent with law, agencies might, for example, implement a regulation on a trial basis, using a randomized controlled trial. Perhaps some firms or locations might be subject to a certain requirement while others are not; the agency could learn about the effects of its action from what emerges. Pilot projects of various sorts have informed the regulatory process, and they could be used more often for this purpose. More generally, OMB recommends careful and continuing steps to reassess existing significant rules.

Chapter III provides an update on agency implementation of the Information Quality Act (IQA) (Section 515 of the Treasury and General Government Appropriations Act, 2001 (Pub. L. No. 106-554, 31 U.S.C. § 3516 note)). The chapter summarizes (a) the current status of correction requests that were received by agencies in FY 2009, along with an update on the status of requests received during FY 2003 through FY 2008 and (b) agency annual reports for the Information Quality Bulletin for Peer Review for FY 2009. In FY 2010, Federal agencies received 27 correction requests and completed 193 peer reviews, 31 of which were highly influential scientific assessments.

This Report is being issued along with OMB's Sixteenth Annual Report to Congress on Agency Compliance with the Unfunded Mandates Reform Act (UMRA) (Pub. L. No. 104-4, 2 U.S.C. § 1538). OMB reports on agency compliance with Title II of UMRA, which requires that each agency conduct a cost-benefit analysis and select the least costly, most cost-effective, or least burdensome alternative before promulgating any proposed or final rule that may result in expenditures of more than $100 million (adjusted for inflation) in any one year by State, local, and tribal governments, or by the private sector. Each agency must also seek input from State, local, and tribal governments.

PART I: 2011 REPORT TO CONGRESS ON THE BENEFITS AND COSTS OF FEDERAL REGULATIONS

Introduction

The Regulatory Right-to-Know Act requires the Office of Management and Budget (OMB) to submit to Congress each year "an accounting statement and associated report" including:

(A) an estimate of the total annual benefits and costs (including quantifiable and nonquantifiable effects) of Federal rules and paperwork, to the extent feasible:
  (1) in the aggregate;
  (2) by agency and agency program; and
  (3) by major rule;
(B) an analysis of impacts of Federal regulation on State, local, and tribal government, small business, wages, and economic growth; and
(C) recommendations for reform.

The statute does not define "major rule." For the purposes of this Report, we define major rules to include all final rules promulgated by an Executive Branch agency that meet any one of the following three conditions:

- Rules designated as "major" under 5 U.S.C. § 804(2);[3]
- Rules designated as meeting the analysis threshold under the Unfunded Mandates Reform Act of 1995 (UMRA);[4] or
- Rules designated as "economically significant" under section 3(f)(1) of Executive Order 12866.[5]

Chapter I summarizes the benefits and costs of major regulations issued between September 2000 and September 2010 and examines in more detail the benefits and costs of major Federal regulations issued in fiscal year 2009. It also discusses regulatory impacts on State, local, and tribal governments, small business, wages, and economic growth. Chapter II offers recommendations for reform. Chapter III provides an update on agency implementation of the Information Quality Act (IQA) (Section 515 of the Treasury and General Government Appropriations Act, 2001 (Pub. L. No. 106-554, 31 U.S.C. § 3516 note)). Chapter IV summarizes agency compliance with UMRA.

I: THE BENEFITS AND COSTS OF FEDERAL REGULATIONS

This chapter consists of two parts: (A) the accounting statement and (B) a brief report on regulatory impacts on State, local, and tribal governments, small business, and wages. Part A revises the benefit-cost estimates in last year's Report by updating the estimates to the end of fiscal year 2010 (September 30, 2010). As in previous Reports, this chapter uses a ten-year look-back. Estimates are based on the major regulations reviewed by OMB from October 1,

2000 to September 30, 2010.[6] For this reason, six rules reviewed from October 1, 1999 to September 30, 2000 (fiscal year 2000) were included in the totals for the 2010 Report but are not included in this Report. A list of these fiscal year 2000 rules can be found in Appendix B (see Table B-1). The removal of the six fiscal year 2000 rules from the ten-year window is accompanied by the addition of 18 fiscal year 2010 rules.

All estimates presented in this chapter are agency estimates of benefits and costs or transparent modifications of agency information performed by OMB.[7] This chapter also includes a discussion of major rules issued by independent regulatory agencies, although OMB does not review these rules under Executive Orders 13563 and 12866.[8] This discussion is based solely on data provided by these agencies to the Government Accountability Office (GAO) under the Congressional Review Act.

Aggregating benefit and cost estimates of individual regulations—to the extent they can be combined—provides potentially valuable information about the effects of regulations. But the resulting estimates are neither precise nor complete. Four points deserve emphasis.

1. Individual regulatory impact analyses vary greatly in rigor and rely on different assumptions, baseline scenarios, methods, and data. To take just one example, agencies offer different monetary valuations for mortality reductions. Summing across estimates involves the aggregation of analytical results that are not strictly comparable. OMB continues to investigate inconsistencies in how agencies answer central regulatory questions and seeks to identify and to promote best practices. Executive Order 13563 emphasizes the importance of such practices and of quantification, directing agencies to "use the best available techniques to quantify anticipated present and future benefits and costs as accurately as possible."
2. As we have noted, it is not always possible, in light of limits in existing information, to quantify or monetize relevant benefits or costs of rules. For purposes of policy, non-monetized benefits and costs may be important. Some regulations have significant non-quantified or non-monetized benefits and costs that are relevant under governing statutes and that may serve as a key factor in an agency's decision to promulgate a particular rule.
3. Prospective analyses may turn out to overestimate or underestimate both benefits and costs; retrospective analysis can be important as a corrective mechanism.[9] Executive Order 13563 specifically calls for such analysis, with the goal of improving relevant regulations through modification, streamlining, expansion, or repeal. The result should be a greatly improved understanding of the accuracy of prospective analyses, as well as corrections to rules as a result of ex post evaluations. A large priority is the development of methods (perhaps including not merely before-and-after accounts but also randomized trials, to the extent feasible and consistent with law) to obtain a clear sense of the effects of rules. In addition, rules should be written and designed, in advance, so as to facilitate retrospective analysis of their effects. In order to promote data-driven regulation, OMB continues to be interested in public suggestions on how to use retrospective analysis to improve regulations, perhaps by expanding them, perhaps by streamlining them, perhaps by reducing or repealing them, perhaps by redirecting them.
4. While emphasizing the importance of quantification, Executive Order 13563 also refers to "values that are difficult or impossible to quantify, including equity, human

dignity, fairness, and distributive impacts." As Executive Order 13563 recognizes, such values may be appropriately considered under relevant law. If, for example, a rule would reduce the incidence of rape, or allow wheelchair-bound workers to have access to bathrooms, a consideration of dignity is involved, and relevant law may require or authorize agencies to take that consideration into account. If a regulation would disproportionately help or hurt those at the bottom of the economic ladder, or those who are suffering from some kind of acute condition or extreme deprivation, relevant law may require or authorize agencies to take that fact into account. (In the recent past, agencies have referred to human dignity, equity, or distributional impacts in the context of proposed or final regulations reducing the risk of prison rape; increasing access by wheelchair-bound people to bathrooms; eliminating the ban on entry into the United States of those who are HIV-positive; barring lifetime limits on health insurance payments; and preventing denial of health insurance to children with preexisting conditions.) So far as we are aware, there is only limited analysis of the distributional effects of regulation in general or in significant domains;[10] such analysis could prove illuminating.

A. Estimates of the Aggregated Annual Benefits and Costs of Regulations Reviewed by OMB over the Last Ten Years

1. In General

Between fiscal years 2001 and 2010, Federal agencies published over 38,000 final rules in the *Federal Register*.[11] OMB reviewed 3,325 of these final rules under Executive Order 12866.[12] Of these OMB-reviewed rules, 540 are considered major rules, primarily due to their anticipated impact on the economy (i.e., estimated benefits or costs were in excess of $100 million in at least one year). We include in our 10-year aggregate of annual benefits and costs of regulations rules that meet two conditions:[13] (1) each rule was estimated to generate benefits or costs of approximately $100 million in any one year; and (2) a substantial portion of its benefits and costs were quantified and monetized by the agency or, in some cases, monetized by OMB. The estimates are therefore not a complete accounting of all the benefits and costs of all regulations issued by the Federal Government during this period.[14] Table 1-1 presents estimates of the total annual benefits and costs of 105 regulations reviewed by OMB over the ten-year period from October 1, 2000, to September 30, 2010, broken down by issuing agency.

As discussed in previous Reports, OMB chose a ten-year period for aggregation because pre-regulation estimates prepared for rules adopted more than ten years ago are of questionable relevance today. The estimates of the benefits and costs of Federal regulations over the period October 1, 2000, to September 30, 2010, are based on agency analyses conducted prior to issuance of the regulation and subjected to public notice and comments and OMB review under Executive Order 12866.

In assembling these tables of estimated benefits and costs, OMB applied a uniform format for the presentation to make agency estimates more closely comparable with each other (for example, annualizing benefit and cost estimates). OMB monetized quantitative estimates where the agency did not do so. For example, for a few rulemakings within the ten-year window of this Report, we have converted agency projections of quantified benefits, such as estimated injuries avoided per year or tons of pollutant reductions per year, to dollars using the valuation estimates discussed in Appendix A of this Report and Appendix B of our 2006 Report.[15]

The aggregate benefits reported in Table 1-1 are comparable to those presented in the 2010 Report. As with previous Reports, the reported monetized benefits continue to be significantly higher than the monetized costs. (In 2009 and 2010, the monetized benefits were also far higher than the monetized costs, as detailed below.) Three agencies -- the Department of Health and Human Services, the Department of Transportation, and the Environmental Protection Agency -- issued a strong majority of total rules (77 of 105). In addition, the Environmental Protection Agency is responsible for a large percentage of both total benefits and total costs.

Table 1-2 provides additional information on aggregate benefits and costs for specific agency programs. A program is included in Table 1-2 only if it finalized three or more major rules in the last ten years with monetized benefits and costs.

The ranges of benefits and costs reported in Tables 1-1 and 1-2 were calculated by adding the lower bounds of agencies' estimates for each of the underlying rules to generate an aggregate lower bound, and similarly adding the upper bounds of agencies' estimates to generate an aggregate upper bound.[17] The range reported by the agency for each rule reflects the agency's uncertainty about the likely impact of the rule. In some cases, this range is a confidence interval based on a formal uncertainty analysis. In most cases, however, the ranges are generated using an informal sensitivity analysis in which input parameters are varied across a "plausible" range.

Table 1-1. Estimates of the Total Annual Benefits and Costs of Major Federal Rules by Agency, October 1, 2000 - September 30, 2010 (billions of 2001 dollars)

Agency	Number of Rules	Benefits	Costs
Department of Agriculture	6	0.9 to 1.3	1.0 to 1.34
Department of Energy	10	8.0 to 10.9	4.5 to 5.1
Department of Health and Human Services	18	18.0 to 40.5	3.7 to 5.2
Department of Homeland Security	1	< 0.1	< 0.1
Department of Housing and Urban Development	1	2.3	0.9
Department of Justice	4	1.8 to 4.0	0.8 to 1.0
Department of Labor	6	0.4 to 1.5	0.4 to 0.5
Department of Transportation (DOT)	26	14.6 to 25.5	7.5 to 14.3
Environmental Protection Agency (EPA)[16]	32	81.8 to 550.7	23.3 to 28.5
Agency	Number of Rules	Benefits	Costs
Joint DOT and EPA	1	3.9 to 18.2	1.7 to 4.7
Total	**105**	**131.7 to 655.0**	**43.7 to 61.7**

The benefits and costs presented in Tables 1-1 and 1-2 are not necessarily correlated. In other words, when interpreting the meaning of these ranges, the reader should not assume that when benefits are in fact on the low end of their range, costs will also tend to be on the low end of their range. This is because, for some rules, there are factors that affect costs that have little correlation with factors that affect benefits (and vice-versa). Accordingly, to calculate the range of net benefits (i.e., benefits minus costs), one should not simply subtract the lower bound of the benefits range from the lower bound of the cost range, and similarly for the upper bound. It is possible that the true benefits are at the lower bound and that the true costs are at the upper bound, as well as vice-versa. Thus, for example, it is possible that the net benefits of Department of Labor rules, taken together, could range from -$30 million to approximately $1.1 billion per year.

2. EPA Air Rules

It should be clear that the rules with the highest benefits and the highest costs, by far, come from the Environmental Protection Agency and in particular its Office of Air. More specifically, EPA rules account for 62 to 84 percent of the monetized benefits and 46 to 53 percent of the monetized costs.[18] The rules that aim to improve air quality account for 95 to 97 percent of the benefits of EPA rules.

Table 1-2. Estimates of Annual Benefits and Costs of Major Federal Rules: Selected Programs and Agencies, October 1, 2000 - September 30, 2010 (billions of 2001 dollars)

Agency	Number of Rules	Benefits	Costs
Department of Agriculture			
Animal and Plant Health Inspection Service	3	0.9 to 1.2	0.7 to 0.9
Department of Energy			
Energy Efficiency and Renewable Energy	10	8.0 to 10.9	4.5 to 5.1
Department of Health and Human Services			
Food and Drug Administration	10	2.6 to 22.3	0.9 to 1.3
Center for Medicare and Medicaid Services	7	15.4 to 18.1	2.7 to 3.9
Department of Labor			
Occupational Safety and Health Administration	4	0.4 to 1.5	0.5
Department of Transportation			
National Highway Traffic Safety Administration	11	11.8 to 21.5	5.2 to 10.8
Federal Aviation Administration	6	0.3 to 1.2	0 to 0.4
Federal Motor Carriers Safety Administration	4	1.3 to 1.5	1.3
Environmental Protection Agency			
Office of Air	20	77.3 to 535.1	19.0 to 24.1
Office of Water	6	1.3 to 3.9	1.1 to 1.2
Office of Chemical Safety and Pollution Prevention	3	3.2 to 11.4	3.4
Office of Solid Waste and Emergency Response	3	0 to 0.3	(0.2)

( ) indicates negative.

It is important to emphasize that the large estimated benefits of EPA rules are mostly attributable to the reduction in public exposure to a single air pollutant: fine particulate matter. Of its 20 air rules, the rule with the highest estimated benefits is the Clean Air Fine Particle Implementation Rule, with benefits ranging from $19 billion to $167 billion per year. While the benefits of this rule far exceed the costs, the cost estimate for the Clean Air Fine Particle Implementation Rule is also the highest at $7.3 billion per year. Because the estimated benefits and costs associated with the clean air rules provide a majority of the total benefits and costs across the Federal Government, and because some of the scientific and economic questions are not resolved, we provide additional information.

With respect to many of these rules, there remains continuing uncertainty in benefits estimates. We note that EPA has invested substantial resources to quantify and reduce some aspects of that uncertainty over the last few years. Even so, significant uncertainty remains in this domain. For this reason, the ranges of benefits and costs presented in Table 1-2 should be treated with caution. If the reasons for uncertainty differ across individual rules, aggregating high-end and low-end estimates can result in totals that may be misleading. In the case of the EPA rules reported here, however, a substantial portion of the uncertainty is similar across several rules, including (1) the uncertainty in the reduction of premature deaths associated with reduction in particulate matter and (2) the uncertainty in the monetary value of reducing mortality risk. EPA continues to improve methods to quantify the degree of technical uncertainty in benefits estimates and to make other improvements to EPA's Regulatory Impact Analyses.

More research remains to be done on several key questions, including analysis of the health benefits associated with reduction of particulate matter, which, as noted, drive a large percentage of aggregate benefits from air pollution controls.[19] Midway through FY 2009, EPA made changes to some underlying assumptions as well as updates to some of the model inputs. These changes are reflected in EPA's more recent Regulatory Impact Analyses. With respect to particulate matter, additional research, to clarify and resolve relevant scientific issues and to make further progress on the relationship between particulate matter and health improvements, would be exceedingly valuable.

3. Rules that Decrease Compliance Costs

We note as well that several regulatory actions have resulted in *decreases* in compliance costs. The net cost savings generated by these actions are included as "negative costs" for those years. In 2004, for example, DOT issued a rule that reduced minimum vertical separation for airspace; this rule resulted in net cost savings. Similarly, in 2009, EPA revised its "Spill Prevention Control and Countermeasures" regulations, among other things to tailor requirements to particular industry sectors and to streamline certain rule requirements, thus producing net cost savings. Executive Order 13563, with its emphasis on retrospective analysis and streamlining burdensome regulations, is designed to promote decreases in compliance costs where appropriate, and many relevant initiatives have been finalized or are in progress.

4. Qualifications

In order for comparisons or aggregations to be meaningful, benefit and cost estimates should correctly account for all substantial effects of regulatory actions, some of which may not be reflected in the available data. Any comparison or aggregation across rules should also consider a number of factors that our presentation is not yet able to take into account. Agencies have adopted somewhat different methodologies—for example, different monetized values for effects (such as mortality[20] and morbidity), different baselines in terms of the regulations and controls already in place, and different treatments of uncertainty. These differences are reflected in the estimates provided in Tables 1-1 and 1-2. While we have generally relied on agency estimates in monetizing benefits and costs, and while those estimates have generally been subject both to public and to interagency review, our reliance on those estimates in this Report should not necessarily be taken as OMB endorsement of all the varied methodologies used by agencies to estimate benefits and costs.

We have noted that many major rules have important non-quantified benefits and costs that may have been a key factor in an agency's decision to select a particular approach. In important cases, agencies have been unable to quantify the benefits of rules, simply because existing information does not permit reliable estimates. These qualitative issues are discussed in Table A-1 of Appendix A, agency rulemaking documents, and previous editions of this Report.

Finally, because these estimates exclude non-major rules and rules adopted more than ten years ago, the total benefits and costs of all Federal rules now in effect are likely to be significantly larger than the sum of the benefits and costs reported in Table 1-1. More research would be necessary to produce comprehensive estimates of total benefits and costs by agency and program. And as noted, it is important to consider retrospective, as opposed to *ex ante*, estimates of both benefits and costs; this topic is a continuing theme of this report.

B. Trends in Annual Benefits and Costs of Regulations Reviewed by OMB over the Last Ten Years

Table 1-3 reports the total benefits and costs of rules issued from October 1, 2000 to September 30, 2010, by fiscal year for which reasonably complete monetized estimates of both benefits and costs are available.[21] For the purposes of showing general trends by fiscal year, Figure 1-1 reports the midpoints of the ranges reported in Table 1-3. As the figure shows, the monetized additional costs of private mandates tend to be around or below $10 billion per year. On average, roughly $5 billion in annual costs have been added each year over this period to the total regulatory burden.

Variability appears greater in benefit estimates than in cost estimates. Note that the three highest years for benefits (2004, 2005, and 2007) are mostly explained by three EPA regulations: the 2004 non-road diesel engine rule, the 2005 interstate air quality rule, and the clean air fine particle implementation rule.[25] Note also that the benefits exceed the costs in every fiscal year; that the highest benefit year, in terms of point estimates, was 2007; that 2007 was also the highest cost year, in those terms; and that the four highest net benefit years, in those terms, were 2004, 2005, 2007, and 2010.

The estimates we report here are prospective ones made by agencies during the rulemaking process. As we have emphasized, it is possible that retrospective studies will show (as they sometimes have) that the benefits and costs were either overestimated or underestimated. As discussed elsewhere in this Report (see Appendix A) as well as previous Reports, the aggregate estimates of benefits and costs derived from estimates by different agencies and over different time periods are subject to significant methodological inconsistencies and differing assumptions.[26] In addition, the groundwork for the regulations issued by one administration is sometimes done in a previous administration.[27]

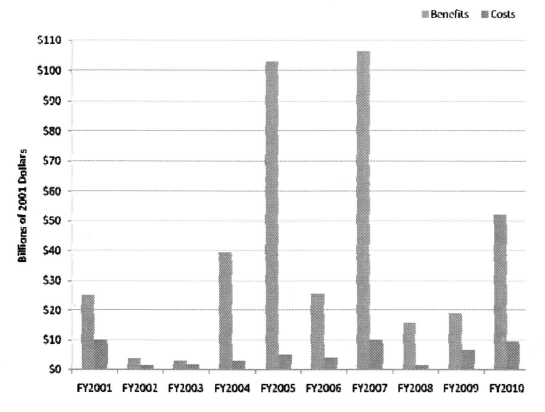

Figure 1-1. Total Annual Benefits and Costs of Major Rules by Fiscal Year.

Table 1-3. Total Annual Benefits and Costs of Major Rules by Fiscal Year, (billions of 2001 dollars)

Fiscal Year	Number of Rules	Benefits	Costs
2001	12	22.5 to 27.8	9.9
2002	2	1.5 to 6.4	0.5 to 2.2
2003	6	1.6 to 4.5	1.9 to 2.0
2004	10[22]	8.8 to 69.8	3.0 to 3.2
2005	12[23]	27.9 to 178.1	3.8 to 6.1
2006	7[24]	6.3 to 44.8	3.7 to 4.3
2007	12	28.6 to 184.2	9.4 to 10.7
2008	11	7.0 to 24.4	1.2 to 1.5
2009	15	8.6 to 28.9	3.7 to 9.5
2010	18	18.8 to 86.1	6.5 to 12.5

C. Estimates of the Benefits and Costs of Major Rules Issued in Fiscal Year 2010

1. Major Rules Issued by Executive Agencies

In this section, we examine in more detail the estimated benefits and costs of the 66 major final rules for which OMB concluded review during the 12-month period beginning October 1, 2009, and ending September 30, 2010.[28] These major rules represent approximately 20 percent of the 328 final rules reviewed by OMB.[29] OMB believes, however, that the benefits and costs of major rules, which have the largest economic effects, account for the majority of the total benefits and costs of all rules subject to OMB review.[30]

Agencies reported monetized benefits and costs of 18 of the 66 regulations in FY2010. These estimates, aggregated by agency in Table 1-4 and listed in Table 1-5(a), are included in the ten-year aggregates in Tables 1-1, 1-2, and 1-3. As with previous years, EPA rules dominate both the benefits and costs of this year's final rules. Nine of the 18 rules are primarily intended to protect health or safety. These include rules from DOL, DOT, and EPA, which affect health and safety through improvements in worker safety, pipeline safety, and environmental quality.

Thirty-two of the rules implement Federal budgetary programs, which primarily caused income transfers, usually from taxpayers to program beneficiaries. Although rules that affect Federal budget programs are subject to Executive Order 12866 and OMB Circular A-4, and are reviewed by OMB, past Reports have focused primarily on regulations that have effects largely through private sector mandates. This focus is justified in part on the ground that agencies typically do not estimate the social costs and benefits of transfer rules. Instead they report the estimated budgetary impacts.

We recognize that markets embed distortions and that the transfers are not lump-sum. Hence, transfer rules may impose real costs on society to the extent that they cause people to change behavior, either by directly prohibiting or mandating certain activities, or, more often, by altering prices and costs. The costs resulting from these behavior changes are referred to as the "deadweight losses" associated with the transfer. The Regulatory Right-to-Know Act requires OMB to report the social costs and benefits of these rules, and OMB encourages agencies to report these costs and benefits for transfer rules; OMB will consider incorporating these estimates into future Reports.

Table 1-4. Estimates, by Agency, of the Total Annual Benefits and Costs of Major Rules: October 1, 2009 - September 30, 2010 (Billions of 2001 dollars)

Agency	Number of Rules	Benefits	Costs
Department of Energy	3	2.0 to 2.7	1.2 to 1.4
Department of Justice	3	1.5 to 3.7	0.7 to 0.9
Department of Labor	1	0.2	0.1
Department of Transportation	4	0.4 to 0.5	0.9 to 1.8
Environmental Protection Agency[31]	6	10.8 to 60.8	1.9 to 3.6
Joint DOT and EPA	1	3.9 to 18.2	1.7 to 4.7
Total	18	18.8 to 86.1	6.5 to 12.5

Table 1-5(a-c) lists each of the 34 "non-budget" rules and, where available, provides information on their monetized benefits, costs, and transfers. It is worth noting that the aggregate benefits far exceed the aggregate costs and that with only two exceptions (Positive Train Control, which involved a clear statutory mandate, and Automatic Dependent Surveillance – Broadcast (ADS-B)), the estimated benefits of individual rules exceeded the costs in nearly every case.[32]

Table 1-5 (a). Major Rules Reviewed with Estimates of Both Annual Benefits and Costs, October 1, 2009 - September 30, 2010 (billions of 2001 dollars)

Agency	RIN[34]	Title	Benefits	Costs
DOJ	1117-AA61	Electronic Prescriptions for Controlled Substances	0.3-1.3	< 0.1
DOJ	1190-AA44	Nondiscrimination on the Basis of Disability in Public Accommodations and Commercial Facilities	1.1 Range: 1.0-2.1	0.6 Range: 0.5-0.7
DOJ	1190-AA46	Nondiscrimination on the Basis of Disability in State and Local Government Services	Range: 0.2-0.3	Range: 0.1-0.2
DOL	1218-AC01	Cranes and Derricks in Construction	0.2	0.1
DOE	1904-AA90	Energy Efficiency Standards for Pool Heaters and Direct Heating Equipment and Water Heaters	1.4 Range: 1.3-1.8	Range: 1.0-1.1
DOE	1904-AB70	Energy Conservation Standards for Small Electric Motors	Range: 0.7-0.8	0.2
DOE	1904-AB93	Energy Efficiency Standards for Commercial Clothes Washers	Range: 0-0.1	< 0.1
EPA	2050-AG16	Revisions to the Spill Prevention, Control, and Countermeasure (SPCC) Rule	0	(0.1)
EPA	2060-AO15	NESHAP: Portland Cement Notice of Reconsideration	Range: 6.1-16.3	Range: 0.8-0.9
EPA	2060-AO48	Review of the National Ambient Air Quality Standards for Sulfur Dioxide[35]	10.5 Range: 2.8-38.6	0.7 Range: 0.3-2.0
EPA	2060-AP36	National Emission Standards for Hazardous Air Pollutants for Reciprocating Internal Combustion Engines (Diesel)	Range: 0.7-1.9	0.3
EPA	2060-AQ13	National Emission Standards for Hazardous Air Pollutants for Reciprocating Internal Combustion Engines--Existing Stationary Spark Ignition (Gas-Fired)	Range: 0.4-1.0	0.2
EPA	2070-AJ55	Lead; Amendment to the Opt-out and Recordkeeping Provisions in the Renovation, Repair, and Painting Program	Range: 0.8-3.0	0.3
DOT	2120-AI92	Automatic Dependent Surveillance—Broadcast (ADS-B) Equipage Mandate to Support Air Traffic Control Service	Range: 0.1-0.2	0.2
DOT	2126-AA89	Electronic On-Board Recorders for Hours-of-Service Compliance	0.2	0.1
DOT	2130-AC03	Positive Train Control	<0.1	0.7 Range: 0.5-1.3
DOT	2137-AE15	Pipeline Safety: Distribution Integrity Management	0.1	0.1
DOT & EPA	2127-AK50; 2060-AP58	Light-Duty Greenhouse Gas Emission Standards and Corporate Average Fuel Economy Standards[36]	11.9 Range: 3.9-18.2	3.3 Range: 1.7-4.7

( ) indicates negative.

Table 1-5 (b). Major Rules Reviewed with Partial Estimates of Annual Benefits or Costs, October 1, 2009 - September 30, 2010 (billions of 2001 dollars)

Agency	RIN	Title	Benefits	Costs
HHS	0920-AA26	Medical Examination of Aliens— Removal of Human Immuno deficiency Virus (HIV) Infection From Definition of Communicable Disease of Public Health Significance	Not Estimated	< 0.1
HHS, DOL & TREAS	093 8-AP65; 1210-AB30	Interim Final Rules Under the Paul Wellstone and Pete Domenici Mental Health Parity and Addiction Equity Act of 2008	Not Estimated	< 0.1
HHS, DOL & TREAS	0991-AB66; 1210-AB41	Interim Final Rules for Group Health Plans and Health Insurance Issuers Relating to Dependent Coverage of Children to Age 26 under the Patient Protection and Affordable Care Act	Not Estimated	< 0.1
HHS, DOL & TREAS	0991-AB68; 121 0-AB42	Interim Final Rules for Group Health Plans and Health Insurance Coverage Relating to Status as a Grandfathered Health Plan under the Patient Protection and Affordable Care Act	Not Estimated	< 0.1
HHS, DOL & TREAS	0991-AB69; 1210-AB43	Patient Protection and Affordable Care Act: Preexisting Condition Exclusions, Lifetime and Annual Limits, Rescissions, and Patient Protections	Not Estimated	< 0.1
HHS, DOL & TREAS	0991-AB70; 1210-AB45	Interim Final Rules for Group Health Plans and Health Insurance Issuers Relating to Internal Claims and Appeals and External Review Processes under the Patient Protection and Affordable Care Act	Not Estimated	< 0.1
DOI	1018-AX06	Migratory Bird Hunting; Final Frameworks for Early-Season Migratory Bird Hunting Regulations	Range: 0.2- 0.3	Not Estimated
DOI	1018-AX06	Migratory Bird Hunting; Final Frameworks for Late Season Migratory Bird Hunting Regulations	Range: 0.2- 0.3	Not Estimated
DOL	1210-AB08	Improved Fee Disclosure for Pension Plans	Not Estimated	< 0.1
TREAS	1557-AD23	S.A.F.E. Mortgage Licensing Act	Not Estimated	0.1-0.2

Table 1-5(c). Additional Non-Budget Major Rules Reviewed, October 1, 2009 - September 30, 2010 (billions of 2001 dollars)

Agency	RIN	Title
HHS	0910-AF93	Use of Ozone-Depleting Substances; Removal of Essential Use Designations [Flunisolide, Triamcinolone, Metaproterenol, Pirbuterol, Albuterol and Ipratropium in Combination, Cromolyn, and Nedocromil][37]
HHS	0910-AG33	Regulations Restricting the Sale and Distribution of Cigarettes and Smokeless Tobacco to Protect Children and Adolescents[38]
HHS, DOL & TREAS	093 8-AQ07; 1210-AB44	Interim Final Rules for Group Health Plans and Health Insurance Issuers Relating to Coverage of Preventive Services under the Patient Protection and Affordable Care Act[39]

Table 1-5(c). (Continued)

Agency	RIN	Title
EPA	2060-AO38	Control of Emissions From New Marine Compression-Ignition Engines at or Above 30 Liters per Cylinder[40]
EPA	2060-AO81	Renewable Fuels Standard Program[41]
EPA	2060-AP86	Prevention of Significant Deterioration/Title V Greenhouse Gas Tailoring Rule[42]

Table 1-6 lists each of 32 "budget" rules and provides information on the estimated income transfers. Unless otherwise noted, OMB simply converts to 2001 dollars agencies' own estimates of annualized impacts. For all 66 rules, we summarize the information on the non- monetized impacts, where available, for these regulations in the "other information" column of Table A-1.

Overall, HHS promulgated the largest number of rules: nineteen. Ten of these largely transfer income from one group of entities to another without imposing significant private mandates; the other nine contain private sector mandates.[33] EPA issued the most rules creating or modifying private mandates; all ten of its rules contain significant private sector impacts.

Ten rules partially monetized either benefits or costs and are listed in Table 1-5(b). Two such rules, DOI's Migratory Bird Hunting regulations, assessed only benefits. These regulations are promulgated annually to allow hunting of migratory game birds. The agency assessed the consumer welfare increase associated with these allowances. Ideally, these benefits should take into account the value of recreational alternatives. Administrative costs are of course relevant and could help inform a full analysis.

Eight rules reported only monetized costs and relevant transfers, without monetizing benefits. As noted, quantification and monetization sometimes present serious challenges, especially in terms of benefits; for some rules, it is not feasible to make projections, because of an absence of available information. Four of these eight rules are joint HHS, DOL, and Treasury rules that implement health insurance reforms under the Affordable Care Act. (One additional rule by the three departments implements the Mental Health Parity and Addiction Equity Act.) For these rules, qualitative information with respect to benefits is provided, alongside an explanation of limits in available information. The main purpose of health insurance is to spread financial risk arising from medical care. In addition, some of these rules address equity concerns, for example by preventing denial of health insurance coverage to children with preexisting conditions. The potential transfer effects and non-quantified effects are described in the "other information" column of Table A-1. We continue to work with agencies to improve the quantification of the benefits and costs of these types of regulations.

The regulatory analyses of six of the 34 "non-budget" rules did not provide an estimate of the incremental benefits or costs of the rule. These rules are described in Table 1-5(c), in which footnotes provide further details on the analysis provided for each rule. The potential transfer effects and non-monetized effects are described in the "other information" column of Table A-1.

2. Major Rules Issued by Independent Agencies

The Small Business Regulatory Enforcement Fairness Act of 1996 (SBREFA)[43] requires the Government Accountability Office (GAO) to submit to Congress reports on major rules, including rules issued by agencies not subject to Executive Order 12866 — the independent regulatory agencies. In preparing this Report, we reviewed the information contained in GAO reports on benefits and costs of major rules issued by independent agencies for the period of October 1, 2009 to September 30, 2010.[44] GAO reported that three agencies issued a total of 17 major rules during this period. (Rules by independent agencies are not subject to OMB review under Executive Order 13563 and Executive Order 12866.)

Table 1-6. Major Rules Implementing or Adjusting Federal Budgetary Programs, October 1, 2009 - September 30, 2010 (billions of 2001 dollars)

Agency	RIN	Title	Budget Effects
USDA	0560-AH90	Supplemental Revenue Assistance Payments Program (SURE)	0.1
USDA	0560-AI07	Dairy Economic Loss Assistance Payment Program	0.2
USDA	0578-AA43	Conservation Stewardship Program	2.7-3.2
USDA	0584-AD30	SNAP: Eligibility and Certification Provisions of the Farm Security and Rural Investment Act of 2002	2.2
DOC	0660-ZA28	Broadband Technology Opportunities Program	2.1
DOD	0720-AB17	TRICARE: Relationship Between the TRICARE Pro-gram and Employer-Sponsored Group Health Coverage	> (0.1)
DOD	0790-AI59	Retroactive Stop Loss Special Pay Compensation	0.4
HHS	0938-AP40	Revisions to Payment Policies Under the Physi-cian Fee Schedule For CY 2010 (CMS-1413-FC)	(11.0)
HHS	0938-AP41	Changes to the Hospital Outpatient Prospective Payment System and Ambulatory Surgical Center Payment System for CY 2010 (CMS-1414-F)	0.4
HHS	0938-AP55	Home Health Prospective Payment System and Rate Update for CY 2010 (CMS-1560-F)	(0.1)
HHS	0938-AP57	End Stage Renal Disease Bundled Payment System (CMS-141 8-F)	(0.2)
HHS	0938-AP72	State Flexibility for Medicaid Benefit Packages (CMS 2232-F4)	(0.7)
HHS	0938-AP77	Revisions to the Medicare Advantage and Medicare Prescription Drug Benefit Programs for Contract Year 2011 (CMS-4085-F)	(0.3)
HHS	0938-AP78	Electronic Health Record (EHR) Incentive Program (CMS-0033-F)	1.0-2.5
HHS	0938-AP80	Medicare Program; Changes to the Hospital Inpatient Prospective Payment Systems for Acute Care Hospitals and the Long Term Care Hospital Prospective Payment System and Fiscal Year 2011 Rates	(0.2)
HHS	0991-AB64	Early Retiree Reinsurance Program	1.0
HHS	0991-AB71	Pre-Existing Condition Insurance Plan Program	1.0
STATE	1400-AC58	Schedule of Fees for Consular Services, Department of State and Overseas Embassies and Consulates	0.3-0.4
DHS	1615-AB80	U. S. Citizenship and Immigration Services Fee Schedule	0.2
DHS	1651-AA83	Electronic System for Travel Authorization (ESTA): Fee for Use of the System	0.1-0.2
DHS	1660-AA44	Special Community Disaster Loans Program	0-1.0
ED	1810-AB04	State Fiscal Stabilization Fund Program--Notice of Proposed Requirements, Definitions, and Approval Criteria	9.5

Table 1-6. (Continued)

Agency	RIN	Title	Budget Effects
ED	1810-AB06	School Improvement Grants--Notice of Proposed Requirements Under the American Recovery and Reinvestment Act of 2009; Title I of the Elementary and Secondary Education Act of 1965	2.9
ED	1810-AB07	Race to the Top Fund--Notice of Proposed Priorities, Requirements, Definitions, and Selection Criteria	3.2
ED	1810-AB08	Teacher Incentive Fund--Priorities, Requirements, Definitions, and Selection Criteria	0.4
ED	1840-AC96	Student Assistance General Provisions; TEACH Grant, Federal Pell Grant, and Academic Compe-titiveness Grant, and National Science and Mathe-matics Access To Retain Talent Grant Programs	0.2
ED	1840-AC99	General and Non-Loan Programmatic Issues	0.2
ED	1840-AD0 1	Federal TRIO Programs, Gaining Early Awareness and Readiness for Undergraduate Program, and High School Equivalency and College Assistance Migrant Programs	1.0
ED	1855-AA06	Investing in Innovation--Priorities, Requirements, Definitions, and Selection Criteria	0.5
DOE	1901-AB27	Loan Guarantees for Projects That Employ Innovative Technologies	3.5-4.0
DOE	1904-AB97	Weatherization Assistance Program for Low-Income Persons - Multi-unit Buildings	4.0
VA	2900-AN54	Diseases Associated With Exposure to Certain Herbicide Agents (Hairy Cell Leukemia and Other Chronic B Cell Leukemias, Parkinson's Disease, and Ischemic Heart Disease)	4.1-5.4

( ) indicates savings from the Federal perspective.

Table 1-7 lists each of these rules and the extent to which GAO reported benefit and cost estimates for the rule. All of the rules, except the Nuclear Regulatory Commission's fee recovery rule, were issued to regulate the financial sector. No rule provided complete monetized benefit and cost information. The Federal Reserve System promulgated four rules on electronic fund transfer and two rules on truth-in-lending, and generally did not provide information on benefits and costs. The Federal Reserve System and the Federal Trade Commission issued a joint rule on fair credit reporting for which the agencies provided monetized cost information, but no monetized benefit assessment. The SEC conducts some benefit-cost analysis of its rules, but it generally does not quantify and monetize benefits and costs. OMB does not know whether the rigor of the analyses conducted by these agencies is similar to that of the analyses performed by agencies subject to OMB review.

We emphasize that for the purposes of informing the public and obtaining a full accounting, it would be desirable to obtain better information on the benefits and costs of the rules issued by independent regulatory agencies. The absence of such information is a continued obstacle to transparency, and it might also have adverse effects on public policy. Executive Order 13563 emphasizes the importance of agency use of "the best available techniques to quantify anticipated present and future benefits and costs as accurately as possible." While that Executive Order applies only to executive agencies, independent agencies may wish to consider the use of such techniques. In its February 2, 2011, guidance on Executive Order 13563, OMB encouraged the independent agencies to follow the principles and requirements of the order.[45]

Table 1-7. Major Rules Issued by Independent Regulatory Agencies, October 1, 2009 - September 30, 2010

Agency	Rule	Information Benefits or Costs	Monetized Benefits	Monetized Costs
Federal Reserve System	Electronic Fund Transfers (74 FR 59,033)	Yes	No	No
Federal Reserve System	Electronic Fund Transfers (75 FR 16,580)	No	No	No
Federal Reserve System	Electronic Fund Transfers (75 FR 31,665)	No	No	No
Federal Reserve System	Electronic Fund Transfers (75 FR 50,683)	No	No	No
Federal Reserve System	Truth in Lending (75 FR 7,658)	No	No	No
Federal Reserve System	Truth in Lending (75 FR 37,526)	No	No	No
Federal Reserve System and Federal Trade Commission	Fair Credit Reporting Risk-Based Pricing Regulations	Yes	No	Yes
Nuclear Regulatory Commission	Revision of Fee Schedules; Fee Recovery for FY 2010 (75 FR 34,220)	Yes	No	Yes
Securities and Exchange Commission	Amendments to Form ADV (75 FR 49,234)	Yes	No	Yes
Securities and Exchange Commission	Amendments to Regulation SHO (75 FR 11,232)*	Yes	No	Yes
Securities and Exchange Commission	Amendments to Rules for Nationally Recognized Statistical Rating Organizations (74 FR 63,832)	Yes	No	Yes
Securities and Exchange Commission	Custody of Funds or Securities of Clients by Investment Advisers (75 FR 1,456)	Yes	No	Yes
Securities and Exchange Commission	Facilitating Shareholder Director Nominations (75 FR 56,668)	Yes	No	No
Securities and Exchange Commission	Internal Control over Financial Reporting in Exchange Act Periodic Reports of Non-Accelerated Filers (74 FR 53,628)	Yes	No	No
Securities and Exchange Commission	Money Market Fund Reform (75 FR 10,060)	Yes	No	No
Securities and Exchange Commission	Political Contributions by Certain Investment Advisers (75 FR 41,018)	Yes	No	Yes
Securities and Exchange Commission	Proxy Disclosure Enhancements (74 FR 68,334)	Yes	No	Yes

* Final rule to an interim final rule promulgated in FY 2009.

OMB provides in Appendix C of this Report a summary of the information available on the regulatory analyses for major rules by the independent agencies over the past ten years. This summary is similar to the ten-year look-back for regulation included in recent Reports. It examines the number of major rules promulgated by independent agencies as reported to the GAO from 2000 through 2010, which are presented in Table C-1.[46] Information is also presented on the extent to which the independent agencies reported benefit and cost information for these rules in Tables C-2 through C-4.

D. The Impact of Federal Regulation on State, Local, and Tribal Governments, Small Business, Wages, and Economic Growth

Section 624 (a)(2) of the Regulatory Right-to-Know Act requires OMB to present an analysis of the impacts of Federal regulation on State, local, and tribal governments, small business, wages, and economic growth. In addition, Presidential Memorandum: Administrative Flexibility (attached as Appendix H) calls for a series of measures to promote flexibility for State, local, and tribal governments; these measures include reduced reporting burdens and streamlined regulation.

1. Impacts on State, Local, and Tribal Governments

Over the past ten years, only four rules have imposed costs of more than $100 million per year ($2001) on State, local, and tribal governments (and thus have been classified as public sector mandates under the Unfunded Mandates Reform Act of 1995):[47]

- *EPA's National Primary Drinking Water Regulations; Arsenic and Clarifications to Compliance and New Source Contaminants Monitoring* (2001): This rule reduces the level of arsenic that is allowed to be in drinking water from 50 ppb to 10 ppb. It also revises current monitoring requirements and requires non-transient, non-community water systems to come into compliance with the standard. This rule may affect State, local, or tribal governments or the private sector at an approximate annualized cost of $189 million for a 3 percent discount rate, and $216 for a 7 percent discount rate. The monetized benefits of the rule range from $146 million to $206 million per year.[48] Qualitative benefits may include reductions in skin and kidney cancer where the skin cancer endpoints are well-established.
- *EPA's National Primary Drinking Water Regulations: Long Term 2 Enhanced Surface Water Treatment* (2005): The rule protects against illness due to cryptosporidium and other microbial pathogens in drinking water and addresses risk-risk trade-offs with the control of disinfection byproducts. It requires the use of treatment techniques, along with monitoring, reporting, and public notification requirements, for all public water systems that use surface water sources. The monetized benefits of the rule range from approximately $260 million to $1.8 billion. The monetized costs of the rule range from approximately $80 million to $130 million.
- *EPA's National Primary Drinking Water Regulations: Stage 2 Disinfection Byproducts Rule* (2006): The rule protects against illness due to drinking water disinfectants and disinfection byproducts (DBPs).[49] The rule effectively tightens the existing standards by making them applicable to each point in the drinking water distribution system individually, rather than only on an average basis to the system as a whole. EPA has determined that this rule may contain a Federal mandate that results in expenditures by State, local, and tribal governments, and the private sector,

of $100 million or more in any one year. While the annualized costs fall below the $100 million threshold, the costs in some future years may be above the $100 million mark as public drinking water systems make capital investments and finance these through bonds, loans, and other means.
- *DHS's Chemical Facility Anti-Terrorism Standards Rule* (2007): This rule establishes risk-based performance standards for the security of our nation's chemical facilities. It requires covered chemical facilities to prepare Security Vulnerability Assessments (SVAs), which identify facility security vulnerabilities, and to develop and implement Site Security Plans (SSPs), which include measures that satisfy the identified risk-based performance standards. The rule also provides DHS with the authority to seek compliance through the issuance of Orders, including Orders Assessing Civil Penalty and Orders for the Cessation of Operations. DHS has determined that this rule constitutes an unfunded mandate on the private sector. In the regulatory impact assessment published with this rule, DHS estimates that there are 1,500 to 6,500 covered chemical facilities. DHS also assumes that this rule may require certain municipalities that own and/or operate power generating facilities to purchase security enhancements. Although DHS is unable to determine if this rule will impose an enforceable duty upon State, local, and tribal governments of $100 million (adjusted annually for inflation) or more in any one year, it has been included in this list for the sake of completeness.

Although these four rules were the only ones over the past ten years to require expenditures by State, local, and tribal governments exceeding $100 million (adjusted for inflation), they were not the only rules with impacts on other levels of governments. For example, many rules have monetary impacts lower than the $100 million threshold, and agencies are also required to consider the federalism implications of rulemakings under Executive Order 13132.

2. Impact on Small Business

The Regulatory Right-to-Know Act calls for an analysis of the effects of regulations on small business. Consistent with that direction, Executive Order 12866, "Regulatory Planning and Review," recognizes the need to attend to such effects. That Executive Order, reaffirmed by and incorporated in Executive Order 13563, "Improving Regulation and Regulatory Review," calls on agencies to tailor their regulations by business size in order to impose the least burden on society, consistent with the achievement of regulatory objectives. It also calls for the development of short forms and other efficient regulatory approaches for small businesses and other entities. In the findings section of SBREFA, Congress states that "small businesses bear a disproportionate share of regulatory costs and burdens."[50] When relevant regulations are issued, each firm must determine whether a regulation applies, how to comply, and whether it is in compliance. As firms increase in size, fixed costs of regulatory compliance are spread over a larger revenue and employee base, which often results in lower regulatory costs per unit of output.

In recognition of these principles, many statutes and regulations explicitly attempt to reduce burdens on small businesses, in part to promote economic growth, in part to ensure against unnecessary or unjustified costs, in part to avoid adverse effects on employment and wages. For example, agencies frequently tailor regulations to limit the costs imposed on small business and to offer regulatory relief, including explicit exemptions for small businesses and slower phase-in schedules, allowing adequate periods of transition. Moreover, the Regulatory Flexibility Act (RFA) requires agencies to assess the effect of regulations on small businesses.[51] Under the RFA, whenever an agency concludes that a particular regulation will have a significant economic effect on a substantial number of small entities, the agency must conduct both an initial and final regulatory flexibility analysis. This analysis must include (among other things) an assessment of the likely burden of the rule on small entities and an analysis of alternatives that may afford relief to small entities while achieving the regulatory goals. OMB works closely with agencies to promote compliance with RFA and to tailor regulations to reduce unjustified costs and to create appropriate flexibility.

On January 18, 2011, the President issued a memorandum to underline the requirements of the RFA and to direct agencies to offer an explanation of any failure to provide flexibility to small businesses in proposed or final rules. Such flexibility may include delayed compliance dates, simplified reporting requirements, and partial or total exemptions. The President's memorandum emphasizes the relationship between small and new businesses and economic growth and job creation; he has directed agencies to ensure, to the extent feasible and consistent with law, that regulatory initiatives contain flexibility for small businesses. This memorandum is attached as Appendix F.

The empirical evidence of the effects of regulation on small business remains less than entirely clear. We have cited in previous Reports research by the Small Business Administration (SBA) Office of Advocacy, suggesting that small entities disproportionately shoulder regulatory and paperwork burdens. In a study sponsored by SBA (and cited in our 2010 Report), for example, Dean, et al., concludes that environmental regulations act as barriers to entry for small firms.[52]

Becker offers a more complex view, focusing on the effect of air pollution regulation on small business.[53] He finds that although "progressively larger facilities had progressively higher unit abatement costs, ceteris paribus,"[54] the relationship between firm size and pollution abatement costs varies depending on the regulated pollutant. For troposphere ozone, the regulatory burden seems to fall substantially on the smallest three quartiles of plants. For SOx, the relationship between regulatory burden and the firm size seems to be U-shaped. For total suspended particles, new multi-unit emitting plants in the smallest size class had $265 more capital expenditure (per $10,000 of value added) in non-attainment counties than similar plants in attainment counties, while "those in the larger size classes had an additional $5 11-687 in expenditure... though the rise was not monotonic."[55]

The evidence in the literature, while suggestive, remains preliminary, inconclusive, and mixed. OMB continues to investigate the evolving literature on the relevant questions in order to obtain a more precise picture. It is clear, however, that some regulations have significant adverse effects on small business, and that it is appropriate to take steps to create flexibility in the event that those adverse effects cannot be justified by commensurate benefits. As the President's 2011 memorandum directs, agencies should specifically explain any refusal to take such steps, especially in light of the importance of small businesses and startups for economic growth and job creation.

3. *Impact on Wages and Employment*

Regulations of many different markets and areas of activity can ultimately affect labor markets, producing changes in wages and employment levels. Some regulations can have adverse effects on both dimensions, especially if they significantly increase costs; other regulations might produce benefits, especially if they significantly decrease costs. The relevant effects can be quite complex, since in general equilibrium, regulation in one market can have ripple effects across many markets, making it difficult to generalize. In addition, some regulations require or promote activities that may have beneficial effects on job creation.

We discuss here the effect of labor market regulations, environmental regulations, and economic regulations on wages and employment. OMB continues to investigate the possibility that certain kinds of regulations can have adverse effects on job creation in particular, and is interested both in empirical work and in taking steps to reduce or eliminate such adverse effects. Under Executive Order 13563, job creation is a relevant consideration in regulatory review ("Our regulatory system must promote public health, welfare, safety, and our environment while promoting economic growth, innovation, competitiveness, and job creation.").

a. Labor market regulations

It is perhaps simplest to analyze the effects of direct regulation of labor markets, as they can be plausibly analyzed using a relatively simple partial equilibrium framework—i.e., one that focuses exclusively on the labor market, ignoring the effects through other markets. There are many different types of labor market regulations. Perhaps the most obvious are direct price controls, such as minimum wage laws.[56] Another form of labor market regulation consists of regulations that mandate particular employer-provided benefits, such as the requirement under the Family and Medical Leave Act (FMLA) to provide unpaid leave to care for a new child; in the same category are rules that affect working conditions, such as workplace safety regulations under the Occupational Safety and Health Act. Another category of labor market regulation is anti-discrimination law, which protects certain classes of workers from discrimination in hiring and wage-setting decisions. Still another form of labor market regulation governs the ability of workers and firms to bargain collectively; in general, U.S. competition law prohibits collusion among employers and allows collective bargaining by workers.

The effects of these approaches must be analyzed separately. Here we outline the theory and evidence on the effect of mandated benefits regulations on wages and employment levels. To be concrete, consider a workplace safety regulation. Summers provides the standard price-theoretic treatment of such regulations.[57] Such a regulation will shift the labor supply curve down by the amount that workers value the increase in safety, so that workers are willing to supply more labor for a given wage than in the absence of the regulation. Because it imposes compliance costs on employers, the regulation also shifts the labor demand curve down by the amount of the compliance cost.

If workers value the mandated benefit at more than it costs employers to provide the benefit, then both the employment level and net wages (i.e., monetary compensation plus the value of non-monetary benefits such as safety) will rise. Under standard assumptions, employers have incentives to provide such benefits, but various market failures may result in suboptimal provision of such benefits. Conversely, if workers value the mandated benefit at less than its cost, then the employment level and net wages will fall. This simple model assumes that wages can indeed perfectly adjust downwards in response to the mandated benefits—but if wages are sticky, then the regulation could result in a decrease in employment levels and an increase in net wages.

In the case of group-specific mandated benefits, which are targeted at identifiable groups of workers in the population, the theoretical analysis is more complicated. Jolls provides the leading account and emphasizes that the interaction of group-specific mandated benefits regulation with anti-discrimination law determines its consequences for labor markets.[58] Consider, for instance, regulations under the Americans with Disabilities Act (ADA) that require that employers accommodate the special needs of disabled employees—a group-specific mandated benefit. The law also forbids employers from discriminating against disabled workers in hiring and compensation decisions. To the extent that it is easier to enforce the prohibition of discrimination in wage setting than in hiring decisions, Jolls argues that the law will result in no reduction in wages for disabled workers but a reduction in their employment level, because employers will prefer to hire (cheaper) non-disabled workers.

In contrast, group-specific mandates that target women, such as maternity leave mandates, are more likely to have an effect on wages because women are disproportionately represented in a few occupations, and hence their wages can more easily be adjusted downward without triggering anti-discrimination enforcement. These mandates can be analyzed in the standard framework provided by Summers described above, and because wages adjust down, are less likely to have a negative effect on employment.

The empirical literature does not offer unambiguous conclusions, but some studies provide support for the predictions of these simple partial equilibrium models. Acemoglu and Angrist find that the ADA resulted in no decrease in relative wages of disabled people but a decrease in employment levels.[59] In contrast, Gruber finds that regulations that require employers to provide comprehensive coverage for childbirth in health insurance plans result in a decrease in women's wages but have no effect on their employment levels.[60] Studies examining the effect of the FMLA in the US, however, find little effect on either relative employment levels or wages of women, perhaps because the mandated leave is short and unpaid and many employers provided maternity leave prior to the law.[61] OMB continues to investigate the growing literature on these topics; the references here are meant to be illustrative rather than exhaustive.

b. Environmental Regulation

The effects of environmental regulation on the labor market can be difficult to assess, in part because they are not easy to disentangle from the effects of other economic changes over time and across industries. The underlying questions require careful and continuing empirical study. In this section we summarize some of the leading articles that are often cited in the academic literature.

Surveying the early studies, Goodstein (1994) finds that seven of nine relevant studies showed increases in employment as a result of environmental regulation, one showed a decrease, and one was inconclusive. He states that "on balance, the available studies indicate that environmental spending... has probably led to a net increase in the number of jobs in the U.S. economy ... although if it exists, this effect is not large." A more recent discussion finds that the research thus far has "yielded mixed results" with respect to "the over-all employment effects of environmental regulation" in the short- or medium-term.[62]

In an influential treatment, Morgenstern, Pizer, and Shih (2002) explore four highly polluting, regulated industries to examine the effects on employment of higher abatement costs from regulation.[63] The authors conclude that increased abatement expenditures generally do not cause a significant change in employment. In reaching this conclusion, they provide a general framework, identifying three sources of potential effects, both beneficial and adverse, that regulation could have on employment:

- *Demand effect:* higher production costs raise market prices and hence reduce consumption (and production), thus reducing demand for output, with potentially negative effects on employment; in the authors' words, the "extent of this effect depends on the cost increase passed on to consumers as well as the demand elasticity of industry output"
- *Cost effect:* As costs go up, plants add more capital and labor (holding other factors constant), with potentially positive effects on employment; in the authors' words, as "production costs rise, more inputs, including labor, are used to produce the same amount of output"
- *Factor-shift effect:* Post-regulation production technologies may be more or less labor intensive (i.e., more/less labor is required per dollar of output); in the authors' words, "environmental activities may be more labor intensive than conventional production," meaning that "the amount of labor per dollar of output will rise," though it is also possible that "cleaner operations could involve automation and less employment, for example"

Isolating these elements, the authors expect, and find, positive employment effects in industries (such as petroleum and plastics) where environmental activities are labor-intensive and demand is relatively inelastic. Where the pollution abatement activities required or encouraged by regulation are not labor-intensive, and where demand is elastic, positive employment effects would not be expected and negative effects should be anticipated to occur; in such cases, the demand effect will dominate the outcome. The authors find that in those industries where labor already represents a large share of production costs and where demand is relatively more elastic (such as steel and pulp and paper), there is nonetheless little evidence of any statistically significant employment consequence. They also state that "increased environmental spending generally does *not* cause a significant change in industry-level employment. Our average across all four industries is a net gain of 1.5 jobs per $1 million in additional environmental spending, with a standard error of 2.2 jobs—an insignificant effect."

In another study, Berman and Bui (2001) use direct measures of regulation and plant data to estimate the employment effects of sharply increased air quality regulation in Los Angeles. They compare changes in employment in affected plants to those in other plants in the same industries but in regions not subject to the local regulations. The authors find that "while regulations do impose large costs, they have a limited effect on employment" – even when exit and dissuaded entry effects are considered.[64] Their conclusion is that local air quality regulation "probably increased labor demand slightly." In their view, the limited effects likely arose because (1) the regulations applied disproportionately to capital-intensive plants with relatively little employment; (2) the plants sold to local markets where competitors were subject to the same regulations (so that sales were relatively unaffected); and (3) abatement inputs served as complements to employment.

In a related paper, Cole and Elliott (2007) study the impact of UK environmental regulations on sectoral employment using panel data spanning 27 different industries over 5 years. They find that environmental regulation costs did not have a statistically significant effect on employment, regardless of whether such costs were treated as exogenous or endogenous. The authors suggest that regulation costs could generate "competing effects on employment and cancel each other out" or simply have no discernable impact at all.

By contrast, other sectoral studies – generally focusing on the manufacturing sector – have found negative effects on employment.[65] The 2010 Report states that OMB is also exploring the risk that domestic regulation might lead companies to do business abroad as a result of domestic regulation in the environmental area, resulting in depressed wages and employment. The economic literature has for some time examined firms' decisions to locate new plants or relocate existing plants in response to environmental regulations.

In this context, the evidence is both suggestive and mixed. In their review of the literature on the effect of environmental regulation on the manufacturing sector, Jaffe et al. find that "although the long-run social costs of environmental regulation may be significant, including adverse effects on productivity, studies attempting to measure the effect of environmental regulation on net exports, overall trade flows, and plant-location decisions have produced estimates that are either small, statistically insignificant, or not robust to tests of model specification."[66]

Using 17-year panel data, Keller and Levinson (2002) find that the stringency of environmental regulation (expressed in terms of pollution abatement costs) has "small deterrent effects" on states competing for foreign direct investment.[67] By contrast, Xing and Kolstad state that "using instruments for the unobserved variables, the statistical results show that the laxity of environmental regulations in a host country is a significant determinant of F[oreign] D[irect] I[nvestment] from the US for heavily polluting industries and is insignificant for less polluting industries."[68]

A recent study by Hanna (2010) measured the response of the foreign direct investment decisions of U.S.-based multinationals to the Clean Air Act Amendments, using a panel of firm- level data over the period 1966-1999. Consistent with the theory that regulation causes firms to substitute foreign for domestic production, the authors find that in the environmental area, domestic regulation has led US-based multinational companies "to increase their foreign assets in polluting industries by 5.3 percent and their foreign output by 9 percent."[69] The authors also find that these results are more robust for firms that manufactured within an industry for which imports had historically accounted for a large percentage of US consumption (see also Greenstone (2002) discussed below). Like Hanna (2010), Brunnermeier and Levinson (2004), using panel data, also find "statistically significant pollution haven effects of reasonable magnitude."[70] Levinson and Taylor's (2008) results in examining trade flows and environmental regulation are consistent with these other studies.[71]

c. Economic regulation

Rate regulations and restrictions on entry in product markets—commonly referred to as "economic regulation"—can have important effects on labor markets. As emphasized by Peoples,[72] restrictions on entry into an industry can make unionization of the industry easier because as a result the industry is dominated by a few large firms, which lowers the cost of organizing workers. The resulting high unionization rates give unions in the regulated industries substantial bargaining power, and as a result wages in regulated industries, which historically include trucking, electricity, and airlines, are higher. Moreover, rate regulations that allow firms in these industries to pass costs on to customers may make it easier for unions to bargain for relatively high wages.

If economic regulation also results in higher prices in the product market, consumers, including workers, will of course have to pay those prices. Blanchard and Giavazzi show in theoretical terms that the increased markups in the product market caused by widespread economic regulation can result in both lower real wages of workers, measured in terms of purchasing power, and lower employment levels.[73] The theoretical negative effect of entry regulation on employment was supported empirically by Bertrand and Kramarz,[74] who examine entry restrictions in the French retail industry and find that they have reduced employment growth in France.

4. Impact on Economic Growth

Measuring the effects of regulation on economic growth is a complex task. Some forms of regulation may have a positive effect on growth, perhaps by promoting stable and efficient operation of financial markets, by improving educational outcomes, by promoting innovation, or by upgrading the operation of the transportation system. Excessive and unnecessary regulations, on the other hand, place undue burdens on companies, consumers, and workers and may cause growth and overall productivity to slow. As we have noted, there is some evidence that domestic environmental regulation has led some US-based multinationals to invest in other nations (especially in the domain of manufacturing), and in that sense, such regulation may have an adverse effect on domestic growth. At the same time, the direct impacts of particular regulations, or categories of regulations, on the overall economy may be difficult to establish because causal chains are uncertain and because it is hard to control relevant variables.

a. *Some conceptual challenges and the nature of growth.* One difficulty with measuring the relationship between regulation and economic growth is identifying the appropriate measure of output. Economists frequently look at Gross Domestic Product (GDP), which is also our principal emphasis here (see below), but GDP may not adequately account for the effects of some regulations. For example, GDP does not capture directly relevant benefits of regulation, such as environmental protection, that do not result in increases in goods or services produced.[75] Some important benefits, improving people's actual welfare, are not adequately captured by GDP. Efforts to expand the national accounts to incorporate omitted factors – such as improvements in environmental quality in satellite accounts – suggest the incompleteness of existing measures.[76]

A detailed literature explores some of the potentially deeper limitations of national income and product accounting. There is a complex and not fully understood relationship between GDP growth and subjective well-being (insofar as a rapidly growing literature suggests that the latter may be measured).[77] Some studies, for example, conclude that, on average, increases in subjective well-being are clearly and consistently associated with rising levels of GDP across different countries.[78] Studies find that the positive relationship between wealth and subjective well-being is especially clear when comparing the subjective well-being of richer and poorer people within the same country at a single point in time; in brief, the subjective wellbeing of richer people is higher.[79] Other studies point to cross-country data suggesting that as income per capita increases, subjective well-being increases steeply but only up to a certain threshold. Afterwards, levels of happiness are only weakly correlated with further increases in income per capita; that is, some studies suggest that above some threshold level, GDP growth may have little effect on subjective well-being.[80] The precise relationship between GDP growth and subjective well-being has yet to be settled.

A more general observation is that there may be a significant difference between self-reported life satisfaction and self-reported day-to-day experience; the measure of "life satisfaction" evidently captures judgments that are not captured in day-to-day experience, and vice-versa.[81] Some studies, for example, find that life satisfaction generally increases with income but that experienced well-being does not.[82]

In this vein, Krueger, et al, offer an alternative measure of well-being—National Time Accounting—that proposes to measure and analyze how people spend and experience their time.[83] One claim is that such measures provide important information that is not fully or adequately captured in GDP or other existing measures. This approach provides an extension to regular time use surveys, and uses what the authors call the Day Reconstruction Method (DRM) to ask respondents what they were doing, and how they felt, at different times during the day.

Federal statistical initiatives are currently underway that are influenced by and build upon this approach. The National Institute on Aging (NIA) is supporting the inclusion of well-being measures in a number of large population-based surveys, both nationally and internationally. Specifically, a module of questions, designed by Krueger with funding from NIA, was fielded in the 2010 American Time Use Survey (ATUS). The ATUS, which is conducted by the U.S. Census Bureau for the Bureau of Labor Statistics (BLS), is a continuous survey about how individuals age 15 and over spend their time doing various activities, such as work, childcare, housework, watching television, volunteering, and socializing. In the module, up to three activities that a respondent reports are randomly selected, and respondents are asked how happy, tired, sad, stressed, and in pain they felt during each of those activities. Data from this module will become available mid-2011. NIA currently intends to fund this module again in 2012, and OIRA continues to support these efforts.

In November 2010, the NIA and the U.K. Economic and Social Research Council sponsored a workshop that was held at the National Academy of Sciences on the role of well-being measures in public policy. This meeting brought together leading academic and policy experts from the U.S. and U.K to explore research needs and practical challenges surrounding the integration of subjective well-being measures into policy planning and evaluation process of local and national governments and agencies. The NIA has further commissioned a National Academy of Sciences panel on development of nonmarket satellite National Accounts of Wellbeing. In addition, NIA, along with the National Center for Complementary and Alternative Medicine, is funding a series of research grants on both experienced and evaluative well-being.

Meanwhile, a rapidly developing literature continues to explore the relationship between economic growth and well-being, and this literature may turn out to have implications for regulatory policy and uses of cost-benefit analysis.[84] For example, a regulatory initiative may have effects on subjective well-being, or actual experience, that cost-benefit analysis does not fully capture. Consider, just for purposes of illustration, a few of many examples from the relevant literature:

- Contributing to the extensive literature on the relevance of relative (as opposed to absolute) economic position, Luttmer reports that higher earnings of neighbors are associated with lower levels of self-reported happiness, suggesting that subjective well-being may be partly a function of relative income.[85] Another study suggests that the impact of relative income levels matters more at higher levels of income.[86]
- Testing for the differences between experienced well-being and life satisfaction, Kahneman and Deaton analyze more than 450,000 responses to the Gallup-Healthways Well-Being Index, a daily survey of 1,000 US residents conducted by the Gallup Organization They find that income and education are more closely related to life satisfaction, but that health, care-giving, loneliness, and smoking are relatively stronger predictors of day-to-day emotions.[87]
- Biswas-Diener et al. compare subjective well-being measures from the U.S. and Denmark. They find that although the Danish claim higher life satisfaction, Americans are higher in both positive and negative affect; they are more "emotional." Their study also suggests that poor Danes are happier than their American counterparts.[88]
- Kahneman et al. use the Day Reconstruction Method in a study of women conducted concurrently during one day in Columbus, Ohio and Renne, France. The authors find that the specific sources from which the women draw happiness vary between the two cities, "reflecting differing cultural norms and social arrangements."[89]
- Examining changes over time in the United States and Britain, Blanchflower and Oswald find that in the last quarter-century, reported levels of well-being have declined in the United States and remained flat in Britain and are affected by such factors as relative income and age. They estimate the monetary values of events such as unemployment and divorce and find that both impose the welfare equivalent of large losses in monetary terms.[90]
- Expanding their investigation to 31 European countries, Blanchflower and Oswald examine data from the 2007 European Quality of Life Survey and find that the statistical structure of well-being in European nations looks "almost exactly the same as in the United States."[91] That is, the "same variables enter, and in almost identical ways." They conclude that, across nations, "[h]appy people are disproportionately the young and old (not middle-aged), rich, educated, married, in work, healthy, exercise- takers, with high fruit-and-vegetable diets, and slim."
- Responding to critics who claim that subjective well-being measures fail to provide valid measures of well-being, Oswald and Wu examine reported life satisfaction among a recent random sample of 1.3 million U.S. inhabitants. They observe a high (0.6) correlation across states between these measures of subjective well-being and objective quality-of-life rankings (calculated from, among other things, state indicators such as crime, air quality, taxes, and cost-of-living).[92] Oswald and Wu conclude that "subjective well-being data contain genuine information about the quality of human lives."
- Using African data collected from the Gallup World Poll and African Demographic and Healthy Surveys, Deaton et al. show that the death of an immediate family member has little effect on life evaluation, but a sizeable impact on measures of emotion, such as depression or sadness. They suggest that the amount of money

- necessary to compensate for the emotional effects of a death is larger than that required to compensate one's resulting life evaluation.[93]
- Harter and Arora investigate the relationship between hours worked and perceived job fit, and their impact on both life satisfaction and experienced measures of well-being.[94] Using data drawn from the Gallup World Poll, they find that perceived job fit was a robust predictor of life satisfaction across various regions, and increased in importance as the hours worked increased. This conclusion adds to prior studies, which show meaningful relationships between the subjective experience of work and objective outcomes, such as employee productivity and turnover.[95]
- Though a random-assignment experiment (supported by General Social Survey data), Ifcher and Zarghamee find that individuals in a happier mood are less likely to prefer present over future utility. In other words, compared to neutral affect, mild positive affect significantly decreases time preference over money.[96] According to the authors, one practical implication is that individuals may benefit from awareness that their mood affects their behavior. For example, a new employee may want to postpone pension plan contribution decisions until he or she is in a happy mood.
- Examining data collected from fifty-eight countries, Engelbrecht finds that natural capital per capita across those countries is correlated with subjective life-satisfaction measures, especially in high-income nations.[97] He concludes that debates about sustainable development – which often seek to ensure that future generations will have a similar level of wealth per capita available to them as current generations do – should incorporate subjective well-being measures.

OMB continues to investigate the relevant literature and to explore, in a preliminary way, its possible implications for improving regulatory policy in ways that promote the goals of economic growth, innovation, competitiveness, and job creation.

b. *Regulation and economic activity.* While identifying the appropriate measure of output is a difficult task, debate also continues about how to evaluate the impact of regulations on the standard indicators of economic activity. Exploration of that impact continues to be centrally important, as Executive Order 13563 makes clear. At the same time, regulatory impacts on economic growth may be difficult to demonstrate because of other simultaneous changes in the economy.

Many regulations affect economic growth indirectly through their effects on intermediate factors. There is a growing consensus specifying these intermediate drivers of growth, including increased human capital, capital investment, research and development, economic competition, physical infrastructure, and good governance.[98] Some evidence strongly suggests that regulations promoting educational attainment may improve human capital accumulation, thereby increasing economic growth.[99] Other studies show a positive link between increased life expectancy and growth.[100]

Regulations can also impose significant costs on businesses, dampening economic competition and capital investment. Djankov et. al. (2002) find that increased regulations on entry into markets—such as licensing and fees—create higher costs of entry and thus adversely affect economic outcomes.[101] By contrast, van Stel et. al. (2007) find that entry regulations actually have little impact on entrepreneurship, but that regulations creating greater labor rigidity have a discernible negative impact.[102]

Relatively few studies attempt to measure the economic impact of regulations in the aggregate; the literature focuses instead on particular regulatory arenas.[103] The literature examining the economic impact of environmental regulations in particular is extensive. Here are a few examples:[104]

- Jorgenson and Wilcoxen modeled dynamic simulations with and without environmental regulation on long-term growth in the US to assess the effects and reported that the long-term cost of regulation is a 2.59% reduction in Gross National Product.[105]
- Berman and Bui find that during a period of aggressive environmental regulation, productivity *increased* among the petroleum refineries located in the Los Angeles from 1987 to 1992, suggesting that "[a]batement costs may severely overstate the true cost of environmental regulation"[106] and that "abatement associated with the SCAQMD regulations was productivity enhancing."[107]
- Greenstone, List, and Syverson (2011) analyze plant-level production data to estimate the effects of environmental regulations on manufacturing plants' total factor productivity (TFP) levels. Using the Clean Air Act Amendments' division of counties into pollutant-specific nonattainment and attainment categories, they find that among surviving polluting plants, a nonattainment designation is associated with a roughly 2.6 percent decline in TFP.
- Gray and Shadbegian examine the investment activity of paper mills from 1979 to 1990,[108] and they find that "plants with relatively high pollution abatement capital expenditures over the period invest less in productive capital. The reduction in productive investment is greater than the increase in abatement investment, leading to lower total investment at high abatement cost plants. The magnitude of this impact is quite large, suggesting that a dollar of pollution abatement investment reduces productive investment by $1.88 at that plant. This seems to reflect both environmental investment crowing out productive investment within a plant, and firms shifting investment towards plants facing less stringent abatement requirements. Estimates placing less weight on within-firm reallocation of investment indicate approximate dollar-for-dollar ($0.99) crowding out of productive investment."[109]
- Becker and Henderson[110] find that in response to ground-level ozone regulation, in polluting industries the births of plants "fall dramatically in nonattainment counties, compared to attainment counties... This shift in birth patterns induces a reallocation of stocks of plants toward attainment areas. Depending on the interpretation of reduced- form coefficients, net present value for a typical new plant in a nonattainment area could fall by 13-22 percent."[111]
- Greenstone[112] finds that "in the first 15 years after the [Clean Air Act Amendments] became law (1972-1987, nonattainment counties (relative to attainment ones) lost approximately 590,000 jobs, $37 billion in capital stock and $75 billion (1987 dollars) of output in polluting industries."[113] However, Greenstone notes that these impacts remain modest in comparison to the size of the national manufacturing sector. Further, these results indicate statistically significant economic costs associated with carbon monoxide regulations, but not with ozone or sulfur dioxide regulations.

- List, et al., examined the effects of air quality regulation stringency and location decisions of new plants in New York State from 1980 to 1990, and found that regulatory stringency and the decision to locate is negatively correlated, and the current parametric estimates of this negative correlation may be understated.[114]
- As noted above, Hanna[115] finds that domestic environmental regulation has had an effect in increasing the outbound foreign direct investment of US-based multinational firms. The results include an increase in foreign investments in polluting industries by 5.3 percent and in foreign output by 9 percent; the results are concentrated in manufacturing.
- Jaffe and Palmer[116] find that increases in compliance costs generated by environmental regulations lead to a lagged effect of increases in research and development expenditures, as measured by patents of new environmental technologies. This corroborates other studies[117] with similar findings. These studies suggest that there may be positive economic effects related to technological innovation in the years following increased environmental regulatory compliance costs. As Jaffe and Palmer argue, "in the aggregate, the disincentives for R&D attributed to a command-and-control approach to environmental regulation may be overcome by the high returns that regulation creates for new pollution-control technology."[118] These results, however, are noted to be sensitive to the definitions of the time lag and difficulties in specifying research and development models, coding patent types, and linking research and development to overall economic growth.
- Chay and Greenstone[119] find that improvements in air quality induced by Clean Air Act regulations resulted in increased housing values at the county level between 1970 and 1980. This finding suggests possible economic gains in asset values resulting from improved environmental conditions, which may have had longer-term impacts on economic growth. Again, these overall impacts are difficult to quantify.
- Kahn examines census and state data and finds that better educated, wealthier populations experienced cleaner air, but that poorer, less educated populations experienced a greater overall improvement in air quality between 1980 and 1998 in California. During this time period, the exposure of the Hispanic population to pollution also fell sharply along with exposure differentials between richer and poorer people. The author concludes that, "[g]iven the overall trend in improvements for certain demographic groups, it appears that regulation under the Clean Air Act has helped, and not economically harmed, the 'have nots.'"[120]

Outside of the context of environmental regulation, a number of studies find that some regulations have promoted economic growth. For example, Carpenter (2009) finds that certain approaches to entry regulation – such as the discretionary approval regimes used by the Food and Drug Administration – can actually increase economic activity by establishing credible expectations of fairness and product safety.[121] Similarly, Greenstone et al. (2006) find that disclosure rules in the securities industry can reduce the adverse effects of informational asymmetries and increase market confidence. Their study finds that the 1964 Securities Act Amendments generated $3-6 billion of asset value for shareholders as a result of increased investment activity. According to their evidence, higher levels of investor protection and disclosure requirements are associated with the higher valuation of equities.[122]

Regulations aimed at managing risks can also have significant economic benefits by increasing the willingness of market actors to participate in market transactions.[123]

Another body of work focuses more specifically on behaviorally informed approaches to regulation, including setting appropriate default rules, using disclosure as a regulatory tool, improving framing, or making relevant information more salient. Such approaches might improve market functioning or reduce the economic costs associated with more aggressive regulatory efforts. Such work suggests that when examining the economic effects of regulation, analysts should be mindful of the importance of considering flexible regulatory approaches. Executive Order 13563 refers in particular to the importance of flexible approaches, stating that with relevant qualifications, "each agency shall identify and consider regulatory approaches that reduce burdens and that maintain flexibility and freedom of choice for the public." In some cases, carefully chosen forms of regulation may yield the same social benefits as existing regulatory approaches, while imposing lower costs. In other cases, well-designed regulatory approaches may actually improve market functioning, increase economic activity, and promote economic growth.[124]

OMB continues to investigate the underlying questions; no clear consensus has emerged on all of the answers. Further work of the sort outlined here might ultimately make it possible to connect regulatory initiatives to changes in GDP and also to changes in subjective well-being under various measures.

II: RECOMMENDATIONS FOR REFORM

Careful analysis of benefits and costs has long been designed to ensure that regulations are grounded in the best available evidence about their likely consequences. Such analysis can reduce the risk that decisions will be made on the basis of intuition, anecdote, or guesswork. Armed with such evidence, regulators will be in a position to increase benefits, reduce burdens, or both. Careful consideration of benefits and costs is especially important in a period of economic difficulty, in which regulatory safeguards must be designed so as to be consistent with the central goals of economic growth, innovation, job creation, and competitiveness. If a regulation would cost a great deal, it may well impose significant burdens on consumers and employees (including prospective employees). It is important to see that even if the immediate incidence of costs is imposed on companies, costly regulations do not merely burden some abstraction called "business"; the ultimate effects will frequently be felt by consumers and workers as well. (See the discussion above of the incidence of regulatory burdens.) Of course numerous regulations have significant social benefits as well.

As OMB Circular A-4 suggests, regulations often respond to conventional market failures, including asymmetric information, monopoly power, and negative externalities from production and consumption (such as pollution); regulations might also respond to problems of myopia and inertia and to difficulties in understanding risks. When properly designed and responsive to a market failure of one or another sort, regulations are likely to make society better off, in some cases as measured by GDP and in other cases as measured by a full accounting of social and economic effects, including those that may not be adequately measured by standard measures (see the discussion in the previous chapter).

Analysis of costs and benefits serves two important roles in this process.[125] First, it can inform the design and consideration of various options, so that relevant officials and members of the public are able to understand the opportunities for both minimizing the costs of achieving a social goal (cost-effectiveness) and maximizing net social benefits (efficiency). Analysis of costs and benefits may show, for example, that an alternative approach can achieve the social goal at lower cost; that an intuitively preferable approach, or one supported by particular groups or relevant anecdotes, actually has net costs; that an intuitively disfavored approach would actually produce benefits far in excess of costs; or that one of the alternatives has by far the highest net benefits. If so, the relevant analysis can help to reveal and to motivate the choice of the superior option. Second, such analysis can identify cases in which poorly defined regulatory choices might substitute government failure for market failure and impose net costs on society.

This analysis can inspire better solutions and new approaches by the executive branch or inform proposals for legislative reform.

The Regulatory Right-to-Know Act charges OMB with making "recommendations for reform." In its 2009 Report, OMB made three principal recommendations. First, OMB recommended consideration of behaviorally informed approaches to regulation. For example, properly designed disclosure policies, appropriate default rules (as in the context of retirement savings), and simplification (as in the context of the Free Application for Federal Student Aid) may have significant and beneficial results. Recent social science research, including work in behavioral economics, provides valuable insight into the design of effective, low-cost methods for achieving regulatory goals. In some contexts, small, inexpensive, seemingly modest steps can produce significant benefits.[126]

Second, OMB recommended that significant regulations should be accompanied with clear, tabular presentations of both benefits and costs, including both quantifiable and nonquantifiable variables; that analysis should take account, where relevant, of the effects of the regulation on future generations and the least well-off; and that continuing efforts should be made to meet some difficult challenges posed by regulatory impact analysis, including treatment of variables that are difficult to quantify and monetize. Third, OMB recommended that regulatory impact analysis should be seen and used as a central part of open government.

In its 2010 Report, OMB recommended four additional reforms that might improve regulatory policy and analysis. First, OMB identified several measures designed to meet analytical challenges, involving increased transparency. Second, OMB offered a brief discussion of disclosure as a regulatory tool, with particular emphasis on the need to attend to how people process information and on the importance of empirical testing of disclosure strategies.[127] Third, and with an emphasis on disclosure, OMB recommended exploration of certain low-cost approaches to the problem of childhood obesity; those approaches offer potential lessons for other programs and problems. Fourth, OMB drew on principles of open government to invite public suggestions about improvements in existing regulations, with particular reference to economic growth. With each of these recommendations, OMB offered concrete suggestions for possible improvements.

OMB continues to support the recommendations from its 2009 and 2010 reports. In recent years, significant progress has been made with respect to all of them. The 2010 report outlined some of that progress,[128] and in the recent past, far more has occurred, with particular emphasis on sensible disclosure strategies and on simplification. To offer a few examples:

- The U.S. Department of Agriculture (USDA) recently unveiled a new and far simpler food icon, *MyPlate*, to replace the *MyPyramid* image as the primary food group symbol. Responding to many complaints about the usefulness of the Food Pyramid, the Department described the new symbol as "an easy-to-understand" visual cue to help consumers adopt healthy eating habits."[129] One of the advantages of the symbol is that it has far more clarity, and far less ambiguity, than did the Food Pyramid in helping consumers to make healthy choices. In this respect, the new symbol responds to research suggesting that disclosure policies often work poorly when they leave people uncertain about what, exactly, they should act to avoid risks.
- EPA and DOT have issued a joint final rule entitled "Revisions and Additions to Motor Vehicle Fuel Economy Label," establishing new requirements for a fuel economy and environment label that will be posted on the window sticker of all new automobiles sold in the United States.[130] The principal goal of the new label is to provide, in clear form, relevant information about the effects of fuel economy – prominently including monetary savings and costs.

  Among other things, the labels provide (1) useful estimates of how much consumers will save or spend on fuel over the next five years with a particular car compared to the average new vehicle; (2) clear descriptions of annual fuel costs; (3) easy-to-read ratings of how a model compares to others for smog emissions and emissions of pollution that contribute to climate change; (4) estimates of how much fuel or electricity it takes to drive 100 miles; and (5) information on the driving range and charging time of an electric vehicle. One of the central advantages of the information on the new label is that it overcomes some of the limitations of the MPG measure, which is subject to the well-known "MPG illusion." The MPG illusion refers to the fact that many people think that the savings of greater fuel economy increase linearly with MPG, whereas far larger savings occur with increases from low MPG levels to somewhat higher ones than from high MPG levels to still higher ones.
- Illustrating how sensible default rules (including automatic enrollment) can simplify people's choices and have significant benefits, USDA recently issued an interim final rule entitled, "Direct Certification and Certification of Homeless, Migrant and Runaway Children for Free School Meals." Under this rule, children who are eligible for benefits under certain programs will be categorically eligible for free lunches and free breakfasts, thus reducing paperwork and increasing participation. As a result, as many as 270,000 additional children may qualify for meals.
- An agency checklist for regulatory impact analysis (see Appendix I), has been produced with the goal of promoting the link between careful analysis and open government. The checklist simplifies and clarifies the central requirements for such analysis.

Executive Order 13563 underlines and codifies several of the recent recommendations, with its emphasis on careful consideration of costs and benefits, on public participation, on measurement and improvement of "the actual results of regulatory requirements," and on use of flexible, freedom-preserving approaches (including appropriate default rules and disclosure) -- and also with its clear direction to each agency "to use the best available techniques to quantify anticipated present and future benefits and costs as accurately as possible." The Presidential Memorandum on Regulatory Compliance, attached as Appendix F, also emphasizes the importance of disclosure.

Our principal and most general recommendation in this Chapter is that, consistent with Executive Order 13563, regulatory decisions and priority-setting should be made in a way that is attentive to the importance of promoting economic growth, innovation, job creation, and competitiveness. The simplest method for achieving that goal is to continue to engage in careful analysis of both costs and benefits and as a general rule and to the extent permitted by law, to proceed only if the benefits justify the costs. To achieve that goal, it is important to ensure careful analysis in advance and also to explore the actual effects of significant rules now on the books, to see if their benefits justify their costs, and to explore whether they might be simplified, streamlined, or otherwise improved.

In the past two years, agencies and OMB have worked together to issue a number of rules for which the benefits exceed the costs, and by a large margin. Consider the following figure and tables:

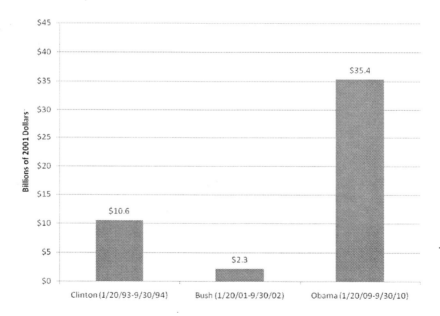

Figure 2-1. Annual Net Benefits of Major Rules through the Second Fiscal Year of an Administration[131].

Table 2-1. Annual Benefits and Costs of Major Rules through the Second Fiscal Year of an Administration (billions of 2001 dollars)[132]

Administration	Benefits	Costs
Obama (1/20/09-09/30/10)	$22.7 to $102.2	$8.2 to $16.5
Bush (1/20/01-09/30/02)	$1.9 to $7.4	$1.3 to $3.4
Clinton (1/20/93-09/30/94)	$5.8 to $24.9	$4.5 to $5.0

Table 2-2. Major Rules with the Highest Net Benefits through the Second Fiscal Year of the Obama Administration (billions of 2001 dollars) [133]

Agency	Rule	Net Benefits
EPA/AR	Review of the National Ambient Air Quality Standards for Sulphur Dioxide	$9.9
EPA/AR	NESHAP: Portland Cement Notice of Reconsideration	$9.4
DOT/ NHTSA & EPA/AR	Passenger Car and Light Truck Corporate Average Fuel Economy Standards MYs 2012 to 2016	$8.6
DOE/EE	Energy Efficiency Standards for General Service Fluorescent Lamps and Incandescent Lamps	$1.4
HHS/FDA	Prevention of Salmonella Enteritidis in Shell Eggs	$1.2

Table 2-3. Major Rules with the Highest Benefits through the Second Fiscal Year of the Obama Administration (billions of 2001 dollars) [134]

Agency	Rule	Benefits
DOT/NHTSA	Passenger Car and Light Truck Corporate Average Fuel Economy Standards MYs 2012 to 2016	$11.9
EPA/AR	Review of the National Ambient Air Quality Standards for Sulphur Dioxide	$10.5
EPA/AR	NESHAP: Portland Cement Notice of Reconsideration	$10.3
DOE/EE	Energy Efficiency Standards for General Service Fluorescent Lamps and Incandescent Lamps	$1.9
DOT/NHTSA	Passenger Car and Light Truck Corporate Average Fuel Economy Model Year 2011	$1.7

Table 2-4. Major Rules with the Highest Costs through the Second Fiscal Year of the Obama Administration (billions of 2001 dollars) [135]

Agency	Rule	Costs
DOT/NHTSA & EPA/AR	Passenger Car and Light Truck Corporate Average Fuel Economy Standards MYs 2012 to 2016	$3.3
DOE/EE	Energy Efficiency Standards for Pool Heaters and Direct Heating Equipment and Water Heaters	$1.1
DOT/NHTSA	Passenger Car and Light Truck Corporate Average Fuel Economy Model Year 2011	$1.0
DOT/NHTSA	Roof Crush Resistance	$0.9
EPA/AR	NESHAP: Portland Cement Notice of Reconsideration	$0.9

In the remainder of this Chapter, our main emphasis is on Executive Order 13563, which is designed to reconcile regulatory goals with objectives associated with economic growth in general and the economic recovery in particular. We also offer brief discussions of (1) three pressing analytic challenges; (2) e-rulemaking; and (3) regulatory cooperation.

A. Executive Order 13563

On January 18, 2011, President Obama issued Executive Order 13563, which emphasizes the importance of protecting "public health, safety and our environment while promoting economic growth, innovation, competitiveness, and job creation."[136] Executive Order 13563 explicitly points to the need for predictability and for certainty, and for use of the least burdensome tools for achieving regulatory ends. It indicates that agencies "must take into account benefits and costs, both quantitative and qualitative." As noted, it draws explicit attention to the need to measure and to improve "the actual results of regulatory requirements" – a clear reference to the importance of retrospective evaluation.

Executive 13563 reaffirms the principles, structures, and definitions in Executive Order 12866, which has long governed regulatory review. In addition, it endorses, and quotes, a number of provisions of that Executive Order that specifically emphasize the importance of considering costs. Importantly, Executive Order 13563 directs agencies "to use the best available techniques to quantify anticipated present and future benefits and costs as accurately as possible." This direction reflects a strong emphasis on quantitative analysis as a means of improving regulatory choices and increasing transparency.

Among other things, Executive Order 13563 elaborates five new sets of requirements to guide regulatory decisionmaking:

- *Public participation.* Agencies are directed to promote public participation, in part by making supporting documents available on Regulations.gov to promote transparency and public comment. In this way, Executive Order 13563 attempts to move rulemaking into the era of the Internet. It also directs agencies, where feasible and appropriate, to engage the public, including affected stakeholders, before rulemaking is initiated.
- *Integration and innovation.* Agencies are directed to attempt to reduce "redundant, inconsistent, or overlapping requirements," in part by working with one another to simplify and harmonize rules. This important provision is designed to reduce confusion, redundancy, and excessive cost. An important goal of simplification and harmonization is "to promote rather than to hamper innovation," which is a foundation of both growth and job creation. Different offices within the same agency might work together to harmonize their rules; different agencies might work together to achieve the same objective. Such steps can also promote predictability and certainty
- *Flexible approaches.* Agencies are directed to identify and consider flexible approaches to regulatory problems, including warnings, appropriate default rules, and disclosure requirements. Such approaches may "reduce burdens and maintain flexibility and freedom of choice for the public." In certain settings, they may be far preferable to mandates and bans, precisely because they maintain freedom of choice and reduce costs.[137] Consistent with the recommendations in previous Reports, and in particular the recommendation for use of empirically informed, freedom-preserving, low-cost tools, this provision emphasizes the importance of considering appropriate default rules and ensuring that disclosure is "clear and intelligible."
- *Science.* Agencies are directed to promote scientific integrity, and in a way that ensures a clear separation between judgments of science and judgments of policy.

- *Retrospective analysis of existing rules.* Agencies are directed to produce preliminary plans to engage in retrospective analysis of existing significant regulations to determine whether they should be modified, streamlined, expanded, or repealed. This provision, calling for careful evaluation of existing practices, fits closely with the suggestion in the first section of the Executive Order that our regulatory system "must measure, and seek to improve, the actual results of regulatory requirements."

Executive Order 13563 should be seen as addressing both the "flow" of new regulations and the "stock" of existing regulations. With respect to the flow, Executive Order 13563 emphasizes the importance of promoting predictability, of carefully considering costs, of choosing the least burdensome approach, and of selecting the most flexible, least costly tools.

With respect to the stock, Executive Order 13563 calls for careful reassessment, based on empirical analysis. It is understood that the purely prospective analysis required by Executive Order 13563 may depend on a degree of speculation and that both costs and benefits may be lower or higher than what was anticipated. After retrospective analysis has been undertaken, agencies will be in a position to reconsider existing rules and to streamline, modify, or eliminate those that do not make sense in their current form.

Retrospective analysis has long been recommended by informed observers. Consider this suggestion from Professor Michael Greenstone (recently Chief Economist at the Council of Economic Advisers): "The single greatest problem with the current system is that most regulations are subject to a cost-benefit analysis only in advance of their implementation. This is the point when the least is known and any analysis must rest on many unverifiable and potentially controversial assumptions."[138] By contrast, retrospective analysis can help show what works and what does not, and in the process can help to promote repeal or streamlining of less effective rules and strengthening or expansion of those that turn out to do more good than harm. Greenstone thus urges a series of reforms designed to "instill a culture of experimentation and evaluation."[139] These reforms include an effort to ensure that regulations are written and implemented in ways that lend themselves to experimental evaluation and creation of independent review to assess the effectiveness of regulations.

One of Greenstone's principal themes involves the importance of experimentation with respect to the likely effects of regulation. Such experimentation can take place in advance. It might, where feasible and consistent with law, take the form of advance testing of regulatory alternatives, perhaps through pilot projects or randomized controlled trials, followed by study of their consequences.[140] Pilot projects and randomized experiments may well provide valuable information about what interventions are likely to be most useful.

For example, the Department of Transportation's National Highway Traffic Safety Administration has initiated distracted driving demonstration programs in two communities to test whether a high visibility enforcement (HVE) model could reduce two specific instances of distracted driving – talking or texting using a hand-held cell phone.[141] Syracuse, New York, and Hartford, Connecticut, (a combination of three contiguous cities – East Hartford, Hartford, and West Hartford) conducted the demonstrations. Before and after each enforcement wave, NHTSA conducted observations of driver cell phone use and collected public awareness surveys at driver licensing offices in each test and comparison site.

According to early analysis, observed cell phone use decreased at both sites by the end of the second wave of the NHTSA's program. Before the distracted driving programs began, observed cell phone use in Syracuse was about half that of the rest of the Nation and

Connecticut was close to average.[142] After the second wave of the high visibility enforcement campaign, hand-held cell phone use decreased 38% in Syracuse (from 3.7% to 2.3%) and 58% in Hartford (from 6.8% to 3.1%).

Consistent with Executive Order 13563, we recommend that agencies create long-term structures and processes for analyzing the actual effects of significant rules, with special attention to those that are most expensive or burdensome. OIRA is now working closely with agencies to promote compliance with the retrospective analysis requirements of Executive Order 13563. The preliminary plans for retrospective review, released on May 26, 2011, demonstrate that the relevant process is well under way. In those plans, agencies identify hundreds of possible reforms, with immediate savings in the hundreds of millions of dollars and with potential savings in the billions of dollars.[143] Notably, many of the ideas on the plans are a product of public input, following a request for comments on potential reforms.

To offer just a few examples:

- The Occupational Safety and Health Administration (OSHA) issued a final rule that will remove over 1.9 million annual hours of redundant reporting burdens on employers and save more than $40 million in annual costs.[144]
- Since the 1970s, milk has been defined as an "oil" and subject to costly rules designed to prevent oil spills. In response to objections from the agriculture community and the President's directive, EPA concluded that the rules placed unjustifiable burdens on dairy farmers and exempted them. The projected annual savings are $140 million.[145]
- OSHA plans to finalize a proposed rule projected to result in an annualized $585 million in estimated savings for employers. This rule would harmonize U.S. hazard classifications and labels with those of a number of other nations by requiring the adoption of standardized terms.[146]
- To eliminate unjustified economic burdens on railroads, the Department of Transportation is reconsidering parts of a rule that requires railroads to install equipment on trains. DOT expects initial savings of up to $400 million, with total 20 year savings of up to $1 billion.[147]
- The Environmental Protection Agency will propose to eliminate the obligation for many states to require air pollution vapor recovery systems at local gas stations, on the ground that modern vehicles already have effective air pollution control technologies. The anticipated annual savings are about $67 million.[148]
- The Departments of Commerce and State are undertaking a series of steps to eliminate unnecessary barriers to exports, including duplicative and unnecessary regulatory requirements, thus reducing the cumulative burden and uncertainty faced by American companies and their trading partners.[149]
- To reduce administrative burdens and increase certainty, the Department of the Interior is reviewing outdated regulations under the Endangered Species Act to streamline the process, to reduce requirements for written descriptions, and to clarify and expedite procedures for approval of conservation agreements.[150]
- To promote flexibility, the Department of Health and Human Services will be reconsidering burdensome regulatory requirements now placed on hospitals and

doctors, to ask whether these requirements are redundant and whether they really benefit patients.[151]

To create a process of retrospective analysis, and a continuing culture of both prospective and retrospective evaluation, OMB recommends that agencies use the best available techniques to assess the consequences of regulation, both as part of retrospective review and in the initial design of rules. As we have noted, a possible approach involves randomized controlled trials, in which regulatory initiatives are used in some domains but not in similarly situated others, thus allowing a careful analysis of their effects.[152] Of course there are constraints – involving law, resources, and feasibility – in using randomized control trials in the regulatory context, but in some cases, they may be both appropriate and highly useful.

The preliminary plans offer relevant discussion. For example, DHS states that it will "build in retrospective review at the earliest stages of regulatory development."[153] Its plan calls for the Department's component agencies to "incorporate a discussion of retrospective analysis goals into their rulemaking project planning" in order "to ensure that the component considers retrospective analysis through the lifespan of the regulation."[154] The Department of Labor provides that it "is contemplating how to incorporate the use of experimental designs to determine the impact of various regulations."[155] The Department of Interior states that it "will consider" the use of "experimental or quasi-experimental designs, including randomized controlled trials."[156] Similarly, the Department of Treasury states that it will work to "develop and incorporate experimental designs into retrospective analysis, when appropriate."[157]

More generally, retrospective review of regulations should be conducted so as to provide a transparent and credible process for evaluating both costs and benefits. Agencies might, for example, announce in advance that they are conducting a retrospective evaluation; they might specify the measures of costs and benefits that they will use; they might work with outside experts to promote objectivity. Disclosure policies are an obvious candidate for such evaluations. Consistent with the goals of open government, agencies might post the materials that underlie and follow the analysis so as to promote assessment and scrutiny by others.

The larger point is that the retrospective analysis required by Executive Order 13563 should by no means be regarded as a one-shot endeavor. It should be seen as an effort to produce a consistent culture of experimentation and reassessment and careful, objective evaluation of existing requirements.

It is worth observing that there is an incipient literature on the practice of regulatory "look back." A recent study by Harrington, building on previous work, explores 61 rules for which benefit-cost ratios could be compared ex ante and ex post.[158] The author identifies various reasons that agency and OMB estimates could leave some benefits and costs uncounted.[159] For the 61 rules analyzed, he finds that both benefits and costs were overestimated "with about equal frequency."[160] Specifically, in sixteen of the cases, the ratios were found to be accurate (plus or minus 25%).[161] In twenty-four cases, the rules showed a better benefit-cost ratio than anticipated. In twenty-one cases, the rules showed a worse benefit-cost ratio than anticipated. Harrington's general conclusion is that while both costs and benefits turn out to be lower than prospective estimates, there is "no bias in estimates of benefit-cost ratios."[162]

While Harrington focuses on benefit-cost ratios (and does not specify the degree to which these costs or benefits were separately misestimated), he refers to other studies that offer more disaggregated evaluations, at least of regulatory costs. One study, for example, compares ex post costs to ex ante estimates for eleven energy efficiency standards for household appliances issued between 1982 and 1995.[163] Of those, the researchers found that ex ante costs were overestimated for five of the rules and accurate for the remaining six (using the same 25% range).[164] Another study analyzed 25 environmental and occupational safety regulations for which ex post data could be located. It found that total costs were overestimated for twelve rules; accurate in five; underestimated in two; and indeterminate for six.[165] The authors argue that the overestimation of total costs were often due to errors in the quantity of emission reductions achieved, driven by both baseline and compliance issues.

A study by the Office of Technology Assessment examined six regulations of the Occupational Safety and Health Administration (OSHA) and found that four rules had lower actual compliance costs than anticipated, while two were "reasonably" accurate. Overall, the report concluded that "the actual compliance response that was observed included advanced or innovative control measures that had not been emphasized in the rulemaking analyses, and the actual cost burden proved to be considerably less than what OSHA had estimated."[166]

In its 2005 Report, OMB provided an overview of various retrospective analyses, based on an examination of 47 case studies.[167] There were three key conclusions. First, agencies accurately estimated benefits over one-third of the time, and they were more likely to overestimate benefits than to underestimate them.[168] More particularly, agencies overestimated benefits 40% of the time, whereas they underestimated benefits only 2% of the time. Second, agencies tended to overestimate the benefit-cost ratio; agency estimates were accurate 23% of the time, while the ratio was overestimated 47% of the time and underestimated 30% of the time. Third, agencies were slightly more likely to overestimate than to underestimate costs; agencies were accurate 26% of the time, overestimated 34% of the time, and underestimated 26% of the time. At least from this study, it does not appear correct to conclude that agencies have systematically underestimated the ratio of benefits to costs, or that the benefits of rules usually turn out to be higher than anticipated.

Consistent with Executive Order 13563, we believe that a great deal more should be done to improve prospective analysis through empirical research, to compare prospective to retrospective estimates, to improve prospective analysis accordingly, and to streamline, expand, modify, or repeal regulations in accordance with what was been learned. There are many opportunities for undertaking and improving retrospective analysis. As part of the effort to promote transparency by sharing more data online, agencies could enable external experts to undertake ex post analyses of the benefits and costs of regulations. For example, a number of agencies have external boards of technical experts. These boards could be asked to provide guidance to the regulatory agencies on how they should collect, compile, and post online data that would enable non-governmental experts to estimate the realized benefits and costs of regulations. This information could be organized and presented so as to facilitate full benefit-cost analyses where feasible, and where not feasible, to generate appropriate measures of cost-effectiveness.

We have previously observed that on January 18, 2011, President Obama signed a memorandum emphasizing agency obligations under the Regulatory Flexibility Act.[169] Drawing attention to the job-creating function of small businesses, and their centrality to economic growth, the Memorandum asks agencies to justify any decision not to provide flexibility for small business – in the form, for example, of delayed compliance dates and partial or total exemptions. A central goal of this Memorandum is to direct agencies to pursue regulatory objectives with careful attention to the risk of imposing excessive or unjustified burdens on small businesses.

B. Improving Analysis

With its emphasis on accounting for both costs and benefits and for minimizing costs, Executive Order 13563 stresses the need for sound analysis. OMB Circular A-4 continues to provide governing principles.[170] The "Agency Checklist for Regulatory Impact Analysis," issued on November 3, 2010, and provided as an appendix to this Report, briefly summarizes the central requirements.[171] Executive Order 13563 explicitly highlights the importance of quantification of both costs and benefits and of using the best available techniques for increasing accuracy. We briefly discuss several issues here.

1. Quantification, nonquantifiable variables, and breakeven analysis

a. Quantification and its limits

A significant goal of Executive Order 13563 is to promote quantification of both benefits and costs and to ensure, to the extent permitted by law, that agencies proceed only after a reasoned determination that the benefits justify the costs. To that end, Section 1(c) states, "each agency is directed to use the best available techniques to quantify anticipated present and future benefits and costs as accurately as possible." Past practice suggests that quantification of the central benefits and costs is often possible and that such quantification permits a reasoned judgment about the approach that maximizes net benefits. But the same section adds, "Where appropriate and permitted by law, each agency may consider (and discuss qualitatively) values that are difficult or impossible to quantify, including equity, human dignity, fairness, and distributive impacts."

It should be clear that such values, where relevant, come in different (if sometimes overlapping) categories.

- The issue may involve *specifying the magnitude of relevant effects*. An agency may know, for example, that a rule will reduce the risk of a terrorist attack, but it may not be able to quantify the reduction and thus be unable to convey the extent of the reduced risk. Alternatively, a technology-based rule may inhibit innovation and impose unknowably higher costs than an equivalent performance-based rule. The direction of an effect may be clear, but the magnitude may be difficult or impossible to specify.
- The issue may involve *monetization*. An agency may know, for example, that a particular rule will have a beneficial effect on ecosystems and likely will preserve a known number of a certain species of fish, but it might not be able to translate that effect into monetary equivalents.
- A rule may have significant beneficial or adverse *distributional effects on lower income groups*. Those effects may or may not themselves be quantifiable; perhaps the agency is aware that poor people will be particularly affected, but perhaps it is

unable to say to what degree. Even when quantification of the relevant effects is possible, they are not easily used as part of a standard analysis of costs and benefits.

- A rule might be designed to protect *human dignity*. It might, for example, reduce the incidence of rape, or allow wheelchair-bound employees to have easier access to bathrooms. Alternatively, an adverse effect on human dignity may be an unintended cost of a rule. For example, a security rule might involve body searches or scans that some might consider to be an invasion of dignity or privacy.
- A rule might be designed to protect *fairness*. It might, for example, prohibit discrimination on the basis of sexual orientation with respect to certain government benefits, or it might ban sexual harassment.
- A rule might be designed to protect *equity*. It might, for example, prohibit insurance companies from declining health insurance to children with preexisting conditions.

An effect might, of course, fall in more than one category. For example, the line between "fairness" and "equity" is not always simple or sharp. A rule that is meant to protect lower income groups may have relevant distributive impacts; it might also be an effort to promote equity. A rule that forbids deception may have a standard economic justification as well as a justification in terms of equity. A rule may also have nonquantifiable effects that run counter to each other. For example, a rule that is intended to promote fairness of a certain kind may have adverse economic consequences for lower-income individuals.[172]

b. Transparency

It is not always easy to decide how to treat variables of this kind as part of the analysis required by Executive Orders 13563 and 12866. The appropriate initial step is to promote transparency. OMB has previously recommended that the best practice is to accompany all significant regulations with (1) a tabular presentation, placed prominently and offering a clear statement of qualitative and quantitative benefits and costs of the proposed or planned action, together with (2) a presentation of uncertainties and (3) similar information for reasonable alternatives to the proposed or planned action.[173]

A key advantage of this approach is that it promotes transparency for the public. If, for example, it is possible to quantify certain benefits (such as protection of water quality) but not to monetize them, then the public should be made aware of that fact. At the same time, qualitative discussion of nonquantifiable benefits and costs should help the public, and relevant decisionmakers, to understand the goal of the regulation and how it might achieve that goal.

The focus on transparency should help in the implementation of Section 1(c) of Executive Order 13563. Suppose, for example, that a regulation will have especially high benefits for lower income groups, or will impose especially high costs on them. It may be appropriate for agencies to offer such information in connection with proposed or final rules. And if a rule would promote human dignity – by reducing the incidence of sexual violence or by increasing the independence of disabled people – and if that effect is relevant under existing law, agencies should so state.

Executive Order 13563, echoing Executive Order 12866, specifically states that agencies must "select, in choosing among alternative regulatory approaches, those approaches that maximize net benefits (including potential economic, environmental, public health and safety, and other advantages; *distributive impacts; and equity*)" (emphasis added). In assessing the approach that maximizes net benefits, quantified benefits and quantified costs are generally the relevant variables. But in some cases, the benefits and costs of a rule may include distributive impacts, fairness, equity, and dignity; agencies are entitled to refer to that fact and to consider the relevant effects.

c. Prioritization and breakeven analysis

Transparency is important, but even when it exists, agencies face serious challenges in resolving the question when and how to proceed when important effects cannot be quantified. We have noted that in some cases, various effects can be quantified even if they cannot be monetized. We have also noted that distributional effects can sometimes be quantified even if they are not part of standard analysis of costs and benefits.

For agencies to know how to weigh the relevant values, the governing law is crucial, and it is important for agencies to try to evaluate and rank such values to give a sense of their relative significance. In terms of the relevant values, a rule may have significant benefits or relatively small ones. For example, a water pollution rule might cover a large or small number of ecosystems, and those systems may or may not be ecologically significant. To the extent feasible, and with close reference to governing law, agencies should give a sense of the relative magnitude and importance of nonquantifiable variables.

When quantification and monetization are not possible, many agencies have found it both useful and informative to engage in "breakeven analysis." Under this approach, agencies specify how high the unquantified or unmonetized benefits would have to be in order for the benefits to justify the costs. Suppose, for example, that a regulation that protects water quality costs $105 million annually, and that it also has significant effects in reducing pollution in rivers and streams. It is clear that the regulation would be justified if and only if those effects could reasonably be valued at $105 million or more. Once the nature and extent of the water quality benefits are understood, it might well be easy to see whether or not the benefits plausibly justify the costs – and if the question is difficult, at least it would be clear why it is difficult. Breakeven analysis is an important tool, and it has analytical value when quantification is speculative or impossible.

Executive Order 13563 places a strong emphasis on quantification, and it is hoped that it will be increasingly possible to use improving available techniques both to quantify and to monetize relevant variables. But where this is not possible, breakeven analysis can help to produce both transparency and informed judgment. We also recommend that to the extent feasible, agencies make efforts to rank and prioritize nonquantifiable variables, so that such variables can be properly evaluated and used to supplement and inform judgment, and not as a freestanding, ex post justification of rules.

2. Cost-per-life-saved of Health and Safety Regulation

For regulations intended to reduce mortality risks, an important analytic tool that can be used to assess regulations, and to help avoid unjustified burdens, is cost-effectiveness analysis. Some agencies develop estimates of the "net cost per life saved" for regulations intended to improve public health and safety. To calculate this figure, the costs of the rule minus any monetized benefits other than mortality reduction are placed in the numerator, and the expected reduction in mortality in terms of total number of lives saved is placed in the denominator. This measure avoids any assignment of monetary values to reductions in mortality risk. It does reflects, however, a concern for economic efficiency, insofar as choosing a regulatory option that reduces a particular mortality risk at a lower net cost to society would conserve scarce resources compared to choosing an option that would reduce the same risk at greater net cost.

Table 2-5 presents the net cost per life saved for twelve recent health and safety rules for which calculation is possible. The net cost per life saved is calculated using a 3 percent discount rate and using the agencies' best estimates for costs and expected mortality reduction. As is apparent, there is substantial variation in the net cost per life saved by these rules.

This table is designed to be illustrative rather than definitive, and continuing work must be done to ensure that estimates of this kind are complete and not misleading. For example, some mortality-reducing rules have a range of other benefits, including reductions in morbidity, and it is important to include these benefits in cost-effectiveness analysis. Other rules have benefits that are exceedingly difficult to quantify but nonetheless essential to consider; consider rules that improve water quality or have aesthetic benefits. Nonetheless, it is clear that some rules are far more cost-effective than others, and it is valuable to take steps to catalogue variations and to increase the likelihood that scarce resources will be used as effectively as possible.

In evaluating cost-effectiveness, it is important to note that OMB Circular A-4 observes that the majority of estimates of a value of a statistical life (VSL) fall within a $1 million-$10 million range,[174] and that agency practice generally falls within the upper half of that range.[175] While considerable progress has been made since 2000, and while some analysts believe that significant narrowing has occurred, the literature has not "settled" on any single number. There are, however, recent accounts of the appropriate range. That range includes estimates in the vicinity of $8.86 million from what may well be the most influential meta-analysis,[176] as well as $6.84 million and $6.4 million (all in 2010 dollars) from two other recent meta-analyses.[177] It is generally agreed, of course, that numbers should be updated for annual income growth. The relevant numbers should be taken into account when considering cost-effectiveness analysis.

Our emphasis on this section is on decreased mortality rates, but we note that some observers[178] have suggested the importance of analyzing and reporting lost life expectancy. Commentators have noted the possibility that for some rules, measures of decreased mortality rates may well capture cases in which people have died a few days or a few weeks before they would have in the absence of regulatory controls. OMB Circular A-4 authorizes the use of lost life-years as one way of analyzing the effects of regulation.

3. *Private vs. social benefits and losses*

As emphasized by OMB Circular A-4, a standard argument for regulation of private markets points to social benefits that cannot readily be produced by such markets. For example, firms may fail to internalize the health damages caused by the air pollution that they emit. Many regulations provide such social benefits. Insofar as they reduce air pollution, fuel economy rules and energy efficiency rules are examples.

Table 2-5. Estimates of the Net Costs per Life Saved of Selected Health and Safety Rules Reviewed by OMB in Fiscal Year 2009-2010 (millions of 2001 dollars)

Agency	Rule	Net Cost per Life Saved	Notes
HHS/FDA	Prevention of Salmonella Enteritidis in Shell Eggs	Negative	Morbidity benefits exceed costs.
DOL/OSHA	Cranes and Derricks in Construction	$4.9	The agency estimates that the rule will prevent 22 fatalities and 175 nonfatal injuries annually. Total costs associated with the rule are $150 million annually at 3%. The monetized value of the injuries prevented is $11 million and the property damage prevented is valued at $7 million. If we subtract the injury and property benefits from costs, the net cost per life saved is thus approximately $6 million (2010 dollars). Adjusting to 2001 dollars yields roughly $5 million.
DOT/FMCSA	New Entrant Safety Assurance Process	Negative	Property damage and morbidity benefits exceed costs.
DOT/FRA	Positive Train Control	$235.1	The agency estimates the present value of fatality reduction benefits is $267 million over 20 years using a VSL of $6 million, implying the prevention of approximately 3 fatalities per year. The agency also estimates the total non-fatality related benefits over 20 years of $407 million implying annual value of $27.3 million. Total costs associated with the rule are $880 million annually. If we subtract the non-fatality related benefits from costs, the net cost per life saved is roughly $284.2 million in 2009 dollars. Adjusting to 2001 dollars yields $235.1 million per life saved.
DOT/NHTSA	Reduced Stopping Distance Requirements for Truck Tractors	Negative	Property damage benefits exceed costs.
DOT/NHTSA	Roof Crush Resistance	$6.4 to $11.0	The agency estimates that the rule will prevent 135 fatalities and 1065 nonfatal injuries annually. These figures translate into 156 equivalent fatalities. The main estimates value equivalent fatalities prevented at $6.1 million. It follows that the value of nonfatal injuries prevented is $6.1 million* (156 - 135) = $128.1 million annually. Total costs associated with the rule range from $875 million to $1400 million annually. If we subtract the injury benefits from costs, the range of net cost

Agency	Rule	Net Cost per Life Saved	Notes
DOT/ PHMSA	Pipeline Safety: Distribution Integrity Management	Negative	Benefits from reduced injuries, reduced property damages, and reduced lost gas exceeds costs. per life saved is thus $5.5 million to $9.4 million (2007 dollars). Adjusting to $2001 yields $6.4 million to $11.0 million.
EPA/ AR	NESHAP: Portland Cement Notice of Reconsideration	Negative	Morbidity benefits exceed costs.
EPA/ AR	Review of the National Ambient Air Quality Standards for Sulphur Dioxide	Negative	Morbidity benefits exceed costs.
EPA/AR	National Emission Standards for Hazardous Air Pollutants for Reciprocating Internal Combustion Engines (Diesel)	$0.9 to $2.2	The agency estimates that the rule will prevent 110 to 270 fatalities annually. Total costs associated with the rule are $355 million annually at 3%. The monetized value of the morbidity benefits is $66 million. If we subtract the morbidity benefits from costs, the net cost per life saved is approximately $1.1 $2.2 million (2008 dollars). Adjusting to 2001 dollars yields roughly $0.9 million to $2.2 million.
EPA/ AR	National Emission Standards for Hazardous Air Pollutants for Reciprocating Internal Combustion Engines-- Existing Stationary Spark Ignition (Gas- Fired)	$1.2 to $1.5	The agency estimates that the rule will prevent 56 to 140 fatalities in 2013. Total costs associated with the rule are $244 million annually at 3%. The monetized value of the morbidity benefits is $36 million. If we subtract the morbidity benefits from costs, the net cost per life saved is approximately $1.5- $3.1 million (2008 dollars). Adjusting to 2001 dollars yields roughly $1.2 million to $1.5 million.
EPA/ OPPTS	Lead; Amendment to the Opt-out and Recordkeeping Provisions in the Renovation, Repair, and Painting Program	Negative	Morbidity benefits exceed costs.

Such rules also provide private benefits. They may increase the cost of products at the point of purchase, but also reduce costs on balance by, for example, reducing the cost of operating a vehicle. In principle and sometimes in practice, the resulting benefits to consumers are substantial. In some cases, the economic benefits to consumers far exceed the costs of the relevant rule.

As agencies have recognized, however, the existence of such "private benefits" creates certain puzzles, at least on standard economic assumptions. If consumers are informed, they should, on those assumptions, seek and purchase the relevant products, simply because it is in their economic interest to do so. And to the extent that this is so, regulations that require products to have increased levels of (say) energy efficiency may cause consumers to purchase products that they have knowingly rejected. In this case, there is at least a question whether it is appropriate to count fuel or energy savings as a benefit. Such regulations may also reduce consumer welfare by causing individuals to purchase products that they would otherwise reject. For example, such products may lack features that consumers prefer, or may have features that consumers do not like, in which case the regulations impose a welfare loss that should be counted in the overall assessment. If regulations that produce economic savings through energy efficiency also produce a loss to consumer welfare, that loss should be taken into account in the analysis.

A departure from the standard economic analysis of these problems is appropriate when consumers lack relevant information or suffer from some kind of bias at the time of decision. It is possible, for example, that energy efficiency, and the savings from energy efficient products, are not sufficiently clear or salient to consumers at the time of purchase; a literature on "shrouded attributes" explores this possibility.[179] It is also possible that consumers are focusing unduly on the short-term and that they do not take sufficient account of long-term gains. And indeed, a growing literature, focusing on the Energy Paradox,[180] attempts to explain why consumers are not purchasing certain goods even though it is in their economic interest to do so. To the extent that a lack of information or a relevant bias accounts for consumer behavior, it is appropriate to include private savings as a benefit, and there may be little or no accompanying consumer welfare loss.

The empirical literature on this topic, while suggestive, remains in its preliminary stages. We recommend continued exploration of these issues, with particular attention to the circumstances in which a lack of information and potential errors or biases on the part of consumers are likely to support regulatory interventions and to justify an accounting of private savings. We also recommend that agencies should clearly separate social and private savings in their Regulatory Impact Analyses, and that when private savings are included, agencies should give careful attention to the conceptual and empirical issues.

C. E-Rulemaking: Improving the Regulatory Process

Under Executive Order 13563, agencies are directed to promote public participation and in particular to provide the public with "timely online access to the rulemaking docket on Regulations.gov, including relevant scientific and technical findings, in an open format that can be easily searched and downloaded." OIRA remains committed to using technology to improve transparency and to increase public participation in the regulatory process. Among other things, OIRA has issued a series of memoranda to provide agencies with practical guidance for improving access to regulatory actions and their supporting justifications. These memoranda should be seen as a beginning of more ambitious efforts, consistent with Executive Order 13563, to promote understanding of and participation in rulemaking, with the ultimate goal of improving the substance of rules through tapping the diverse perspectives and dispersed knowledge of the American people.

- In April 2010, OMB published "Increasing Openness in the Rulemaking Process – Use of the Regulation Identifier Number (RIN), " a memorandum that aims to promote greater openness by requiring Federal agencies to use the Regulation Identifier Number (RIN) on all relevant documents throughout the entire "lifecycle" of a rulemaking.[181] By using the RIN as the key identifier on all related docket materials, the government will be better able to use technology to assemble electronic dockets and will help the public to have easier and more comprehensive access to regulatory information.
- In May 2010, OMB published "Increasing Openness in the Rulemaking Process – Improving Electronic Dockets," to improve public access to regulatory information by requiring Federal agencies to compile and maintain comprehensive electronic regulatory dockets on Regulations.gov.[182] This memorandum states that to the extent that they are part of rulemaking, supporting materials (such as notices, significant guidance documents, environmental impact statements, regulatory impact analyses, and information collections) should be made available during the notice-and-comment period by being uploaded and posted as part of the electronic docket. These materials should be in machine-readable format to enable the public to perform full-text searches of the documents and to extract information. (This memorandum is consistent with Executive Order 13563, which specifically emphasizes the importance of providing the public with relevant information, including scientific and technical findings, on Regulations.gov, with an opportunity for comment.)
- In November 2010, OIRA worked with the eRulemaking Program Management Office (PMO) and Federal agencies to publish a best practices document, titled "Improving Electronic Dockets on Regulations.gov and the Federal Docket Management System – Best Practices for Federal Agencies." The document outlines strategic goals and best practices to improve agency use of the Federal Docket Management System (FDMS) and Regulations.gov. The document also seeks to establish a common taxonomy and adoption of data protocols for the various rulemaking and non-rulemaking docket and document types.[183]

The two memoranda and the best practices document establish a new commitment to improving the public's ability to find regulatory documents and inclusive docket information— thus promoting public participation in the Federal regulatory process and collaboration between the Federal agencies and the public. Efforts to measure compliance with these initiatives continue. An ultimate goal of this emphasis on participation is to improve the content of rules by bringing diverse perspectives to bear. In his Memorandum on Open Government, President Obama noted, "Knowledge is widely dispersed in society, and public officials benefit from having access to that dispersed knowledge." A central purpose of increased participation is to tap that widely dispersed knowledge in the rulemaking process.

If, for example, a proposal would create special hardships for small business, or deliver important benefits to disadvantaged groups, it is important for officials to obtain that information.

OIRA's work with the Regulatory Information Service Center (RISC) has also led to many recent enhancements to Reginfo.gov, a website that displays regulatory actions and information collections currently at OIRA for review. In February 2010, RISC launched an OIRA "dashboard" and redesigned Reginfo.gov. The OIRA dashboard uses an interactive display to present information about rulemakings under review and allows the public to sort rules by agency, length of review, stage of rulemaking, and economic significance. During the 2010 calendar year, Reginfo.gov received a cumulative total of nearly one million page views; since the addition of the OIRA dashboard, the website has seen a 28 percent increase in the number of site visitors, totaling 169,549 visitors.[184]

As a result of recent improvements, Regulations.gov provides the public with easier access to regulatory documents and the regulatory process. The improvements include the ability to conduct searches within a docket, a regulatory topics index, and posting of public comments, as well as a link to helpful videos on the YouTube channel and other sites.[185] In May 2009, and again in January 2010, the eRulemaking PMO launched Regulations.gov/ Exchange, an on-line forum to promote interaction with the public and to foster open dialogue among all users, including industry, public interest groups, trade associations, and state and local governmental entities. During the 2010 calendar year, Regulations.gov received a cumulative total of 123 million page views; since the addition of these new site features and functions, the site has seen a 31 percent increase in the number of site visitors, totaling 190 million. The site also received approximately 306,000 web form comments in 2010.[186]

OMB continues to support these and other efforts to use technological advances to facilitate transparency and increase public participation in the regulatory process. We recommend continued efforts to improve them, with the central goal of improving the understanding and substance of rules.

D. Regulatory Cooperation

In the current economic climate, and consistent with the President's emphasis on promoting exports, the Administration recognizes the importance of increased trade and exports to economic growth, job creation, entrepreneurship, and innovation. To promote those goals, OIRA is participating in a number of regulatory cooperation initiatives with key trading partners. For example:

- Since 2005, OIRA has co-chaired the European Commission-United States High-Level Regulatory Cooperation Forum, which reports to the Cabinet-level Transatlantic Economic Council.
- In May 2010, President Obama and Mexican President Felipe Calderón established a High-Level Regulatory Cooperation Council, which is also co chaired by OIRA and is comprised of senior-level regulatory, trade, and foreign affairs officials from the U.S. and Mexico.
- On February 4, 2011, President Obama and Prime Minister Harper announced the creation of a Regulatory Cooperation Council, which is also co-chaired by OIRA and

is comprised of senior-level regulatory, trade, and foreign affairs officials from the U.S. and Canada.

These and other collaborative efforts are focused, in significant part, on promoting exports and on discouraging and addressing unnecessary or unjustified restrictions on trade. In addition, such efforts are focused, where feasible and appropriate, on bridging current areas of divergence among relevant regulators, as well as preventing unjustified or harmful divergences from occurring in emerging areas of regulation. Because of the importance of promoting trade and exports, we recommend that serious consideration should be given to preventing such unjustified divergences.

In this regard, OIRA recognizes that an adverse impact on trade is possible when countries apply different standards or technical requirements to address common environmental, health, safety, or other concerns. In some cases, such divergences can lead to additional costs and burdens on U.S. suppliers, particularly small and medium-sized enterprises (SMEs), and, in some cases, can make it difficult or impossible for U.S. suppliers to penetrate foreign markets. Such divergences can also increase regulatory burdens for governments and costs for consumers.

Cooperative efforts—including regulator-to-regulator dialogue, information exchange, mutual recognition arrangements, and similar initiatives—could have significant domestic benefits, including increasing the safety and quality of other countries' exports to the U.S. and thus helping to protect U.S. consumers. Regulatory cooperation can also help lower costs and burdens for businesses (especially SMEs), as well as for governments and consumers, and stimulate U.S. exports, which can promote job creation and economic growth. When regulators in different countries share data, studies, and other information on specific regulatory issues, they may be more likely to reach similar conclusions on relevant questions, including the risks associated with a particular product, appropriate measures to mitigate those risks, and the costs and benefits of alternative regulatory approaches. Such steps can lead regulators to adopt regulations that are more aligned and allow producers to develop economies of scale, to reduce costs associated with complying with divergent regulations, and to pass cost savings on to consumers.

Of course, it is critical that any alignment in regulatory approaches continues to promote national health, safety, environmental, and other legitimate policy objectives. To promote the relevant goals, we recommend that regulatory cooperation should be based, to the extent feasible and appropriate, on an open exchange of information and perspectives among the U.S. government, foreign governments, affected domestic and foreign stakeholders in the private sector, and the public at large.

With that objective in mind, the United States Trade Representative and the OIRA issued a relevant memorandum to heads of executive agencies and departments on May 19, 2011.[187] The memorandum is designed to promote exports and trade by ensuring a high degree of openness and public participation in the rulemaking process, with an emphasis on international cooperation.

E. Public Recommendations on Retrospective Analysis

In its 2009 and 2010 Reports, OMB emphasized the importance of public participation and in particular of obtaining access to "dispersed knowledge" about how to improve regulation. The 2009 Report said, "[i]f members of the public have fresh evidence or ideas about improvement of existing regulations – including expansion, redirection, modification, or repeal – it is important to learn about that evidence or those ideas. A general goal is to connect the interest in sound analysis with the focus on open government, in part by promoting public engagement and understanding of regulatory alternatives.

Consistent with Executive Order 13563, OMB is especially interested in how to improve retrospective analysis of existing rules. In the draft of this Report, OMB requested information about published and unpublished studies (both conceptual and empirical) involving such retrospective analysis. OMB also requested suggestions about how to improve understanding of the accuracy of prospective analyses of rules and how to undertake retrospective analysis. OMB will carefully consider these suggestions.

III: UPDATE ON THE IMPLEMENTATION OF OMB'S INFORMATION QUALITY INITIATIVES

Objective and high-quality analysis can improve regulatory decisions. OMB and the regulatory agencies have taken a number of steps to improve the rigor and transparency of analysis supporting their decisions. Of particular importance in the context of regulatory analysis is OMB's Circular A-4, "Regulatory Analysis," which was issued in 2003 after public comment, interagency review, and peer review. Circular A-4 defines good regulatory analysis and standardizes how benefits and costs of Federal regulatory actions are measured and reported.[188]

In this chapter of the Report, we highlight recent developments in OMB's continuing efforts to improve government information quality and transparency, as well as provide a brief update on the 2010 Agency reporting under the Government-Wide Information Quality Guidelines ("IQ Guidelines") and the Information Quality Bulletin for Peer Review ("Peer Review Bulletin"). The Government-Wide Information Quality Guidelines, issued in 2002 after an extensive public comment process, provide policy and procedural guidance to Federal agencies for ensuring and maximizing the quality of the information they disseminate.[189] The Information Quality Bulletin for Peer Review, issued in 2004 after an extensive public comment process, provides further guidance for pre-dissemination review of influential scientific information.[190]

A. Recent Developments in Information Quality

The Obama Administration's strong commitment to ensuring information quality has been recently reinforced in a variety of contexts. The President's March 9, 2009 Memorandum on Scientific Integrity[191] refers to the need for each agency to:

- have appropriate rules and procedures to ensure the integrity of the scientific process within the agency;
- use scientific and technological information that has been subject to well-established scientific processes such as peer review when considered in policy decisions;
- appropriately and accurately reflect scientific and technological information in complying with and applying relevant statutory standards; and
- make available to the public the scientific or technological findings or conclusions considered or relied upon in policy decisions.

Since that time, the Director of the Executive Office's Office of Science and Technology Policy (OSTP) issued a Memorandum to the Heads of Departments and Agencies that provides further guidance to Executive Branch leaders as they implement Administration policies on scientific integrity.[192] The OSTP Director's December 17, 2010, memorandum emphasizes that "the accurate presentation of scientific and technological information is critical to informed decision making by the public and policymakers." Several passages in the memorandum specifically reinforce the goals of OMB's ongoing information quality initiatives. Specifically:

- Consistent with the Bulletin on Peer Review, the OSTP Director's Memorandum asks that agencies develop policies to ensure that data and research used to support policy decisions undergo independent peer review by qualified experts, where feasible and appropriate, and consistent with law (Sec I.2(b)).
- Consistent with the emphasis on transparency in the Information Quality Guidelines (as well Circular A-4), the OSTP Director's Memorandum asks agencies to develop policies that:
    - Expand and promote access to scientific and technical information by making it available online in open formats. Where appropriate, this should include data and models underlying regulatory proposals and policy decisions (Sec I.3).
    - Communicate scientific findings by including a clear explication of underlying assumptions; accurate contextualization of uncertainties; and a description of the probabilities associated with both optimistic and pessimistic projections, including best-case and worst-case scenarios where appropriate (Sec I.4).

Consistent with this Administration's current efforts to ensure the quality of information on which public policy is based, OMB will continue to work with Executive departments and agencies over the next year to ensure that they have in place comprehensive processes for pre-dissemination review of information quality, including the independent peer review of scientific information. We note that such efforts may be especially important in agencies where staff turnover may have affected agency familiarity with the types of internal processes necessary to implement the IQ Guidelines and the Peer Review Bulletin.

B. Government-Wide Information Quality Guidelines

Section 515 of the Treasury and General Government Appropriations Act, 2001 (Pub. L. No. 106-554, 44 U.S.C. § 3516 note), commonly known as the "Information Quality Act" (IQA), requires OMB to develop government-wide standards "for ensuring and maximizing" the quality of information disseminated by Federal agencies.

To implement the IQA, OMB issued final government-wide guidelines on February 22, 2002 (67 FR 8452), and each Federal agency is charged with promulgating its own Information Quality Guidelines. OMB has facilitated the development of these agency guidelines, working with the agencies to ensure consistency with the principles set forth in the government-wide guidelines. By October 1, 2002, almost all agencies released their final guidelines, which became effective immediately. The OMB government-wide guidelines require agencies to report annually to OMB providing information on the number and nature of complaints received by the agency and how such complaints were resolved.

In August 2004, the OIRA Administrator issued a memorandum to the President's Management Council requesting that agencies post all Information Quality correspondence on agency web pages to increase the transparency of the process.[193] In their FY 2004 Information Quality Reports to OMB, agencies provided OMB with the specific links to these web pages and OMB began providing this information to the public in our 2005 update on Information Quality.[194] This increase in transparency allows the public to view all correction requests, appeal requests, and agency responses to these requests. The web pages also allow the public to track the status of correction requests that may be of interest. An updated list of agency web pages is provided in Appendix I of this Report.

In our 2003 Report, OMB presented a detailed discussion of the IQA and its implementation, including a discussion of perceptions and realities, legal developments, methods for improving transparency, suggestions for improving correction requests, and the release of the OMB Information Quality Bulletin for Peer Review.[195]

This section of the chapter provides a summary of the current status of correction requests received in FY 2010, as well as an update on the status of requests received in FY 2004, FY 2005, FY 2006, FY 2007, FY 2008 and FY 2009. An update on legal developments is also provided. Our discussion of the individual correction requests and agency responses is minimal because all correspondence between the public and agencies regarding these requests is publicly available on the agencies' Information Quality web pages.

1. Request for Correction Process

a. New Correction Requests and Appeal Requests Received by the Agencies in FY 2010

Table 3-1 below lists the departments and agencies that received requests for correction in FY 2010. In FY 2010, a total of 27 requests for correction were sent to 10 different departments and agencies. FY 2010 was the first year correction requests were sent to the Department of Housing and Urban Development (HUD) and the Federal Reserve Board. In addition, four appeals associated with these 27 requests were filed in FY 2010. One appeal was sent to the Environmental Protection Agency (EPA), one appeal was sent to the National

Oceanic and Atmospheric Administration (NOAA), within the Department of Commerce (DOC), and two appeals were sent to the Department of the Interior (DOI). Within DOI one appeal was sent to the U.S. Geological Survey (USGS) and the other appeal was sent to the Fish and Wildlife Service (FWS). As some of the agencies' 27 responses to initial correct requests were sent at the end of FY 2010, or were still pending at the end of FY 2010, there is a possibility that additional appeals may have since been filed or will be filed in the future.

Further, as shown below in Table 3-2, two additional appeals were filed in FY 2010 that related to correction requests from FY2009. One was sent to the Bureau of Land Management (BLM), within DOI, regarding a 2009 BLM leasing report. The other request was sent to the Environmental Protection Agency (EPA) regarding the scientific assessment for oxides of nitrogen. Both appeal responses are being deferred until related litigation is complete; to the extent the litigation addresses the information quality concerns, a further response to the appeal may not be required from the agencies.

Table 3-1. Departments and Agencies that Received Information Quality Correction Requests in FY 2010

Agency	Number of FY10 Correction Requests
Department of Agriculture	2
Department of Commerce	1
Department of Health and Human Services	2
Department of the Interior	4
National Aeronautics and Space Administration	1
Environmental Protection Agency	11
Department of Labor	1
Department of Housing and Urban Development	1
Federal Communications Commission	3
Federal Reserve Board	1
Total	**27**

Table 3-2. Departments and Agencies that Received Information Quality Appeals Requests in FY 2010, Following Responses to Requests Initiated in FY 2009

Agency	Number of FY10 Appeals
Department of the Interior	1
Environmental Protection Agency	1
Total	**2**

The correction requests received in FY 2010 were quite diverse. For instance, the American Coatings Association requested that both EPA and HUD withdraw participation and sponsorship of public service announcements disseminated to raise awareness of the consequences of lead poisoning; the Center for Regulatory Effectiveness asked the Food and

Drug Administration, within the Department of Health and Human Services (HHS), to correct information relating to presentations and statements discussing scientific information on the impacts of smoking menthol cigarettes; and the US Association of Reptile Keepers and the Pet Industry Joint Advisory Council asked the USGS to correct information in a report relating to the biological and management profiles for nine large species of pythons, anacondas and the boa constrictor.

Figure 3-1 shows the status of the 27 FY 2010 correction requests and four appeals. For further details, links to all the correction requests, and the complete agency responses, we encourage readers to visit the agency Information Quality web pages.[196] OMB continues to use the "different processes" category to describe responses that were handled by other pre-existing processes at the agencies. For instance, comments sent to the Fish and Wildlife Service regarding information on the Sage Grouse were handled as public comments under another existing review process related to the listing determination.

As noted in previous reports, OMB cautions readers against drawing any conclusions about trends or year-to-year comparisons because agency procedures for classifying correction requests are still evolving. However, we note that in FY 2003 there were 48 correction requests; in FY 2004, there were 37 correction requests; in FY 2005, there were 24 correction requests; in FY 2006, there were 22 correction requests; in FY 2007, there were 21 correction requests; in FY 2008, there were 14 correction requests; and in FY 2009, there were 17 correction requests.

b. Status of Outstanding Correction Requests Received by the Agencies in FY 2003-2009

At the close of FY 2009, 11 Information Quality correction request responses and 3 appeal responses remained pending from the agencies. The pending correction requests were initiated in FY 2004, FY 2005, FY 2006, FY 2007, FY 2008, and FY 2009. Figure 4-2 shows the status of those outstanding correction request responses at the close of FY 2010. Agencies responded to 4 of these correction requests and continued to work on responses to the remaining 7 at the end of FY 2010. Six of the pending requests are requests to the Army Corps of Engineers, within the Department of Defense, and one of the pending requests is to the Centers for Disease Control, within HHS. As is shown below, there was one appeal that was sent after the agencies responded. This appeal was sent to BLM and the response was handled through another process.

Figure 3-3 below gives the status of the 4 appeal requests pending at the close of FY 2009. The Forest Service, within USDA, denied an outstanding appeal regarding the naming of a location in a draft environmental impact statement, and the Bureau of Reclamation, within DOI, denied an appeal regarding information in a biological assessment. In responding to an outstanding appeal regarding sampling at a landfill, in lieu of removing maps, EPA clarified that many of the documents in the file were interim documents and added clarifying footnotes and disclaimers to the maps. In addition, the Federal Communications Commission continued to work on the appeal it received in FY 2007 regarding line charges. Correspondence showing the agencies' responses to these requests is publicly available on the agencies' Information Quality web pages.

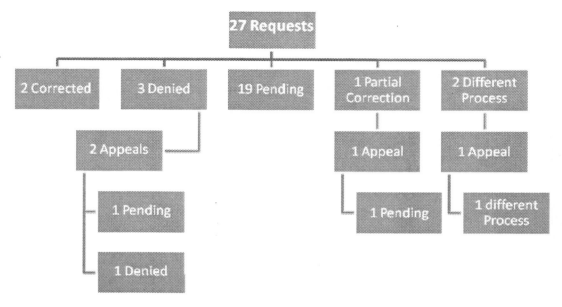

Figure 3-1. Status of IQ Correction Requests Received in FY 2010.

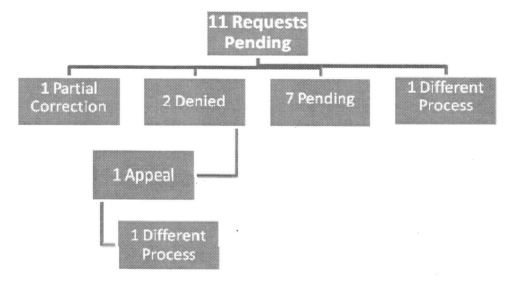

Figure 3-2. FY 2010 Status of Pending Correction Requests from FY 2004, FY 2005, FY 2006, FY 2007, FY 2008, and FY 2009.

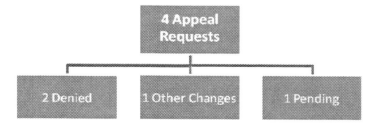

Figure 3-3. FY 2010 Status of Pending Appeal Requests from FY 2009.

2. Legal update

As discussed in previous reports, there has been litigation under the Information Quality Act (IQA), as well as regarding the scope of judicial review under the Administrative Procedure Act (APA) in those challenges. During calendar year 2010, there were two judicial developments. First, the United States Court of Appeals for the Ninth Circuit affirmed the district court's dismissal of the case for lack of jurisdiction under the APA. See *Americans for Safe Access* v. *United States Dep't of Health and Human Servs.*, No. 07-17388, 2010 U.S. App. LEXIS 21282,* 5 (9th Cir. 2010) (holding that HHS's decision was not a reviewable final agency action). Second, the United States Court of Appeals for the District of Columbia Circuit declined to find that the IQA had been violated based on its determination that OMB's interpretation regarding "dissemination" (and, in particular, the exclusion from the definition of dissemination of documents "prepared and distributed in the context of adjudicative proceedings") was a reasonable interpretation of the statute. *Prime Time* v. *Vilsack*, 599 F.3d 678, 685 (D.C. Cir. 2010). These recent decisions follow other cases that have dismissed IQA challenges, including on other grounds. See, e.g., *Salt Institute* v. *Leavitt*, 440 F.3d 156, 159 (4th Cir. 2006); *In re Operation of the Missouri River System Litigation*, 363 F. Supp. 2d 1145, 117475 (D. Minn. 2004), vacated in part and aff'd in part on other grounds, 421 F.3d 618 (8th Cir. 2005).

C. Information Quality Bulletin for Peer Review

In keeping with the goal of improving the quality of government information, on December 16, 2004, OMB issued the Final Information Quality Bulletin for Peer Review (the "Peer Review Bulletin").[197] The Peer Review Bulletin requires executive agencies to ensure that all "influential scientific information" they disseminate after June 16, 2005, is peer-reviewed.

"Influential scientific information" is defined as "scientific information the agency reasonably can determine will have or does have a clear and substantial impact on important public policies or private sector decisions."[198] The term "influential" is to be interpreted consistently with OMB's government-wide Information Quality Guidelines and the information quality guidelines of each agency.

One type of scientific information is a scientific assessment. For the purposes of the Peer Review Bulletin, the term "scientific assessment" means an evaluation of a body of scientific or technical knowledge, which typically synthesizes multiple factual inputs, data, models, assumptions, and/or applies best professional judgment to bridge uncertainties in the available information.[199]

The Peer Review Bulletin describes the factors that should be considered in choosing an appropriate peer review mechanism and stresses that the rigor of the review should be commensurate with how the information will be used. It directs agencies to choose a peer review mechanism that is adequate, giving due consideration to the novelty and complexity of the science to be reviewed, the relevance of the information to decision making, the extent of prior peer reviews, and the expected benefits and costs of additional review. When deciding what type of peer review mechanism is appropriate for a specific information product, agencies should consider at least the following issues: individual versus panel review; timing;

scope of the review; selection of reviewers; disclosure and attribution; public participation; disposition of reviewer comments; and adequacy of prior peer review.

The Peer Review Bulletin specifies the most rigorous peer review requirements for "highly influential scientific assessments," which are a subset of "influential scientific information." To ensure that implementation of the Peer Review Bulletin is not too costly, these requirements for more intensive peer review apply only to the more important scientific assessments disseminated by the Federal Government – those that could have a potential impact of more than $500 million in any one year on either the public or private sector, or are novel, controversial, or precedent-setting, or have significant interagency interest.

Under the Peer Review Bulletin, agencies are granted broad discretion to weigh the benefits and costs of using a particular peer review mechanism for a specific information product. In addition to the factors noted above, agencies also have the option of employing "alternative processes" for meeting the peer review requirement (e.g., commissioning a National Academy of Sciences' panel). Moreover, to ensure that peer review does not unduly delay the release of urgent findings, time-sensitive health and safety determinations are exempted from the requirements of the Peer Review Bulletin. There are also specific exemptions for national security, individual agency adjudication or permit proceedings, routine statistical information, and financial information. The Peer Review Bulletin does not cover information disseminated in connection with routine rules that materially alter entitlements, grants, user fees, or loan programs, or the rights and obligations of recipients thereof.

The Peer Review Bulletin provides two mechanisms for monitoring the progress of the agencies in meeting these peer-review requirements: a transparent peer review planning process and annual reporting, described below.

The good science and good government requirements of the Peer Review Bulletin should assist in improving the accuracy and transparency of agency science. Additionally, the peer review planning process described in the Peer Review Bulletin, which includes posting of plans on agency websites, enhances the ability of the government and the public to track influential scientific disseminations made by agencies.

On June 16, 2005, the Peer Review Bulletin became effective for all influential scientific information, including highly-influential scientific assessments. The peer review planning component of the Bulletin, discussed below, became fully effective on December 16, 2005. By the end of FY 2009, the Bulletin had been implemented for four full years.

1. Peer Review Planning

The Peer Review Planning component of the Peer Review Bulletin (Section V) requires agencies to engage in a systematic process of peer review planning for influential scientific information (including highly influential scientific assessments) that the agency plans to disseminate in the foreseeable future.

A key feature of the agency's peer review plan is a web-accessible listing (an "agenda") of forthcoming influential scientific disseminations that is updated on a regular basis. These postings are designed to allow the public to participate in the peer review process by providing data and comments to the sponsoring agencies, as well as to external peer reviewers. By making these agendas publicly available, agencies increase the level of transparency in their peer review processes, and also have a mechanism to gauge the extent of public interest in their proposed peer reviews.

The agenda is designed to encourage planning for peer review early in the information-generation process. Thus, the agenda should cover all information subject to the Peer Review Bulletin that the agency plans to disseminate in the foreseeable future. For instance, once an agency has established a timeline for the generation of a scientific report, the agency should include that report in its agenda. Thus, although the Peer Review Bulletin specifies that agencies should update their peer review agendas every six months, the agenda is not a six-month forecast (i.e., it should not be limited to information (documents) that the agency plans to peer review in the next six months).

Readers are encouraged to visit the agendas for agencies of interest. OMB asks agencies to ensure that there is an easily identifiable hyperlink to the peer review agenda from the agency's Information Quality home page. For cabinet-level departments that have a central information quality page but do not have a central peer review agenda, OMB requests that a hyperlink to each agency agenda be provided. Section B in Appendix I provides the URLs for most agencies' peer review agendas.

Cabinet-level departments and agencies that have institutionalized processes for proactively identifying documents subject to the Bulletin include the Departments of Agriculture,[200] Commerce,[201] Health and Human Services,[202] Housing and Urban Development, Interior,[203] Labor, Transportation, and the Environmental Protection Agency. Other agencies with processes in place for proactively identifying documents subject to the Peer Review Bulletin include the Consumer Product Safety Commission, the Small Business Administration, and the Federal Communications Commission.

Table 3-3. Peer Reviews Conducted Subject to the Bulletin in FY2010

Department/ Agency**	Total Peer Reviews Completed	Reviews of Highly Influential Scientific Assessments	Waivers, Deferrals, or Exemptions	Potential Reviewer Conflicts
Department of Agriculture	74	7	None	None
Department of Commerce	24	1	None	None
Department of Energy	1	0	None	None
Department of Health and Human Services	22	17	None	None
Department of the Interior	32	0	7 (Waiver)	None
Department of Labor	2	0	None	None
Department of Transportation	7	2	None	None
Environmental Protection Agency	28	4	None	None
Federal Communications Commission	1	0	None	None
Small Business Administration	2	0	None	None
Total	193	31	7	None

While this draft document is available for public comment, OMB is following up on incomplete reports from the Departments of Defense and Education.

From time to time, other agencies produce or sponsor influential scientific information, but do not identify forthcoming information products subject to the Peer Review Bulletin this fiscal year. OMB reminds these agencies to ensure that they maintain processes for determining when documents are subject to the Bulletin, and to ensure that the peer review plans for those documents are listed on the agency's agenda in a timely manner. These agencies include the Departments of Defense, Education, Energy, Homeland Security, Justice, State, and Veterans Affairs, as well as the National Aeronautics and Space Administration, the Nuclear Regulatory Commission, the Federal Trade Commission, and the Tennessee Valley Authority.

Several agencies have determined that they do not currently produce or sponsor information subject to the Peer Review Bulletin. Most of these agencies produce primarily financial information or routine statistical information for which the Bulletin provides specific exemptions. Others primarily engage in management, oversight, or granting activities. A list of these agencies can be found in Section C in Appendix I.

Although the Peer Review Planning section of the Bulletin lays out the specific items that should be included in each peer review plan, OMB does not specify the format that agencies should use, thereby giving agencies the flexibility to incorporate their agendas into existing e-government and science planning initiatives.[204] As such, some agencies house their peer review agendas within a research arm of the agency, whereas others operate out of the office of the chief information officer or the policy and planning office. Some departments provide an integrated agenda across the agencies,[205] while other departments have chosen to have individual agencies host their own agendas.[206] Furthermore, some agencies have chosen to provide a single agenda for both influential scientific information and highly influential scientific assessments,[207] while others provide two separate agendas.[208]

The Peer Review Bulletin specifically requires that agencies provide a link from the agenda to each document made public pursuant to the Bulletin, including the completed peer review report. Although some agencies routinely provide such links,[209] agendas at other agencies do not yet have this capability. Agencies have advised that provision of these links is not always straightforward when the peer review is nested within a more complicated preexisting public process.[210] OMB is currently working with the agencies to ensure that the required information is posted, and that the web sites are easy to locate and navigate.

Table Details

- The Department of Agriculture agencies reporting peer reviews in FY 2010 were the Food Safety Inspection Service, the Agricultural Research Service, the Economic Research Service, and the Forest Service.
- The only Department of Commerce agency reporting peer reviews in this fiscal year was the National Oceanic and Atmospheric Administration.
- The only Department of Energy peer review reported in this fiscal year was associated with the Energy Efficiency & Renewable Energy, Vehicle Technologies Program.
- The Department of Health and Human Services agencies reporting peer reviews in FY 2010 were the Centers for Disease Control and Prevention and the National Toxicology Program at the National Institute for Environmental Health Sciences.

- The Department of the Interior agencies reporting peer reviews in FY 2010 were the Fish and Wildlife Service, the Geological Survey, and the National Park Service.
- The Department of Labor agencies reporting peer reviews in FY 2010 were the Occupational Health and Safety Administration and the Mine Safety and Health Administration.
- The Department of Transportation agencies reporting peer reviews in FY 2010 were the Federal Highway Administration, the Federal Motor Carrier Safety Administration, and the National Highway Traffic Safety Administration.

PART II: FIFTEENTH ANNUAL REPORT TO CONGRESS ON AGENCY COMPLIANCE WITH THE UNFUNDED MANDATES REFORM ACT

Introduction

This report represents OMB's fifteenth annual submission to Congress on agency compliance with the Unfunded Mandates Reform Act of 1995 (UMRA). This report on agency compliance with the Act covers the period of October 2009 through September 2010; the rules published before October 2009 are described in last year's report.

In recent years, this report has been included along with our final Report to Congress on the Benefits and Costs of Federal Regulations. This is done because the two reports together address many of the same issues, and both highlight the need for regulating in a responsible manner that accounts for the benefits and costs of rules and takes into consideration the interests of our intergovernmental partners. This year, OMB is again publishing the UMRA report with the Report to Congress on the Benefits and Costs of Federal Regulations.

State and local governments have a vital constitutional role in providing government services. They have the major role in providing domestic public services, such as public education, law enforcement, road building and maintenance, water supply, and sewage treatment. The Federal Government contributes to that role by promoting a healthy economy and by providing grants, loans, and tax subsidies to State and local governments. However, over the past two decades, State, local, and tribal governments increasingly have expressed concerns about the difficulty of complying with Federal mandates without additional Federal resources.

In response, Congress passed the Unfunded Mandates Reform Act of 1995 (UMRA, or "the Act"). Title I of the Act focuses on the Legislative Branch, addressing the processes Congress should follow before enactment of any statutory unfunded mandates. Title II addresses the Executive Branch. It begins with a general directive for agencies to assess, unless otherwise prohibited by law, the effects of their rules on the other levels of government and on the private sector (Section 201). Title II also describes specific analyses and consultations that agencies must undertake for rules that may result in expenditures of over $100 million (adjusted annually for inflation) in any year by State, local, and tribal governments in the aggregate, or by the private sector.

Specifically, Section 202 requires an agency to prepare a written statement for intergovernmental mandates that describes in detail the required analyses and consultations on the unfunded mandate. Section 205 requires that for all rules subject to Section 202, agencies must identify and consider a reasonable number of regulatory alternatives, and then generally select from among them the least costly, most cost-effective, or least burdensome option that achieves the objectives of the rule. Exceptions require the agency head to explain in the final rule why such a selection was not made or why such a selection would be inconsistent with law.

Title II requires agencies to "develop an effective process" for obtaining "meaningful and timely input" from State, local and tribal governments in developing rules that contain significant intergovernmental mandates (Section 204). Title II also singles out small governments for particular attention (Section 203). OMB's guidelines assist Federal agencies in complying with the Act and are based upon the following general principles:

- Intergovernmental consultations should take place as early as possible, beginning before issuance of a proposed rule and continuing through the final rule stage, and be integrated explicitly into the rulemaking process;
- Agencies should consult with a wide variety of State, local, and tribal officials;
- Agencies should estimate direct benefits and costs to assist with these consultations;
- The scope of consultation should reflect the cost and significance of the mandate being considered;
- Effective consultation requires trust and significant and sustained attention so that all who participate can enjoy frank discussion and focus on key priorities; and
- Agencies should seek out State, local, and tribal views on costs, benefits, risks, and alternative methods of compliance, and whether the Federal rule will harmonize with and not duplicate similar laws in other levels of government.

Federal agencies have been actively consulting with States, localities, and tribal governments in order to ensure that regulatory activities were conducted consistent with the requirements of UMRA.

The remainder of this report lists and briefly discusses the regulations meeting the Title II threshold and the specific requirements of Sections 202 and 205 of the Act from October 1, 2009 to September 30th, 2010.

IV: REVIEW OF SIGNIFICANT REGULATORY MANDATES

In FY 2010, Federal agencies issued thirteen final rules that were subject to Sections 202 and 205 of the Unfunded Mandate Reform Act of 1995 (UMRA), as they require expenditures by State, local or tribal governments, in the aggregate, or by the private sector, of at least $100 million in any one year (adjusted annually for inflation). The Environmental Protection Agency has five, Department of Energy has three, Department of Transportation has three, Department of Health and Human Services has one, and the Environmental Protection Agency and Department of Transportation issued one joint rule.[211]

OMB worked with the agencies to ensure that the selection of the regulatory options for these rules fully complied with the requirements of Title II of the Act. Descriptions of the rules in addition to agency statements regarding compliance with the Act are included in the following section.

A. Environmental Protection Agency

1. Renewable Fuels Standard Program

This final rule implements provisions in title II of the 2007 Energy Independence and Security Act (EISA) that amend section 211(o) of the Clean Air Act. The amendments revise the National Renewable Fuels Standard Program in the United States, increasing the national requirement to a total of 36 billion gallons of total renewable fuel in 2022.

EPA did not estimates annual costs for this rule but did determine that this rule was economically significant and would likely create an UMRA mandate. This final rule does not contain mandates under UMRA on State, local, and tribal governments. The overall impact on the private sector does exceed the $100 million threshold in the aggregate. Consequently, the provisions of this rule constitute a private sector mandate under the UMRA.

2. National Emission Standards for Hazardous Air Pollutants for Reciprocating Internal Combustion Engines

In this final rule, EPA established national emission standards for hazardous air pollutants from existing stationary compression ignition (diesel) engines.

EPA estimates $373 million in annual costs. This final rule does not contain mandates under UMRA on State, local, and tribal governments. The overall impact on the private sector does exceed the $100 million threshold in the aggregate. Consequently, the provisions of this rule constitute a private sector mandate under the UMRA.

3. NESHAP: Portland Cement Notice of Reconsideration

In this final rule, EPA established emissions standards for hazardous air pollutants, such as mercury and acid gases, from existing and new Portland cement facilities. EPA also established revised emissions limits for particulate matter, nitrogen oxide, and sulfur dioxin at new and reconstructed facilities.

EPA estimates $926 to $950 million in annual costs. This final rule does not contain mandates under UMRA on State, local, and tribal governments. The overall impact on the private sector does exceed the $100 million threshold in the aggregate. Consequently, the provisions of this rule constitute a private sector mandate under the UMRA.

4. National Emission Standards for Hazardous Air Pollutants for Reciprocating Internal Combustion Engines--Existing Stationary Spark Ignition (Gas-Fired)

In this final rule, EPA established national emission standards for hazardous air pollutants and nitrogen oxides from existing stationary gas-fired engines.

EPA estimates $253 million in annual costs. This final rule does not contain mandates under UMRA on State, local, and tribal governments. The overall impact on the private sector does exceed the $100 million threshold in the aggregate. Consequently, the provisions of this rule constitute a private sector mandate under the UMRA.

5. Lead; Amendment to the Opt-out and Recordkeeping Provisions in the Renovation, Repair, and Painting Program

This final rule revised the 2008 Lead Renovation, Repair, and Painting Program (RRP) rule that established accreditation, training, certification, and recordkeeping requirements as well as work practice standards on persons performing renovations for compensation in most pre 1978 housing and child-occupied facilities.

EPA estimates $320 million in annual costs. This final rule does not contain mandates under UMRA on State, local, and tribal governments. The overall impact on the private sector does exceed the $100 million threshold in the aggregate. Consequently, the provisions of this rule constitute a private sector mandate under the UMRA.

B. Department of Energy

1. Energy Efficiency Standards for Commercial Clothes Washers

This final rule amends existing standards for commercial clothes washers.

DOE estimates $23 million in annual costs. This final rule does not contain mandates under UMRA on State, local, and tribal governments. The agency believes the overall impact on the private sector likely does not exceed the $100 million threshold in the aggregate; however, based on the possibility of crossing the threshold, the agency provided an UMRA analysis.

2. Energy Conservation Standards for Small Electric Motors

This final rule establishes energy conservation standards for small electric motors.

DOE estimates $264 million in annual costs. This final rule does not contain mandates under UMRA on State, local, and tribal governments. The overall impact on the private sector does exceed the $100 million threshold in the aggregate. Consequently, the provisions of this rule constitute a private sector mandate under the UMRA.

3. Energy Efficiency Standards for Pool Heaters and Direct Heating Equipment and Water Heaters

This final rule establishes energy conservation standards for pool heaters and direct heating equipment and amends standards for water heaters.

DOE estimates $1,285 million in annual costs. This final rule does not contain mandates under UMRA on State, local, and tribal governments. The overall impact on the private sector does exceed the $100 million threshold in the aggregate. Consequently, the provisions of this rule constitute a private sector mandate under the UMRA.

C. Department of Transportation

1. Automatic Dependent Surveillance--Broadcast (ADS-B) Equipage Mandate to Support Air Traffic Control Service

This rulemaking would add requirements and performance standards for Automatic Dependent Surveillance-Broadcast (ADS-B) Out equipment on aircraft operating in certain classes of U.S. airspace. This equipment would need to be installed by aircraft owners by 2020. ADS-B Out is an essential piece of a system required to move forward with the Next Generation Air system, which will ultimately increase the capacity and safety of U.S.

airspace. ADS-B will allow planes to fly closer together, to have more precise take-offs and landings, and to have better communications with the FAA's Air Traffic Control centers.

FAA estimates $261 million in annual costs. This final rule does not contain mandates under UMRA on State, local, and tribal governments. The overall impact on the private sector does exceed the $100 million threshold in the aggregate. Consequently, the provisions of this rule constitute a private sector mandate under the UMRA.

Electronic On-Board Recorders for Hours-of-Service Compliance

With this rule, motor carriers that have demonstrated serious noncompliance with existing FMCSA hours of service rules will be subject to mandatory installation of EOBRs meeting the new performance standards. If FMCSA determines, based on HOS records reviewed during a compliance review, that a motor carrier has a 10 percent or greater violation rate for any HOS regulation listed in the new Appendix C to part 385, FMCSA will issue the carrier an EOBR remedial directive. The motor carrier will then be required to install EOBRs in all of its commercial motor vehicles regardless of their date of manufacture and use the devices for HOS recordkeeping for a period of 2 years.

FMCSA estimates this rule will lead to $140 million in annual costs for the private sector. This final rule does not contain mandates under UMRA on State, local, and tribal governments. FMCSA does not indentify private sector mandates in this rule; however it is included in this chapter because the agency's private sector cost estimates may be viewed as crossing the UMRA threshold.[212]

3. Positive Train Control

The final rule, effective March 2010, required certain freight and passenger railroad operations to plan for and install systems on locomotives and on railroad track (among other requirements) – enabling the train to be automatically controlled in certain circumstances.

FRA estimates that this Congressionally mandated regulation has annualized costs of approximately $901 million with mandates on private industry as well as some State and local governments (those that fund and/or operate intercity passenger and commuter rail systems). Consequently, the provisions of this rule constitute a private sector mandate under the UMRA.

D. Department of Health and Human Services

1. Use of Ozone-Depleting Substances; Removal of Essential Use Designations [Flunisolide, Triamcinolone, Metaproterenol, Pirbuterol, Albuterol and Ipratropium in Combination, Cromolyn, and Nedocromil]

This final rule would remove the essential use designations after a specified date for metered-dose inhalers (MDIs) containing flunisolide, triamcinolone, metaproterenol, pirbuterol, albuterol and ipratropium in combination, cromolyn, and nedocromil. Under the provisions of this final rule, these MDIs would have to be removed from the market. This final rule is consistent with obligations under the Clean Air Act and the Montreal Protocol on Substances That Deplete the Ozone Layer.

FDA did not estimate annual costs for this rule but did determine that this rule was economically significant and would likely create an UMRA mandate. This final rule does not contain mandates under UMRA on State, local, and tribal governments. The overall impact on the private sector does exceed the $100 million threshold in the aggregate. Consequently, the provisions of this rule constitute a private sector mandate under the UMRA.

E. Joint Rulemakings

1. EPA/NHTSA Joint Rulemaking to Establish Light-Duty Greenhouse Gas Emission Standards and Corporate Average Fuel Economy Standards

EPA and NHTSA issued this joint Final Rule to establish a National Program consisting of new standards for light-duty vehicles that will reduce greenhouse gas emissions and improve fuel economy. This joint Final Rule is consistent with the National Fuel Efficiency Policy announced by President Obama on May 19, 2009. EPA is finalizing greenhouse gas emissions standards under the Clean Air Act, and NHTSA is finalizing Corporate Average Fuel Economy standards under the Energy Policy and Conservation Act, as amended. These standards apply to passenger cars, light-duty trucks, and medium-duty passenger vehicles, covering model years 2012 through 2016, and represent a harmonized and consistent National Program.

EPA and DOT estimate that the 2012-2016 Model Year lifetime discounted costs are $51.5 billion assuming $21/ton social cost of carbon value. (Neither DOT nor EPA provided annualized values in their RIAs). This final rule does not contain mandates under UMRA on State, local, and tribal governments. The overall impact on the private sector does exceed the $100 million threshold in the aggregate. Consequently, the provisions of this rule constitute a private sector mandate under the UMRA.

APPENDIX A: CALCULATION OF BENEFITS AND COSTS

Chapter I presents estimates of the annual benefits and costs of selected major final regulations reviewed by OMB between October 1, 2000 and September 30, 2010. OMB presents more detailed explanation of these regulations in several documents.

- Rules from April 1, 1999 to September 30, 2001: Table 19 of the 2002 Report.
- Rules from October 1, 2001 to September 30, 2002: Table 19 of the 2003 Report.
- Rules from October 1, 2002 to September 30, 2003: Table 12 of the 2004 Report.
- Rules from October 1, 2003 to September 30, 2004: Tables 1-4 and A-1 of the 2005 Report.
- Rules from October 1, 2004 to September 30, 2005: Tables 1-4 and A-1 of the 2006 Report
- Rules from October 1, 2005 to September 30, 2006: Tables 1-4 and A-1 of the 2007 Report.
- Rules from October 1, 2006 to September 30, 2007: Tables 1-4 and A-1 of the 2008 Report.

- Rules from October 1, 2007 to September 30, 2008: Tables 1-4 and A-1 of the 2009 Report.
- Rules from October 1, 2008 to September 30, 2009: Tables 1-4 and A-1 of the 2010 Report.
- Rules from October 1, 2009 to September 30, 2010: Tables 1-4 and A-1 of this Report.

In assembling estimates of benefits and costs presented in Table 1-4, OMB has:

(1) Applied a uniform format for the presentation of benefit and cost estimates in order to make agency estimates more closely comparable with each other (for example, annualizing benefit and cost estimates); and
(2) Monetized quantitative estimates where the agency has not done so (for example, converting agency projections of quantified benefits, such as estimated injuries avoided per year or tons of pollutant reductions per year, to dollars using the valuation estimates discussed below).

All benefit and cost estimates are adjusted to 2001 dollars using the latest Gross Domestic Product (GDP) deflator, available from the Bureau of Economic Analysis at the Department of Commerce.[213] In instances where the nominal dollar values the agencies use for their benefits and costs is unclear, we assume the benefits and costs are presented in nominal dollar values of the year before the rule is finalized. In periods of low inflation such as the past few years, this assumption does not affect the overall totals. All amortizations are performed using a discount rate of 7 percent unless the agency has already presented annualized, monetized results using a different explicit discount rate.

OMB discusses, in this Report and in previous Reports, the difficulty of estimating and aggregating the benefits and costs of different regulations over long time periods and across many agencies. In addition, where OMB has monetized quantitative estimates where the agency has not done so, we have attempted to be faithful to the respective agency approaches. The adoption of a uniform format for annualizing agency estimates allows, at least for purposes of illustration, the aggregation of benefit and cost estimates across rules; however, agencies have used different methodologies and valuations in quantifying and monetizing effects. Thus, an aggregation involves the assemblage of benefit and cost estimates that are not strictly comparable.

To address this issue in part, the 2003 Report included OMB's new regulatory analysis guidance, also released as OMB Circular A-4, which took effect on January 1, 2004 for proposed rules and January 1, 2005 for final rules. The guidance recommends what OMB considers to be "best practices" in regulatory analysis, with a goal of strengthening the role of science, engineering, and economics in rulemaking. The overall goal of this guidance is a more competent and credible regulatory process, and a more consistent regulatory environment. OMB expects that as more agencies adopt these recommended best practices, the benefits and costs presented in future Reports will become more comparable across agencies and programs. The 2006 Report was the first report that included final rules subject to OMB Circular A-4. OMB will continue to work with the agencies to ensure that their impact analyses follow the new guidance.

Table A-1 below presents information on the impacts of 66 major rules reviewed by OMB from October 1, 2009 through September 30, 2010. Unless otherwise stated, the estimates presented in Table A-1 are unmodified agency estimates of annualized impacts except for an adjustment to 2001 dollars, which is the requested format in OMB Circular A-4.

Table 1-5(a) in Chapter I of this Report presents the estimates for the 1 8 rules finalized in fiscal year 2010 that were added to the Chapter I accounting statement totals. Table A-2 below presents the benefits and costs of previously reported major rules reviewed by OMB from October 1, 2000 through September 30, 2009 that are also included in the Chapter I accounting statement totals.

Chapter I presents estimates of the annual benefits and costs of selected major final regulations reviewed by OMB between October 1, 2000 and September 30, 2010. OMB presents more detailed explanation of these regulations in several documents.

- Rules from April 1, 1999 to September 30, 2001: Table 19 of the 2002 Report.
- Rules from October 1, 2001 to September 30, 2002: Table 19 of the 2003 Report.
- Rules from October 1, 2002 to September 30, 2003: Table 12 of the 2004 Report.
- Rules from October 1, 2003 to September 30, 2004: Tables 1-4 and A-1 of the 2005 Report.
- Rules from October 1, 2004 to September 30, 2005: Tables 1-4 and A-1 of the 2006 Report
- Rules from October 1, 2005 to September 30, 2006: Tables 1-4 and A-1 of the 2007 Report.
- Rules from October 1, 2006 to September 30, 2007: Tables 1-4 and A-1 of the 2008 Report.
- Rules from October 1, 2007 to September 30, 2008: Tables 1-4 and A-1 of the 2009 Report.
- Rules from October 1, 2008 to September 30, 2009: Tables 1-4 and A-1 of the 2010 Report.
- Rules from October 1, 2009 to September 30, 2010: Tables 1-4 and A-1 of this Report.

In assembling estimates of benefits and costs presented in Table 1-4, OMB has:

(1) Applied a uniform format for the presentation of benefit and cost estimates in order to make agency estimates more closely comparable with each other (for example, annualizing benefit and cost estimates); and
(2) Monetized quantitative estimates where the agency has not done so (for example, converting agency projections of quantified benefits, such as estimated injuries avoided per year or tons of pollutant reductions per year, to dollars using the valuation estimates discussed below).

Table A-1. Summary of Agency Estimates for Final Rules October 1, 2009-September 30, 2010
(As of Date of Completion of OMB Review)

RIN	Title	Benefits (2001$)	Costs (2001$)	Other Information
Department of Agriculture				
0560-AH90	Supplemental Revenue Assistance Payments Program (SURE) [74 FR 68480]	Not estimated	Not estimated	Transfers: $713-$718 million The full RIA is available from agency upon request.
0560-AI07	Dairy Economic Loss Assistance Payment Program [74 FR 67805]	Not estimated	Not estimated	Transfers: $238 million The full RIA is available from agency upon request.
0578-AA43	Conservation Stewardship Program [75 FR 31610]	Not estimated	Not estimated	Transfers: $2,710-$3,191 million The full RIA is available from agency upon request.
0584-AD30	SNAP: Eligibility and Certification Provisions of the Farm Security and Rural Investment Act of 2002 [75 FR 4912]	Not estimated	Not estimated	Transfers: $2,221-$2,223 million The full RIA is included as an appendix in the Federal Register publication.
Department of Commerce				
0660-ZA28	Broadband Technology Opportunities Program [75 FR 3792]	Not estimated	Not estimated	Transfers: $2,130 million The full RIA is available from agency upon request.
Department of Defense				
0720-AB17	TRICARE: Relationship Between the TRICARE Program and Employer-Sponsored Group Health Coverage [75 FR 18051]	Not estimated	Not estimated	Transfers: $59 million (payment reductions) The full RIA is available from agency upon request.
0790-AI59	Retroactive Stop Loss Special Pay Compensation [75 FR 19878]	Not estimated	Not estimated	Transfers: $438 million The full RIA is available from agency upon request.
Department of Education				
1810-AB04	State Fiscal Stabilization Fund Program-Notice of Proposed Requirements, Definitions, and Approval Criteria [74 FR 58436]	Not estimated	$31 million Range: $25-$37 million	Transfers: $9,510 million The RIA is included in the preamble.

RIN	Title	Benefits (2001$)	Costs (2001$)	Other Information
1810-AB06	School Improvement Grants--Notice of Proposed Requirements Under the American Recovery and Reinvestment Act of 2009; Title I of the Elementary and Secondary Education Act of 1965 [74 FR 65617]	Not estimated	Not estimated	Transfers: $2,932 million The RIA is included in the preamble.
1810-AB07	Race to the Top Fund--Notice of Proposed Priorities, Requirements, Definitions, and Selection Criteria [74 FR 59688]	Not estimated	$1 million	Transfers: $3,272 million The RIA is included in the preamble.
1810-AB08	Teacher Incentive Fund--Priorities, Requirements, Definitions, and Selection Criteria [75 FR 28714]	Not estimated	Not estimated	Transfers: $358 million The RIA is included in the preamble.
1840-AC96	Student Assistance General Provisions; TEACH Grant, Federal Pell Grant, and Academic Competitiveness Grant, and National Science and Mathematics Access To Retain Talent Grant Programs [74 FR 61239]	Not estimated	Not estimated	Transfers: $185 million The RIA is included in the preamble.
1840-AC99	General and Non-Loan Programmatic Issues [74 FR 55902]	Not estimated	Not estimated	Transfers: $229-$232 million The RIA is included in the preamble.
1840-AD01	Federal TRIO Programs, Gaining Early Awareness and Readiness for Undergraduate Program, and High School Equivalency and College Assistance Migrant Programs [75 FR 65712]	Not estimated	Not estimated	Transfers: $1,010 million The RIA is included in the preamble.
1855-AA06	Investing in Innovation--Priorities, Requirements, Definitions, and Selection Criteria [75 FR 12004]	Not estimated	Not estimated	Transfers: $532 million The RIA is included in the preamble.
Department of Energy				
1901-AB27	Loan Guarantees for Projects That Employ Innovative Technologies [74 FR 63544]	Not estimated	Not estimated	Transfers: $3,457-$3,945 million

Table A-1. (Continued)

RIN	Title	Benefits (2001$)	Costs (2001$)	Other Information
1904-AA90	Energy Efficiency Standards for Pool Heaters and Direct Heating Equipment and Water Heaters [75 FR 20112]	$1,386 million Range: $1,274-$1,817 million	$1,063 million Range: $975-$1,122 million	The RIA is included in the Technical Support Document as Chapter 15 and is available at: http://www1.eere.energy.buildings/appliance_standards/residential/pdfs/reg_impact_direct_heat_standards_tsd.pdf
1904-AB70	Energy Conservation Standards for Small Electric Motors [75 FR 10874]	$707 million Range: $688-$827 million	$218 million	The RIA is included in the Technical Support Document as Chapter 15 and is available at: http://www1.eere.energy.buildings/appliance_standards/commercial/pdfs/reg_impact_small_motors_nopr_tsd.pdf
1904-AB93	Energy Efficiency Standards for Commercial Clothes Washers [75 FR 1122]	$51 million Range: $46-$67 million	$20 million Range: $17-$21 million	The RIA is included in the preamble.
1904-AB97	Weatherization Assistance Program for Low-Income Persons - Multi-unit Buildings [75 FR 3847]	Not estimated	Not estimated	Transfers: $4,097 million The RIA is included in the preamble.

Department of Health and Human Services

RIN	Title	Benefits (2001$)	Costs (2001$)	Other Information
0910-AF93	Use of Ozone-Depleting Substances; Removal of Essential Use Designations [Flunisolide, Triamcinolone, Metaproterenol, Pirbuterol, Albuterol and Ipratropium in Combination, Cromolyn, and Nedocromil] [75 FR 19213]	Quantified	Not monetized	Benefits: Reduction of CFC emissions by 310-365 tons annually. Costs: Possible Change in Use of Asthma and COPD Therapy (0.33-14 million days of therapy) per year. Transfers: $13-$83 million per year in 2001 dollars (from Private Payers, Medicare and Medicaid to Drug Manufacturers). The RIA is included in the preamble.
0910-AG33	Regulations Restricting the Sale and Distribution of Cigarettes and Smokeless Tobacco to Protect Children and	Not estimated	Not estimated	This rule reinstates a 1996 final rule (as required by statute), and points to the original RIA (see 61 FR 44395). It does not provide an incremental analysis

RIN	Title	Benefits (2001$)	Costs (2001$)	Other Information
	Adolescents [75 FR 13225]			of the impacts of the rule compared to a baseline that takes into account current levels of compliance with the rule. Thus, the 1996 RIA very likely overstates both costs as well as benefits. The RIA is included in the preamble.
0920-AA26	Medical Examination of Aliens—Removal of Human Immunodeficiency Virus (HIV) Infection From Definition of Communicable Disease of Public Health Significance [74 FR 56547]	Quantified	$3 million Range: $11-$21 million	Quantified Benefits: 4,000 to 24,000 HIV-positive immigrants present in the U.S. in Year 5 who would not otherwise be able to immigrate. Qualitative Benefits: 1. Will reduce stigmatization of and discrimination against HIV-infected people. 2. Will bring family members together who had been barred from entry, thus strengthening families. 3. Will permit HIV-infected immigrants with skills in high demand would be permitted to enter the U.S. to seek employment and contribute as productive members of U.S. society. 4. Compared to those who don't receive appropriate multi-drug anti-retroviral therapy, those receiving such therapy survive an additional 13 years, with an average life expectancy of approximately 29 years (to age 49 years). This increased life expectancy allows opportunity for longer and improved productivity. Transfers: $71-$513 million (from HIV positive immigrants and health insurance payers to healthcare providers) The RIA is included in the preamble.
0938-AP40	Revisions to Payment Policies Under the Physician Fee Schedule For CY 2010 (CMS1413-FC) [74 FR 61738]	Not estimated	Not estimated	Transfers: $10,999 million (payment reductions) The RIA is included in the preamble.
0938-AP41	Changes to the Hospital Outpatient Prospective Payment System and	Not estimated	Not estimated	Transfers: $441 million The RIA is included in the preamble.

Table A-1. (Continued)

RIN	Title	Benefits (2001$)	Costs (2001$)	Other Information
0938-AP55	Ambulatory Surgical Center Payment System for CY 2010 (CMS-1414-F) [74 FR 60316]	Not estimated	Not estimated	Transfers $116 million (payment reductions) The RIA is included in the preamble.
0938-AP57	Home Health Prospective Payment System and Rate Update for CY 2010 (CMS-1560-F) [74 FR 58077]	Not estimated	Not estimated	Transfers: $164 million (payment reductions) The RIA is included in the preamble.
0938-AP72	End Stage Renal Disease Bundled Payment System (CMS-1418-F) [75 FR 49030]	Not estimated	Not estimated	Transfers: $692-$730 million (payment reductions) The RIA is included in the preamble.
0938-AP77	State Flexibility for Medicaid Benefit Packages (CMS-2232-F4) [75 FR 23068]	Not estimated	$232-$233 million	Transfers: $261-272 million (payment reductions) The RIA is included in the preamble.
0938-AP78	Revisions to the Medicare Advantage and Medicare Prescription Drug Benefit Programs for Contract Year 2011 (CMS4085-F) [75 FR 19677]	Not estimated	$524 million Range: $513-$535 million	Transfers: $851-$2,542 million The RIA is included in the preamble.
0938-AP80	Electronic Health Record (EHR) Incentive Program (CMS-0033-F) [75 FR 44314]	Not estimated	Not estimated	Transfers: $237 million (payment reductions) The RIA is included in the preamble.
0991-AB64	Medicare Program; Changes to the Hospital Inpatient Prospective Payment Systems for Acute Care Hospitals and the Long Term Care Hospital Prospective Payment System and Fiscal Year 2011 Rates [75 FR 50042]	Not estimated	$33 million	Transfers: $1,024 million (Federal government to sponsors/contractors) The RIA is included in the preamble.
	Early Retiree Reinsurance Program [75 FR 24450]			

RIN	Title	Benefits (2001$)	Costs (2001$)	Other Information
0991-AB71	Pre-Existing Condition Insurance Plan Program [75 FR 45010]	Not estimated	$2 million	Transfers: $1,009-$1,018 million (from Federal Government to contractors to administer the program) The agency reports $5 billion in transfers for the period from July 1, 2010 to December 31, 2013. We assumed a uniform distribution of funds over the time period and annualized over the four calendar years, and then converted the estimate to 2001 dollars. The RIA is included in the preamble.
Department of Health and Human Services, Department of Labor and Department of the Treasury					
0938-AP65; 1210-AB30	Interim Final Rules Under the Paul Wellstone and Pete Domenici Mental Health Parity and Addiction Equity Act of 2008 [75 FR 5410]	Not estimated	$10-$12 million	Qualitative Benefits: Benefits of the rule include a possible increase in access to mental health and substance abuse disorder benefits that could lead to improved health, a reduction in overall health expenditures for those with mental health or substance abuse disorders and increased worker productivity and earnings. Parity could also lead to reduced visit limitations and lower cost-sharing and out-of-pocket expenditures providing financial protection. Transfers: $2.2 billion in 2001 dollars (private transfers from those who do not utilize mental health or substance abuse disorder benefits to those that do). The RIA is included in the preamble.
0938-AQ07; 1210-AB44	Interim Final Rules for Group Health Plans and Health Insurance Issuers Relating to Coverage of Preventive Services under the Patient Protection and Affordable Care Act [75 FR 41726]	Not estimated	Not estimated	Qualitative Benefits: By expanding coverage and eliminating cost sharing for the required preventive services, the Departments expect access and utilization of these services to increase. To the extent that individuals increase their use of these

Table A-1. (Continued).

RIN	Title	Benefits (2001$)	Costs (2001$)	Other Information
				services the Departments anticipate several benefits: (1) prevention and reduction in transmission of illnesses as a result of immunization and screening of transmissible diseases; (2) delayed onset, earlier treatment, and reduction in morbidity and mortality as a result of early detection, screening, and counseling; (3) increased productivity and fewer sick days; and (4) savings from lower health care costs. Another benefit of these interim final regulations will be to distribute the cost of preventive services more equitably across the broad insured population. Qualitative Costs: New costs to the health care system result when beneficiaries increase their use of preventive services in response to the changes in coverage and cost-sharing requirements of preventive services. The magnitude of this effect on utilization depends on the price elasticity of demand and the percentage change in prices facing those with reduced cost sharing or newly gaining coverage. Qualitative Transfers: Transfers will occur to the extent that costs that were previously paid out-of-pocket for certain preventive services will now be covered by group health plans and issuers under these interim final regulations. Risk pooling in the group market will result in sharing expected cost increases across an plan or employee group as higher average premiums for all enrollees. However, not all of those covered will utilize

RIN	Title	Benefits (2001$)	Costs (2001$)	Other Information
				preventive services to an equivalent extent. As a result, these interim final regulations create a small transfer from those paying premiums in the group market utilizing less than the average volume of preventive services in their risk pool to those whose utilization is greater than average. To the extent there is risk pooling in the individual market, a similar transfer will occur. The RIA is included in the preamble.
0991-AB66; 1210-AB41	Interim Final Rules for Group Health Plans and Health Insurance Issuers Relating to Dependent Coverage of Children to Age 26 under the Patient Protection and Affordable Care Act [75 FR 27122]	Quantified	$9 million	Quantified Benefits: 190,000 to 1.6 million previously uninsured individuals who gain coverage in 2011. Qualitative Benefits: Expanding coverage options of the 19-25 population should decrease the number uninsured, which in turn should decrease the cost-shifting of uncompensated care onto those with insurance, increase the receipt of preventive health care and provide more timely access to high quality care, resulting in a healthier population. Allowing extended dependent coverage will also permit greater job mobility for this population as their insurance coverage will no longer be tied to their own jobs or student status. Dependants aged 19-25 that have chronic or other serious health conditions would still be able to continue their current coverage through a parent's plan. To the extent there is an increase in beneficial utilization of healthcare, health could improve. Transfers: $2.8-$5.7 billion (if the rule causes family health insurance premiums to increase, there will be a transfer from individuals with family

Table A-1. (Continued)

RIN	Title	Benefits (2001$)	Costs (2001$)	Other Information
				health insurance coverage who do not have dependents aged 19-25 to those individuals with family health insurance coverage that have dependents aged 19-25). The RIA is included in the preamble.
0991-AB68; 1210-AB42	Interim Final Rules for Group Health Plans and Health Insurance Coverage Relating to Status as a Grandfathered Health Plan under the Patient Protection and Affordable Care Act [75 FR 34538]	Not estimated	$21 million Range: $17-$23 million	Qualitative Benefits: These interim final regulations allow plans the choice or retaining or relinquishing grandfather status. Non-grandfathered plans are required to offer coverage with minimum benefit standards and patient protections as required by the Affordable Care Act, while grandfathered plans are only required to comply with certain provisions. The existence of grandfathered health plans could provide individuals with the benefits of plan continuity, which may be have a high value to some. It could potentially prevent premiums from increasing, depending on the extent to which their current plan does not include the benefits and rotections of the new law. It also could prevent the employer from dropping of coverage which would reduce new Medicaid enrollment and spending and lower the number of uninsured individuals. Qualitative costs: Limits on the changes to cost-sharing in grandfathered plans and the elimination of cost-sharing for some services in non-grandfathered plans, leads to transfers of wealth from premiums payers overall to individuals using covered services. Once pre-existing conditions are fully prohibited and other insurance reforms take effect, the extent to which individuals are enrolled

RIN	Title	Benefits (2001$)	Costs (2001$)	Other Information
				in grandfathered plans could affect adverse selection, as higher risk plans relinquish grandfather status to gain new protections while lower risk grandfather plans retain their grandfather status. This could result in a transfer of wealth from non-grandfathered plans to grandfathered health plans. The RIA is included in the preamble.
0991-AB69; 1210–AB43	Patient Protection and Affordable Care Act: Preexisting Condition Exclusions, Lifetime and Annual Limits, Rescissions, and Patient Protections [75 FR 43330]	Not estimated	$4 million	Qualitative Benefits: These patient protections are expected to expand coverage for children with preexisting conditions and individuals who face rescissions, lifetime limits, and annual limits as a result of high health care costs. Expanded coverage is likely to increase access to health care, improve health outcomes, improve worker productivity, and reduce family financial strain and "job lock". Many of these benefits have a distributional component and promote equity in the sense that they will be enjoyed by those who are especially vulnerable as a result of health problems and financial status. Choice of physician will likely lead to better, sustained patient-provider relationships, resulting in decreased malpractice claims and improved medication adherence and health promotion. Removing referrals and prior authorizations for primary care, OB/GYN, and emergency services is likely to reduce administrative and time burdens on both patients and physicians. Qualitative Costs: To the extent these patient protections increase access to health care services, increased health care utilization and costs will

Table A-1. (Continued)

RIN	Title	Benefits (2001$)	Costs (2001$)	Other Information
				result due to increased uptake. Expanding coverage to children with preexisting conditions and individuals subject to rescissions will likely increase overall health care costs, given that these groups tend to have high cost conditions and require more costly care than average. Qualitative Transfers: These patient protections create a transfer of wealth from those paying premiums in the group market to those obtaining the increased patient protections. To the extent there is risk pooling in the individual market, a similar transfer will occur. The RIA is included in the preamble.
0991-AB70; 1210–AB45	Interim Final Rules for Group Health Plans and Health Insurance Issuers Relating to Internal Claims and Appeals and External Review Processes under the Patient Protection and Affordable Care Act [75 FR 43330]	Not estimated	$42 million	Qualitative Benefits: A more uniform, rigorous, and consumer friendly system of claims and appeals processing will provide a broad range of direct and indirect benefits that will accrue to varying degrees to all of the affected parties. These interim final regulations could improve the extent to which employee benefit plans provide benefits consistent with the established terms of individual plans. While payment of these benefits will largely constitute transfers, the transfers will be welfare improving, because incorrectly denied benefits will be paid. Greater certainty and consistency in the handling of benefit claims and appeals and improved access to information about the manner in which claims and appeals are adjudicated should lead to efficiency gains in the system, both in terms of the allocation of spending across plans and

RIN	Title	Benefits (2001$)	Costs (2001$)	Other Information
				enrollees as well as operational efficiencies among individual plans. This certainty and consistency can also be expected to benefit, to varying degrees, all parties within the system, particularly consumers, and to lead to broader social welfare gains. Transfers: $20 million. Qualitative transfers: The Departments estimated the dollar amount of claim denials reversed in the external review process. While this amount is a cost to plans, it represents a payment of benefits that should have previously been paid to participants, but was denied. Part of this amount is a transfer from plans and issuers to those now receiving payment for denied benefits. These transfers will improve equity, because incorrectly denied benefits will be paid. Part of the amount could also be a cost if the reversal leads to services and hence resources being utilized now that had been denied previously. The Departments are not able to distinguish between the two types, but believe that most reversals are associated with a transfer. The RIA is included in the preamble.
Department of Homeland Security					
1615-AB80	U. S. Citizenship and Immigration Services Fee Schedule [75 FR 58961]	Not estimated	Not estimated	Transfers: $173 million The RIA is included in the preamble.
1651-AA83	Electronic System for Travel Authorization (ESTA): Fee for Use of the System [75 FR 47701]	Not estimated	Not estimated	Transfers: $121-$206 million The full RIA is available at:http://www.regulations.govDocument ID: USCBP-2010-0025-0002
1660-AA44	Special Community Disaster Loans Program [75 FR 2800]	Not estimated	<$1 million	Transfers: $0-$1,075 million The RIA is included in the preamble.

Table A-1. (Continued)

RIN	Title	Benefits (2001$)	Costs (2001$)	Other Information
Department of the Interior				
1018-AX06	Migratory Bird Hunting; Final Frameworks for Early-Season Migratory Bird Hunting Regulations [75 FR 52873]	$271 million Range: $234-$309 million	Not estimated	Estimates based on the RIA for the 2008-2009 season. The full RIA is available at: http://www.fws.gov/migratorybirds/NewReportsPublications/SpecialTopics/HuntingRegulations/Mig%20bird%20Regs%20analysis%202008.pdf
Department of Justice				
1117-AA61	Electronic Prescriptions for Controlled Substances [75 FR 16236]	$348-$1,320 million	$35-$36 million	The RIA is available at: http://www.deadiversion.usdoj.gov/ecomm/e_rx/eia_dea_218.pdf
1190-AA44	Nondiscrimination on the Basis of Disability in Public Accommodations and Commercial Facilities [75 FR 56164]	$1,123million Range: $980-$2,056 million	$611million Range: $549-$719 million	The RIA is available at:http://www.ada.gov/regs2010/ADAregs2010.htm
1190-AA46	Nondiscrimination on the Basis of Disability in State and Local Government Services [75 FR 56236]	$173 million Range: $151-$304 million	$138 million Range: $122-$172 million	The RIA is available at: http://www.ada.gov/regs2010/ADAregs2010.htm
Department of Labor				
1210-AB08	Improved Fee Disclosure for Pension Plans [75 FR 41599]	Not estimated	$44-$48 million	Qualitative Benefits: Qualitative: The final regulation will increase the amount of information that service providers disclose to plan fiduciaries. Non-quantified benefits include information cost savings, discouraging harmful conflicts of interest, service value improvements through improved decisions and value, better enforcement tools to redress abuse, and harmonization with other EBSA rules and programs. The RIA is included in the preamble.
1218-AC01	Cranes and Derricks in Construction [75 FR 47906]	$172 million	$123-$126 million	The RIA is included in the preamble.

RIN	Title	Benefits (2001$)	Costs (2001$)	Other Information
Department of State				
1400-AC58	Schedule of Fees for Consular Services, Department of State and Overseas Embassies and Consulates [75 FR 36522]	Not estimated	Not estimated	Transfers: $322-$394 million The RIA is included in the preamble.
Department of Transportation				
2120-AI92	Automatic Dependent Surveillance-Broadcast (ADS-B) Equipage Mandate to Support Air Traffic Control Service [75 FR 30160]	$172 million Range: $149-$195 million	$233 million Range: $153-$292 million	The RIA is available at:http://www.regulations.gov Document ID: FAA-2007-29305-0288.1
2126-AA89	Electronic On-Board Recorders for Hours-of-Service Compliance [75 FR 17208]	$165- $170 million	$126- $129 million	The RIA is available at: http://www.regulations.gov Document ID: FMCSA-2004-18940-1157
2130-AC03	Positive Train Control [75 FR 2597]	$34 million Range: $34-$37 million	$745 million Range: $519-$1,264 million	The RIA is available at:http://www.fra.dot.gov/downloads/safety/PTCRSIAfinalRIA120809.pdf
2137-AE15	Pipeline Safety: Distribution Integrity Management [74 FR 63906]	$97-$145 million	$92-$97 million	The RIA is available at: http://www.regulations.gov Document ID: PHMSA-RSPA-2004-19854-0255
Department of Transportation and Environmental Protection Agency				
2060-AP58; 2127-AK50	Light-Duty Greenhouse Gas Emission Standards and Corporate Average Fuel Economy Standards [75 FR 25323]	$11.9 billion Range: $3.9-$18.2 billion	$3.3 billion Range: $1.7-$4.9 billion	The primary estimates are based on the total cost and benefits estimates for model years 2012-2016 in EPA's RIA and the range of total cost and benefit estimates in DOT's RIA, annualized over the life of the vehicles covered by the rule. DOT and EPA estimates differ somewhat due to programmatic differences between the two rules and differences in estimation modeling. DOT's RIA is available at: http://www.nhtsa.gov/staticfiles/rulemaking/pdf/cafe/CAFE_2012-2016FRIA_04012010.pdf EPA's RIA is available at: http://www.epa.gov/otaq/climate/regulations/420r10009.pdf

Table A-1. (Continued)

RIN	Title	Benefits (2001$)	Costs (2001$)	Other Information
Department of the Treasury				
1557-AD23	S.A.F.E. Mortgage Licensing Act [75 FR 44656]	Not estimated	$148 million Range: $86-$157 million	Qualitative Benefits: Rule enhances bank oversight/OCC supervision of mortgage origination through written policies/procedures and regulatory requirements on national banks and employee loan originators. Qualitative Costs: OCC monetized the cost of compensation but did not attempt to account for any possible reduction in banks' fee or other income due to lower loan originator productivity due to the implementation of the joint interagency Rule. The RIA is available at:http://www.regulations.gov Document ID: OCC-2010-0007-0002
Department of Veterans Affairs				
2900-AN54	Diseases Associated With Exposure to Certain Herbicide Agents (Hairy Cell Leukemia and Other Chronic B Cell Leukemias, Parkinson's Disease, and Ischemic Heart Disease) [75 FR 53202]	Not estimated	Not estimated	Transfers: $4,101-$5,408 million The RIA is available at: http://www.va.gov /ORPM/FY_2010 Published_VA_Regulations.asp (scroll to number 37)
Environmental Protection Agency				
2050-AG16	Revisions to the Spill Prevention, Control, and Countermeasure (SPCC) Rule [74 FR 58784]	$0	($81 million) Range ($78-$85 million)	Cost savings. The RIA is available at: http://www.Regulations.gov Docket ID: EPA-HQ-OPA-2007-0584
2060-AO15	NESHAP: Portland Cement Notice of Reconsideration [75 FR 54970]	$6.1-$16.3 billion	$0.8-$0.9 billion	The RIA is available at: http://www.epa. gov/ttn/atw/pcem/ria_cement.doc
2060-AO38	Control of Emissions From New Marine Compression-Ignition Engines at or Above 30 Liters per Cylinder [75 FR 22897]	Not estimated	Not estimated	The agency presents estimated benefits and costs for the coordinated strategy, both national and international levels, to control emissions from

RIN	Title	Benefits (2001$)	Costs (2001$)	Other Information
				ocean-going vessels. It includes: (1) the engine and fuel controls finalizing under the Clean Air Act; (2) the proposal submitted by the United States Government to the International Maritime Organization to amend MARPOL Annex VI to designate U.S. coasts as an Emission Control Area in which all vessels, regardless of flag, would be required to meet the engine and marine fuel sulfur requirements in Annex VI; and (3) the new engine emission and fuel sulfur limits contained in the amendments to Annex VI that are applicable to all vessels regardless of flag under the Act to Prevent Pollution from Ships. The estimates, although illustrative, do not represent the benefits and costs of the rule. The RIA available at: http://www.epa.gov/otaq/regs/nonroad/marine/ci/420r09019.pdf
2060-AO48	Review of the National Ambient Air Quality Standards for Sulfur Dioxide [75 FR 35519]	$10.5 billion Range: $2.9-$38.6 billion	$0.7 billion Range: $0.3-$2.0 billion	The agency provided benefit and cost estimates for 2020. In order to annualize, as with previous NAAQS rulemakings, OMB assumed that the benefits and costs would be zero in the first year after the rule is finalized, the benefits and costs would increase linearly until year 2020, and the benefit and cost estimates would equal the 2020 estimates thereafter. EPA's RIA is available at: http://www.epa.gov/ttn/ecas/regdata/RIAs/fso2ria100602full.pdf
2060-AO81	Renewable Fuels Standard Program [75 FR 14670]	Not estimated	Not estimated	EPA utilizes a case study approach to assess the consequences of an expansion of renewable fuel use, whether caused by the RFS2 program or by market force. The analytical approach taken by

Table A-1. (Continued)

RIN	Title	Benefits (2001$)	Costs (2001$)	Other Information
				EPA is to predict what the world would be like, in terms of a range of economic and environmental factors, if renewable fuel use increases to the level required by the RFS2 standards. EPA then compares this to two reference cases without the RFS2 program. The estimates, although illustrative, do not represent the benefits and costs of the rule. EPA's RIA is available at: http://www.epa.gov/otaq/renewablefuels/420r10006.pdf
2060-AP36	National Emission Standards for Hazardous Air Pollutants for Reciprocating Internal Combustion Engines (Diesel) [75 FR 9647]	Range: $709-$1,920 million	$311 million Range: $296-$311 million	EPA's RIA is available at: http://www.epa.gov/ttn/atw/rice/rice_neshap_ria2-17-10.pdf
2060-AP86	Prevention of Significant Deterioration/Title V Greenhouse Gas Tailoring Rule [75 FR 31514]	Not estimated	Not estimated	EPA estimated that the Tailoring rule would provide significant regulatory relief to state permitting agencies, because without the rule, the number of permits required would overwhelm the resources of permitting authorities, and severely impair the functioning of the programs. Although EPA estimated savings of $1.5 billion to permitting authorities and $21 billion for facilities, these savings estimates are not included in this report for two reasons. First, in order to count these cost savings, one would have to assume that the joint EPA/DOT greenhouse gas and fuel economy rules imposed an extra $22.5 billion in costs. In such a case, the inclusion of these impacts affects the total net benefits of FY 2010 rulemaking. Furthermore, EPA argued in the Tailoring rule that this level of permitting would be administratively impossible.

RIN	Title	Benefits (2001$)	Costs (2001$)	Other Information
				For example, EPA estimated processing the over 6 million permits needed in the absence this rule may take as long as 10 years, and indicated even this may be an underestimate. In other words, these savings estimates, although illustrative, do not represent a cost that would be imposed in the absence of this rule. EPA's RIA is available at: http://www.epa.gov/ttnecas1/regdata/RIAs/riaghgtailoring092109.pdf
2060-AQ13	National Emission Standards for Hazardous Air Pollutants for Reciprocating Internal Combustion Engines--Existing Stationary Spark Ignition (Gas-Fired) [75 FR 51569]	$380-$992 million	$202-$209 million	EPA's RIA is available at: http://www.epa.gov/ttn/atw/rice/fnl_si_rice_ria.pdf
2070-AJ55	Lead; Amendment to the Opt-out and Recordkeeping Provisions in the Renovation, Repair, and Painting Program [75 FR 24802]	$785-$2,953 million	$267-$290 million	The RIA is available at: http://www.regulations.gov Document ID: EPA-HQ-OPPT-2005-0049-1076.6

Table A-2. Estimates of Annual Benefits and Costs of Major Final Rules October 1, 2000 - September 30, 2009215
(Millions of 2001 Dollars)

RIN	Title	Completed	Published	Benefits	Costs	Source of Estimate
Department of Agriculture						
0579-AB73	Bovine Spongiform Encephalopathy: Minimal Risk Regions and Importation of Commodities	12/29/04	1/4/05	572-639	557-623	2006 Report: Table 1-4
0579-AB81	Mexican Hass Avocado Import Program	11/23/04	11/30/04	122-184	71-114	2006 Report: Table 1-4

Table A-2. (Continued).

RIN	Title	Completed	Published	Benefits	Costs	Source of Estimate
0579-AC01	Bovine Spongiform Encephalopathy; Minimal-Risk Regions and Importation of Commodities	9/14/07	9/18/07	169-340	98-194	2008 Report: Table 1-4
0583-AC46	Performance Standards for Ready-To-Eat Meat and Poultry Products	5/30/03	6/6/03	43-152	17	2004 Report: Table 12
0583-AC88	Prohibition of the Use of Specified Risk Materials for Human Food and Requirements for the Disposition of Non-Ambulatory Disabled Cattle	6/29/07	7/13/07	0	87-221	2008 Report: Table 1-4
0596-AB77	Special Areas; Roadless Area Conservation --36 CFR Part 294	1/5/01	1/12/01	0	184	2002 Report: Table 19
Department of Energy						
1904-AA67	Energy Efficiency Standards for Clothes Washers	1/2/01	1/12/01	2,150	940	2002 Report: Table 19
1904-AA76	Energy Efficiency Standards for Water Heaters	1/9/01	1/17/01	680	510	2002 Report: Table 19
1904-AA77	Energy Efficiency Standards for Central Air Conditioners and Heat Pumps	1/17/01	1/22/01	1,233	1,132	2003 Report: Table 19 (adjusted)[216]
1904-AA78	Energy Efficiency Standards for Residential Furnaces and Boilers	11/6/07	11/19/07	120-182	33-38	2009 Report: Table 1-4
1904-AA92	Energy Efficiency Standards for General Service Fluorescent Lamps and Incandescent Lamps	6/26/09	7/14/09	1,111-2,886	192-657	2010 Report: Table 1-4
1904-AB08	Energy Efficiency Standards for Electric Distribution Transformers	9/27/07	10/12/07	490-865	381-426	2008 Report: Table 1-4
1904-AB59	Energy Efficiency Standards for Commercial Refrigeration Equipment	12/18/08	1/9/09	186-224	69-81	2010 Report: Table 1-4
Department of Health and Human Services						
0910-AA43	Hazard Analysis and Critical Control Point (HACCP); Procedures for the Safe and Sanitary Processing and Importing of Juice	1/10/01	1/19/01	150	30	2002 Report: Table 19

RIN	Title	Completed	Published	Benefits	Costs	Source of Estimate
0910-AB30	Food Labeling: Safe Handling Statements, Labeling of Shell Eggs; Refrigeration of Shell Eggs Held for Retail Distribution Recipients Receiving Blood and Blood Components at Increased Risk of Transmitting HCV Infection (Lookback)	11/29/00	12/5/00	261	15	2002 Report: Table 19
0910-AB88	Current Good Manufacturing Practice in Manufacturing, Packing, or Holding Dietary Ingredients and Dietary Supplements	5/8/07	6/25/07	10-79	87-293	2008 Report: Table 1-4
0910-AC14	Prevention of Salmonella Enteritidis in Shell Eggs	7/2/09	7/9/09	206-8,583	48-106	2010 Report: Table 1-4
0910-AC26	Bar Code Label Requirements for Human Drug Products and Blood Products	2/17/04	2/26/04	1,352-7,342	647	2005 Report: Table 1-4
0910-AC34	Amendments to the Performance Standard for Diagnostic X-Ray Systems and Their Major Components	5/27/05	6/10/05	87-2,549	30	2006 Report: Table 1-4
0910-AC48	Applications for FDA Approval To Market a New Drug Patent Listing Requirements and Application of 30- Month Stays on Approval of Abbreviated New Drug Applications Certifying That a Patent...	6/9/03	6/18/03	226	10	2004 Report: Table 12
0910-AF19	Declaring Dietary Supplements Containing Ephedrine Alkaloids Adulterated Because They Present an Unreasonable Risk of Illness or Injury (Final Rule)	2/5/04	2/11/04	0-130	7-89	2005 Report: Table 1-4
0919-AA01	Patient Safety and Quality Improvement Act of 2005 Rules	11/14/08	11/21/08	69-136	87-121	2010 Report: Table 1-4
0938-AH99	Health Insurance Reform: Standard Unique Health Care Provider Identifier --CMS-0045-F	1/13/04	1/23/04	214	158	2005 Report: Table 1-4
0938-AM50	Updates to Electronic Transactions (Version 5010) (CMS-0009-F)	1/9/09	1/16/09	1,114-3,194	661-1,449	2010 Report: Table 1-4
0938-AN25	Revisions to HIPAA Code Sets (CMS-0013-F)	1/9/09	1/16/09	77-261	44-238	2010 Report: Table 1-4
0938-AN49	Electronic Prescribing Standards(CMS-0011-F)	11/1/05	11/7/05	196-660	82-274	2007 Report: Table 1-4

Table A-2. (Continued)

RIN	Title	Completed	Published	Benefits	Costs	Source of Estimate
0938-AN79	Fire Safety Requirements for Long-Term Care Facilities: Sprinkler Systems (CMS-3191-F)	8/6/08	8/13/08	53-56	45-56	2009 Report: Table 1-4
0938-AN95	Immunization Standard for Long Term Care Facilities (CMS-3198-P)	9/30/05	10/7/05	11,000	6	2006 Report: Table 1-4
0991-AB08	Standards for Privacy of Individually Identifiable Health Information	12/19/00	12/28/00	2,700	1,680	2002 Report: Table 19
Department of Homeland Security						
1651-AA72	Changes to the Visa Waiver Program To Implement the Electronic System for Travel Authorization (ESTA) Program	5/30/08	6/9/08	20-29	13-99	2009 Report: Table 1-4
Department of Housing and Urban Development						
2502-AI61	Real Estate Settlement Procedures Act (RESPA); To Simplify and Improve the Process of Obtaining Mortgages and Reduce Consumer Costs (FR-5180)	11/7/08	11/17/08	2,303	884	2010 Report: Table 1-4
Department of Justice						
1117-AA60	Electronic Orders for Schedule I and II Controlled Substances	3/18/05	4/1/05	275	108-118	2006 Report: Table 1-4
Department of Labor						
1210-AB06	Revision of the Form 5500 Series and Implementing Regulations	8/30/07	11/16/07	0	(83)	2008 Report: Table 1-4
1218-AA65	Safety Standards for Steel Erection	1/8/01	1/18/01	167	78	2002 Report: Table 19
1218-AB45	Occupational Exposure to Hexavalent Chromium (Preventing Occupational Illness: Chromium)	2/17/06	2/28/06	35-862	263-271	2007 Report: Table 1-4
1218-AB77	Employer Payment for Personal Protective Equipment	11/2/07	11/15/07	40-336	2-20	2009 Report: Table 1-4
1219-AB46	Emergency Mine Evacuation	12/5/06	12/8/06	10	41	2008 Report: Table 1-4

RIN	Title	Completed	Published	Benefits	Costs	Source of Estimate
Department of Transportation						
2120-AH68	Reduced Vertical Separation Minimum in Domestic United States Airspace (RVSM)	10/8/03	10/27/03	(60)	(320)	2005 Report: Table 1-4
2120-AI17	Washington, DC, Metropolitan Area Special Flight Rules Area	12/3/08	12/16/08	10-839	89-382	2010 Report: Table 1-4
2120-AI23	Transport Airplane Fuel Tank Flammability Reduction	7/9/08	7/21/08	21-66	60-67	2009 Report: Table 1-4
2120-AI51	Congestion and Delay Reduction at Chicago O'Hare International	8/18/06	8/29/06	153-164	0	2007 Report: Table 1-4
2120-AJ01	Part 121 Pilot Age Limit	6/8/09	7/15/09	30-35	4	2010 Report: Table 1-4
2126-AA23	Hours of Service Drivers; Driver Rest and Sleep for Safe Operation	4/9/03	4/28/03	690	1,318	2004 Report: Table 12
2126-AA59	New Entrant Safety Assurance Process	11/26/08	12/16/08	472-602	60-72	2010 Report: Table 1-4
2126-AA90	Hours of Service of Drivers	8/16/05	8/25/05	19	(235)	2006 Report: Table 1-4
2126-AB14	Hours of Service of Drivers[217]	11/13/08	11/19/08	Not included	Not included	2010 Report: Table 1-4
2127-AG51	Roof Crush Resistance	4/30/09	5/12/09	374-1,160	748-1,189	2010 Report: Table 1-4
2127-AH09	Upgrade of Head Restraints	11/23/04	12/14/04	111-139	83	2006 Report: Table 1-4
2127-AI10	Advanced Air Bags: Response to Petitions Federal Motor Vehicle Safety Standards; Occupant Crash Protection	12/5/01	12/18/01	140-1,600	400-2,000	2002 Report: Table 19
2127-AI33	Tire Pressure Monitoring Systems[218]	5/29/02	6/5/02	Not Included	Not Included	2003 Report: Table 19
2127-AI70	Light Truck Average Fuel Economy Standards, Model Years 2005-2007	3/31/03	4/7/03	255	220	2004 Report: Table 12

Table A-2. (Continued)

RIN	Title	Completed	Published	Benefits	Costs	Source of Estimate
2127-AJ91	Rear Center Lap/Shoulder Belt Requirement--Standard 208	11/30/04	12/8/04	188-236	162-202	2006 Report: Table 1-4
2127-AJ10	Side Impact Protection Upgrade--FMVSS No. 214	8/28/07	9/11/07	736-1,058	401-1,051	2008 Report: Table 1-4
2127-AJ23	Tire Pressure Monitoring Systems	3/31/05	4/8/05	1,012-1,316	938-2,282	2006 Report: Table 1-4
2127-AJ37	Reduced Stopping Distance Requirements for Truck Tractors	7/16/09	7/27/09	1,250-1,520	23-164	2010 Report: Table 1-4
2127-AJ61	Light Truck Average Fuel Economy Standards, Model Year 2008 and Possibly Beyond	3/28/06	4/6/06	847-1,035	666-754	2007 Report: Table 1-4
2127-AJ77	Electronic Stability Control (ESC)	3/23/07	4/6/07	5,987-11,282	913-917	2008 Report: Table 1-4
2127-AK29	Passenger Car and Light Truck Corporate Average Fuel Economy Model Year 2011	3/24/09	3/30/09	857-1,905	650-1,910	2010 Report: Table 1-4
2137-AD54	Pipeline Integrity Management in High Consequence Areas (Gas Transmission Pipelines)	11/26/03	12/15/03	154	288	2005 Report: Table 1-4
2137-AE25	Pipeline Safety: Standards for Increasing the Maximum Allowable Operating Pressure for Gas Transmission Pipelines	10/2/08	10/17/08	85-89	13-14	2010 Report: Table 1-4
2130-AB84	Regulatory Relief for Electronically Controlled Pneumatic Brake System Implementation	8/29/08	10/16/08	828-884	130-145	2009 Report: Table 1-4
Environmental Protection Agency						
2040-AB75	National Primary Drinking Water Regulations, Arsenic, and Clarifications to Compliance and New Source Contaminants Monitoring	1/10/01	1/22/01	140-198	206-206	2002 Report: Table 19
2040-AD19	National Pollutant Discharge Elimination System Permit Regulation and Effluent Guidelines and Standards for Concentrated Animal Feeding Operations (CAFOs)	12/14/02	2/12/03	204-355	360	2004 Report: Table 12
2040-AD37	National Primary Drinking Water Regulations: Long Term 2 Enhanced Surface Water Treatment Rule	6/22/05	1/5/06	262-1,785	80-132	2006 Report: Table 1-4

RIN	Title	Completed	Published	Benefits	Costs	Source of Estimate
2040-AD38	National Primary Drinking Water Regulations: Stage 2 Disinfection Byproducts Rule	11/23/05	1/4/06	598-1,473	74-76	2007 Report: Table 1-4
2040-AD56	Effluent Guidelines and Standards for the Meat and Poultry Products Point Source Category (Revisions)	2/26/04	9/8/04	0-10	41-56	2005 Report: Table 1-4
2040-AD62	Establishing Location, Design, Construction, and Capacity Standards for Cooling Water Intake Structures at Large Existing Power Plants (Final Rule)	2/16/04	7/9/04	72	383	2005 Report: Table 1-4
2050-AG23	Oil Pollution Prevention; Spill Prevention, Control, and Countermeasure (SPCC) Requirements--Amendments	11/15/06	12/26/06	0	(86-148)	2008 Report: Table 1-4
2050-AG31	Definition of Solid Wastes Revisions	9/17/08	10/30/08	16-285	14	2009 Report: Table 1-4
2060-AG52	Plywood and Composite Wood Products	2/26/04	7/30/04	152-1,437	155-291	2005 Report: Table 1-4
2060-AG63	National Emission Standards for Hazardous Air Pollutants for Stationary Reciprocating Internal Combustion Engines	2/26/04	6/15/04	105-1,070	270	2005 Report: Table 1-4
2060-AG69	National Emission Standards for Hazardous Air Pollutants: Industrial/Commercial/Institutional Boilers and Process Heaters[219]	2/26/04	9/13/04	Not Included	Not Included	2005 Report: Table 1-4
2060-AI11	Emissions From Nonroad Spark-Ignition Engines and Standards for Recreational Spark-Ignition Engines	9/13/02	11/8/02	1,330-4,818	192	2003 Report: Table 19
2060-AI34	National Emission Standards for Hazardous Air Pollutants for Chemical Recovery Combustion Sources at Kraft, Soda, Sulfite, and Stand-Alone Semichemical Pulp Mills	12/15/00	1/12/01	293-393	32	2002 Report: Table 19
2060-AI44	Review of the National Ambient Air Quality Standards for Particulate Matter	9/21/06	10/17/06	3,837-39,879	2,590-2,833	2007 Report: Table 1-4
2060-AI69	Heavy-Duty Engine Emission Standards and Diesel Fuel Sulfur Control Requirements 2007	12/21/00	1/18/01	13,000	2,400	2002 Report: Table 19
2060-AJ31	Clean Air Visibility Rule	6/15/05	7/6/05	2,302-8,153	314-846	2006 Report: Table 1-4
2060-AJ65	Clean Air Mercury Rule--Electric Utility Steam Generating Units[220]	3/15/05	5/18/05	Not Included	Not Included	2006 Report: Table 1-4

Table A-2. (Continued)

RIN	Title	Completed	Published	Benefits	Costs	Source of Estimate
2060-AK27	Control of Emissions of Air Pollution From Nonroad Diesel Engines and Fuel (Final Rule)	5/7/04	6/29/04	6,853-59,401	1,336	2005 Report: Table 1-4
2060-AK70	Control of Hazardous Air Pollutants From Mobile Sources	2/8/07	2/26/07	2,310-2,983	298-346	2008 Report: Table 1-4
2060-AK74	Clean Air Fine Particle Implementation Rule	3/28/07	4/25/07	18,833-167,408	7,324	2008 Report: Table 1-4
2060-AL76	Clean Air Interstate Rule Formerly Titled: Interstate Air Quality Rule[221]	3/10/05	5/12/05	11,947-151,769	1,716-1,894	2006 Report: Table 1-4
2060-AM06	Control of Emissions from New Locomotives and New Marine Diesel Engines Less Than 30 Liters per Cylinder	2/14/08	5/6/08	4,145-14,550	295-392	2009 Report: Table 1-4
2060-AM34	Control of Emissions From Nonroad Spark-Ignition Engines and Equipment	8/18/08	10/8/08	899-4,762	196-200	2009 Report: Table 1-4
2060-AM82	Standards of Performance for Stationary Compression Ignition Internal Combustion Engines	6/28/06	7/11/06	679-757	56	2007 Report: Table 1-4
2060-AN24	Review of the National Ambient Air Quality Standards for Ozone[222]	3/12/08	3/27/08	Not Included	Not Included	2009 Report: Table 1-4
2060-AN72	Petroleum Refineries--New Source Performance Standards (NSPS)--Subpart J	4/30/08	6/24/08	176-1,669	27	2009 Report: Table 1-4
2060-AN83	Review of the National Ambient Air Quality Standards for Lead	10/15/08	11/12/08	455-5,203	113-2,241	2010 Report: Table 1-4
2070-AC83	Lead-Based Paint; Amendments for Renovation, Repair and Painting	3/28/08	4/22/08	657-1,611	383-417	2009 Report: Table 1-4
2070-AD38	Lead and Lead Compounds; Lowering of Reporting Thresholds; Community Right-to-Know Toxic Chemical Release Reporting	1/8/01	1/17/01	1,750-6,840	2,700	2002 Report: Table 19

( ) indicates negative.

All benefit and cost estimates are adjusted to 2001 dollars using the latest Gross Domestic Product (GDP) deflator, available from the Bureau of Economic Analysis at the Department of Commerce.[214] In instances where the nominal dollar values the agencies use for their benefits and costs is unclear, we assume the benefits and costs are presented in nominal dollar values of the year before the rule is finalized. In periods of low inflation such as the past few years, this assumption does not affect the overall totals. All amortizations are performed using a discount rate of 7 percent unless the agency has already presented annualized, monetized results using a different explicit discount rate.

OMB discusses, in this Report and in previous Reports, the difficulty of estimating and aggregating the benefits and costs of different regulations over long time periods and across many agencies. In addition, where OMB has monetized quantitative estimates where the agency has not done so, we have attempted to be faithful to the respective agency approaches. The adoption of a uniform format for annualizing agency estimates allows, at least for purposes of illustration, the aggregation of benefit and cost estimates across rules; however, agencies have used different methodologies and valuations in quantifying and monetizing effects. Thus, an aggregation involves the assemblage of benefit and cost estimates that are not strictly comparable.

To address this issue in part, the 2003 Report included OMB's new regulatory analysis guidance, also released as OMB Circular A-4, which took effect on January 1, 2004 for proposed rules and January 1, 2005 for final rules. The guidance recommends what OMB considers to be "best practices" in regulatory analysis, with a goal of strengthening the role of science, engineering, and economics in rulemaking. The overall goal of this guidance is a more competent and credible regulatory process, and a more consistent regulatory environment. OMB expects that as more agencies adopt these recommended best practices, the benefits and costs presented in future Reports will become more comparable across agencies and programs. The 2006 Report was the first report that included final rules subject to OMB Circular A-4. OMB will continue to work with the agencies to ensure that their impact analyses follow the new guidance.

Table A-1 below presents information on the impacts of 66 major rules reviewed by OMB from October 1, 2009 through September 30, 2010. Unless otherwise stated, the estimates presented in Table A-1 are unmodified agency estimates of annualized impacts except for an adjustment to 2001 dollars, which is the requested format in OMB Circular A-4.

Table 1-5(a) in Chapter I of this Report presents the estimates for the 1 8 rules finalized in fiscal year 2010 that were added to the Chapter I accounting statement totals. Table A-2 below presents the benefits and costs of previously reported major rules reviewed by OMB from October 1, 2000 through September 30, 2009 that are also included in the Chapter I accounting statement totals.

APPENDIX B: THE BENEFITS AND COSTS OF 1999-2000 MAJOR RULES

Table B-1 lists the rules that were omitted from the ten-year running totals presented in Chapter I of our Report to Congress. It consists of the annualized and monetized benefits and costs of rules for which OMB concluded review between October 1, 1999 and September 30,

2000. These rules were included in Chapter I of the 2010 Report as part of the ten-year totals, but are not included in the 2011 Report.

While we limit the Chapter I accounting statement to regulations issued over the previous ten years, we have included in this Appendix the benefits and cost estimates provided for the economically significant rulemakings that have been covered in previous Reports in order to provide transparency. These estimates were first included in the 2002 Report (see table 19 in that report).

Table B-1. Estimates of Annual Benefits and Costs of Six Major Federal Rules October 1, 1999 - September 30, 2000 (millions of 2001 dollars)

Agency	RIN	Title	OMB Review Completed	Benefits	Costs
HHS/ CMS	0938-AI58	Health Insurance Reform: Standards for Electronic Transactions	8/11/00	2,720	700
DOE/ EE	1904-AA75	Energy Conservations Standards for Fluorescent Lamp Ballasts	8/31/00	280	70
EPA/ Water	2040-AC82	National Pollutant Discharge Elimination System: Regulations for Revision of the Water Pollution Control Program Addressing Storm Water Discharges	10/15/99	700-1,700	900-1,100
EPA/ AR	2060-AE29	Phase 2 Emission Standards for New Nonroad Small Spark Ignition Handheld Engines At or Below 19 Kilowatts and Minor Amendments to Emission Requirements Applicable to Small Spark Ignition Engines	3/1/00	170-890	190-250
EPA/ AR	2060-AI12	Control of Emissions of Air Pollution from 2004 and Later Model Year Highway Heavy- Duty Engines; Revision of Light-Duty Truck Definition	7/28/00	1,840-12,650	482
EPA/ AR	2060-AI23	Control of Air Pollution from New Motor Vehicle Emissions Standards and Gasoline Sulfur Control Requirements	12/21/99	7,300-13,400	4,000

APPENDIX C: INFORMATION ON THE REGULATORY ANALYSES FOR MAJOR RULES BY INDEPENDENT AGENCIES

Table C-1. Total Number of Rules Promulgated by Independent Agencies October 1, 2000 – September 30, 2010

Agency	2001	2002	2003	2004	2005	2006	2007	2008	2009	2010
Consumer Product Safety Commission (CPSC)	0	0	0	0	0	1	0	0	--	--
Federal Communications Commission (FCC)	2	4	0	1	4	2	2	4	--	--
Federal Energy Regulatory Commission (FERC)	0	0	0	0	0	0	0	1	--	--
Federal Reserve System	0	0	1	1	0	0	0	0	3	7
Federal Trade Commission (FTC)	0	0	0	0	1	0	0	0	--	1
National Credit Union Administration (NCUA)	0	0	0	0	0	0	0	0	--	--
Nuclear Regulatory Commission (NRC)	1	1	1	1	1	1	1	2	2	1
Pension Benefit Guaranty Corporation (PBGC)	0	0	0	0	0	0	0	0	--	--
Securities and Exchange Commission (SEC)	3	3	5	1	5	0	7	4	8	9
Total	6	8	7	4	11	4	10	11	13	17

Table C-2. Total Number of Rules with Some Information on Benefits or Costs[223] Promulgated by Independent Agencies October 1, 2000- September 30, 2010

Agency	2001	2002	2003	2004	2005	2006	2007	2008	2009	2010
Consumer Product Safety Commission (CPSC)	--	--	--	--	--	1	--	--	--	--
Federal Communications Commission (FCC)	0	0	0	1	0	0	0	0	--	--
Federal Energy Regulatory Commission (FERC)	--	--	--	--	--	--	--	1	--	--
Federal Reserve System	--	--	0	1	--	--	--	--	0	2
Federal Trade Commission (FTC)	--	--	--	--	0	--	--	--	--	1
National Credit Union Administration (NCUA)	--	--	--	--	--	--	--	--	--	--
Nuclear Regulatory Commission (NRC)	--	--	--	--	--	--	--	1	1	--
Pension Benefit Guaranty Corporation (PBGC)	--	--	--	--	--	--	--	--	--	--
Securities and Exchange Commission (SEC)	3	3	5	1	5	--	7	4	8	9
Total	3	3	5	3	5	1	7	6	8	11

APPENDIX D: THE BENEFITS AND COSTS OF MAJOR RULES BY ADMINISTRATION

Chapter II presents estimates of the annual benefits and costs of major final regulations reviewed by OMB during the first two fiscal years of three Administrations. The totals presented in chapter 2 are based on aggregation of estimates presented in previous reports. Table D-1 includes major final rules OMB completed review between January 20, 1993 to September 30, 1994 where both benefit and cost estimates were previously reported. Table D-2 includes major final rules OMB completed review between January 20, 2001 to September

30, 2002 where both benefit and cost estimates were previously reported. Table D-3 includes major final rules OMB completed review between January 20, 2009 to September 30, 2009 where both benefit and cost estimates were previously reported. The tables and figure presented in chapter II also include the benefits and costs of 18 major final rules we report in table 1-5(a). OMB presents more detailed explanation of these regulations in several previous documents as noted in the "source" column of the tables.

Table D-1. Estimates of Annual Benefits and Costs of Major Federal Rules January 20, 1993 to September 30, 1994[224] (millions of 2001 dollars per year)

Agency	RIN	Title	OMB Review Completed	Published	Benefits	Costs	Source
HUD	2502-AE66	Manufactured Housing Construction and Safety Standards	9/21/93	10/21/93	$103	$63	2004 Report: Table 13
DOL	1218-AB25	Occupational Exposure to Asbestos	7/1/94	8/10/94	$92	$448	2005 Report: Table C-1
DOT	2105-AE43	Prevention of Alcohol Misuse in the Aviation, Transit, Motor Carrier, Railroad, and Pipeline Industries, Common Preamble	1/25/94	2/15/94	$107	$37	2005 Report: Table C-1
DOT	2125-AC85	Controlled Substances and Alcohol Use and Testing	1/25/94	2/15/94	$1,539	$114	2005 Report: Table C-1
EPA	2050-AD89	Land Disposal Restrictions Phase II, Universal Treatment Standards and Treatment Standards for Organic Toxicity, Characteristic Wastes, and Newly Listed Wastes	7/29/94	9/19/94	$26	$240-$272	2005 Report: Table C-1
EPA	2060-AC19	Hazardous Organic NESHAP (HON) for the Synthetic Organic Chemical Manufacturing Industry (SOCMI) and Other Processes Subject to the Negotiated Regulation for Equipment Leaks	2/28/94	4/22/94	$593-$2,628	$295-$333	2005 Report: Table C-1
EPA	2060-AC64	Control of Air Pollution from New Motor Vehicles and	1/22/94	4/6/94	$167-$760	$33	2003 Report: Table 18

Agency	RIN	Title	OMB Review Completed	Published	Benefits	Costs	Source
		New Motor Vehicle Engines, Refueling Emission Regulations for Light-Duty Vehicles and Trucks and Heavy-Duty Vehicles					
EPA	2060-AC65	Control of Air Pollution from New Motor Vehicles and New Motor Vehicle Engines, Regulations Requiring on-Board Diagnostic Systems on 1994 and Later Model Year Light-Duty Vehicles	1/28/93	2/19/93	$702-$3,423	$226	2004 Report: Table 13
EPA	2060-AD27	Fuel and Fuel Additives: Standards for Reformulated Gasoline	12/15/93	2/16/94	$122-$947	$1,085-$1,395	2005 Report: Table C-1
EPA	2060-AD45	Acid Rain NOX Regulations under Title IV of the Clean Air Act Amendments of 1990	2/25/94	3/22/94	$433-$4,446	$297	2005 Report: Table C-1
EPA	2060-AD54	Determination of Significance for Nonroad Sources and Emission Standards for New Nonroad Compression Ignition Engines At or Above 37 Kilowatts, Control of Air Pollution -- SAN 3112	5/26/94	6/17/94	$647-$6,821	$29-$70	2005 Report: Table C-1
EPA	2060-AD91	Accelerated Phaseout of Ozone Depleting Chemicals and Listing and Phaseout of Methyl Bromide	11/29/93	12/10/93	$1,260 $3,993	$1,681	2005 Report: Table C-1
					$5,791-$24,885	$4,548-$4,969	

Table D-2. Estimates of Annual Benefits and Costs of Major Federal Rules January 20, 2001 to September 30, 2002[225] (millions of 2001 dollars per year)

Agency	RIN	Title	OMB Review Completed	Published	Benefits	Costs	Source
DOE	1904-AA77	Energy Efficiency Standards for Central Air Conditioners and Heat Pumps	1/31/02	5/23/02	Not Included	Not Included	2003 Report: Table 19 with Adjustments[226]
DOT	2127-AI10	Advanced Air Bags: Response to Petitions Federal Motor Vehicle Safety Standards; Occupant Crash Protection	12/5/01	12/18/01	$140-$1,600	$400-$2,000	2002 Report: Table 19
DOT	2127-AI33	Tire Pressure Monitoring Systems	5/29/02	6/5/02	$409-$944	$749-$1,206	2003 Report: Table 19
EPA	2060-AI11	Emissions From Nonroad Spark-Ignition Engines and Standards for Recreational Spark-Ignition Engines	9/13/02	11/8/02	$1,330 $4,818	$192	2003 Report: Table 19[227]
					$1,879-$7,362	$1,341-$3,398	

Table D-3. Estimates of Annual Benefits and Costs of Major Federal Rules January 20, 2009 to September 30, 2009[228] (millions of 2001 dollars per year)

Agency	RIN	Title	OMB Review Completed	Published	Benefits	Costs	Source
HHS	0910-AC14	Prevention of Salmonella Enteritidis in Shell Eggs	7/2/09	7/9/09	$206-$8,583	$48-$106	2010 Report: Table 1-4
DOE	1904-AA92	Energy Efficiency Standards for General Service Fluorescent Lamps and Incandescent Lamps	6/26/09	7/14/09	$1,111 $2,886	$192-$657	2010 Report: Table 1-4
DOT	2120-AJ01	Part 121 Pilot Age Limit	6/8/09	7/15/09	$30-$35	$4	2010 Report: Table 1-4
DOT	2127-AG51	Roof Crush Resistance	4/30/09	5/12/09	$374-$1,160	$748-$1,189	2010 Report: Table 1-4
DOT	2127-AJ37	Reduced Stopping Distance Requirements for Truck Tractors	7/16/09	7/27/09	$1,250 $1,520	$23-$164	2010 Report: Table 1-4
DOT	2127-AK29	Passenger Car and Light Truck Corporate Average Fuel Economy Model Year 2011	3/24/09	3/30/09	$857-$1,905	$650-$1,910	2010 Report: Table 1-4
					$3,828-$16,089	$1,665-$4,030	

Appendix E: Executive Order 13563: Improving Regulation and Regulatory Review

Executive Order 13563 of January 18, 2011
Improving Regulation and Regulatory Review

By the authority vested in me as President by the Constitution and the laws of the United States of America, and in order to improve regulation and regulatory review, it is hereby ordered as follows:

Section 1. *General Principles of Regulation.*
(a) Our regulatory system must protect public health, welfare, safety, and our environment while promoting economic growth, innovation, competitiveness, and job creation. It must be based on the best available science. It must allow for public participation and an open exchange of ideas. It must promote predictability and reduce uncertainty. It must identify and use the best, most innovative, and least burdensome tools for achieving regulatory ends. It must take into account benefits and costs, both quantitative and qualitative. It must ensure that regulations are accessible, consistent, written in plain language, and easy to understand. It must measure, and seek to improve, the actual results of regulatory requirements.
(b) This order is supplemental to and reaffirms the principles, structures, and definitions governing contemporary regulatory review that were established in Executive Order 12866 of September 30, 1993. As stated in that Executive Order and to the extent permitted by law, each agency must, among other things: (1) propose or adopt a regulation only upon a reasoned determination that its benefits justify its costs (recognizing that some benefits and costs are difficult to quantify); (2) tailor its regulations to impose the least burden on society, consistent with obtaining regulatory objectives, taking into account, among other things, and to the extent practicable, the costs of cumulative regulations; (3) select, in choosing among alternative regulatory approaches, those approaches that maximize net benefits (including potential economic, environmental, public health and safety, and other advantages; distributive impacts; and equity); (4) to the extent feasible, specify performance objectives, rather than specifying the behavior or manner of compliance that regulated entities must adopt; and (5) identify and assess available alternatives to direct regulation, including providing economic incentives to encourage the desired behavior, such as user fees or marketable permits, or providing information upon which choices can be made by the public.
(c) In applying these principles, each agency is directed to use the best available techniques to quantify anticipated present and future benefits and costs as accurately as possible. Where appropriate and permitted by law, each agency may consider (and discuss qualitatively) values that are difficult or impossible to quantify, including equity, human dignity, fairness, and distributive impacts.

Sec. 2. *Public Participation.*
(a) Regulations shall be adopted through a process that involves public participation. To that end, regulations shall be based, to the extent feasible and consistent with law, on the open exchange of information and perspectives among State, local, and tribal officials, experts in relevant disciplines, affected stakeholders in the private sector, and the public as a whole.
(b) To promote that open exchange, each agency, consistent with Executive Order 12866 and other applicable legal requirements, shall endeavor to provide the public with an opportunity to participate in the regulatory process. To the extent feasible and permitted by law, each agency shall afford the public a meaningful opportunity to comment through the Internet on any proposed regulation, with a comment period that should generally be at least 60 days. To the extent feasible and permitted by law, each agency shall also provide, for both proposed and final rules, timely online access to the rulemaking docket on Regulations.gov, including relevant scientific and technical findings, in an open format that can be easily searched and downloaded. For proposed rules, such access shall include, to the extent feasible and permitted by law, an opportunity for public comment on all pertinent parts of the rulemaking docket, including relevant scientific and technical findings.
(c) Before issuing a notice of proposed rulemaking, each agency, where feasible and appropriate, shall seek the views of those who are likely to be affected, including those who are likely to benefit from and those who are potentially subject to such rulemaking.

Sec. 3. *Integration and Innovation.* Some sectors and industries face a significant number of regulatory requirements, some of which may be redundant, inconsistent, or overlapping. Greater coordination across agencies could reduce these requirements, thus reducing costs and simplifying and harmonizing rules. In developing regulatory actions and identifying appropriate approaches, each agency shall attempt to promote such coordination, simplification, and harmonization. Each agency shall also seek to identify, as appropriate, means to achieve regulatory goals that are designed to promote innovation.

Sec. 4. *Flexible Approaches.* Where relevant, feasible, and consistent with regulatory objectives, and to the extent permitted by law, each agency shall identify and consider regulatory approaches that reduce burdens and maintain flexibility and freedom of choice for the public. These approaches include warnings, appropriate default rules, and disclosure requirements as well as provision of information to the public in a form that is clear and intelligible.

Sec. 5. *Science.* Consistent with the President's Memorandum for the Heads of Executive Departments and Agencies, "Scientific Integrity" (March 9, 2009), and its implementing guidance, each agency shall ensure the objectivity of any scientific and technological information and processes used to support the agency's regulatory actions.

Sec. 6. *Retrospective Analyses of Existing Rules.*
(a) To facilitate the periodic review of existing significant regulations, agencies shall consider how best to promote retrospective analysis of rules that may be outmoded,

ineffective, insufficient, or excessively burdensome, and to modify, streamline, expand, or repeal them in accordance with what has been learned. Such retrospective analyses, including supporting data, should be released online whenever possible.

(b) Within 120 days of the date of this order, each agency shall develop and submit to the Office of Information and Regulatory Affairs a preliminary plan, consistent with law and its resources and regulatory priorities, under which the agency will periodically review its existing significant regulations to determine whether any such regulations should be modified, streamlined, expanded, or repealed so as to make the agency's regulatory program more effective or less burdensome in achieving the regulatory objectives.

Sec. 7. *General Provisions.*
(a) For purposes of this order, "agency" shall have the meaning set forth in section 3(b) of Executive Order 12866.
(b) Nothing in this order shall be construed to impair or otherwise affect:
   (i) authority granted by law to a department or agency, or the head thereof; or
   (ii) functions of the Director of the Office of Management and Budget relating to budgetary, administrative, or legislative proposals.
(c) This order shall be implemented consistent with applicable law and subject to the availability of appropriations.
(d) This order is not intended to, and does not, create any right or benefit, substantive or procedural, enforceable at law or in equity by any party against the United States, its departments, agencies, or entities, its officers, employees, or agents, or any other person.

APPENDIX F: PRESIDENTIAL MEMORANDUM: REGULATORY COMPLIANCE

Memorandum of January 18, 2011
Regulatory Compliance
Memorandum for the Heads of Executive Departments and Agencies

My Administration is committed to enhancing effectiveness and efficiency in Government. Pursuant to the Memorandum on Transparency and Open Government, issued on January 21, 2009, executive departments and agencies (agencies) have been working steadily to promote accountability, encourage collaboration, and provide information to Americans about their Government's activities.

To that end, much progress has been made toward strengthening our democracy and improving how Government operates. In the regulatory area, several agencies, such as the Department of Labor and the Environmental Protection Agency, have begun to post online (at ogesdw.dol.gov and www.epa-echo.gov), and to make readily accessible to the public, information concerning their regulatory compliance and enforcement activities, such as information with respect to administrative inspections, examinations, reviews, warnings, citations, and revocations (but excluding law enforcement or otherwise sensitive information about ongoing enforcement actions).

Greater disclosure of regulatory compliance information fosters fair and consistent enforcement of important regulatory obligations. Such disclosure is a critical step in encouraging the public to hold the Government and regulated entities accountable. Sound regulatory enforcement promotes the welfare of Americans in many ways, by increasing public safety, improving working conditions, and protecting the air we breathe and the water we drink. Consistent regulatory enforcement also levels the playing field among regulated entities, ensuring that those that fail to comply with the law do not have an unfair advantage over their law-abiding competitors. Greater agency disclosure of compliance and enforcement data will provide Americans with information they need to make informed decisions. Such disclosure can lead the Government to hold itself more accountable, encouraging agencies to identify and address enforcement gaps.

Accordingly, I direct the following:

First, agencies with broad regulatory compliance and administrative enforcement responsibilities, within 120 days of this memorandum, to the extent feasible and permitted by law, shall develop plans to make public information concerning their regulatory compliance and enforcement activities accessible, downloadable, and searchable online. In so doing, agencies should prioritize making accessible information that is most useful to the general public and should consider the use of new technologies to allow the public to have access to real-time data. The independent agencies are encouraged to comply with this directive.

Second, the Federal Chief Information Officer and the Chief Technology Officer shall work with appropriate counterparts in each agency to make such data available online in searchable form, including on centralized platforms such as data.gov, in a manner that facilitates easy access, encourages cross-agency comparisons, and engages the public in new and creative ways of using the information.

Third, the Federal Chief Information Officer and the Chief Technology Officer, in coordination with the Director of the Office of Management and Budget (OMB) and their counterparts in each agency, shall work to explore how best .to generate and share enforcement and compliance information across the Government, consistent with law. Such data sharing can assist with agencies' risk-based approaches to enforcement: A lack of compliance in one area by a regulated entity may indicate a need for examination and closer attention by another agency. Efforts to share data across agencies, where appropriate and permitted by law, may help to promote flexible and coordinated enforcement regimes.

This memorandum is not intended to, and does not, create any right or benefit, substantive or procedural, enforceable at law or in equity by any party against the United States, its departments, agencies, or entities, its officers, employees, or agents, or any other person. Nothing in this memorandum shall be construed to impair or otherwise affect the functions of the Director of the Office of Management and Budget relating to budgetary, administrative, or legislative proposals.

The Director of OMB is authorized and directed to publish this memorandum in the *Federal Register.*

APPENDIX G: PRESIDENTIAL MEMORANDUM: REGULATORY FLEXIBILITY, SMALL BUSINESS, AND JOB CREATION

Memorandum of January 18, 2011
Regulatory Flexibility, Small Business, and Job Creation
Memorandum for the Heads of Executive Departments and Agencies

Small businesses play an essential role in the American economy; they help to fuel productivity, economic growth, and job creation. More than half of all Americans working in the private sector either are employed by a small business or own one. During a recent 15-year period, small businesses created more than 60 percent of all new jobs in the Nation.

Although small businesses and new companies provide the foundations for economic growth and job creation, they have faced severe challenges as a result of the recession. One consequence has been the loss of significant numbers of jobs.

The Regulatory Flexibility Act (RFA), 5 U.S.C. 601–612, establishes a deep national commitment to achieving statutory goals without imposing unnecessary burdens on the public. The RFA emphasizes the importance of recognizing "differences in the scale and resources of regulated entities" and of considering "alternative regulatory approaches . . . which minimize the significant economic impact of rules on small businesses, small organizations, and small governmental jurisdictions." 5 U.S.C. 601 note.

To promote its central goals, the RFA imposes a series of requirements designed to ensure that agencies produce regulatory flexibility analyses that give careful consideration to the effects of their regulations on small businesses and explore significant alternatives in order to minimize any significant economic impact on small businesses. Among other things, the RFA requires that when an agency proposing a rule with such impact is required to provide notice of the proposed rule, it must also produce an initial regulatory flexibility analysis that includes discussion of significant alternatives. Significant alternatives include the use of performance rather than design standards; simplification of compliance and reporting requirements for small businesses; establishment of different timetables that take into account the resources of small businesses; and exemption from coverage for small businesses.

Consistent with the goal of open government, the RFA also encourages public participation in and transparency about the rulemaking process. Among other things, the statute requires agencies proposing rules with a significant economic impact on small businesses to provide an opportunity for public comment on any required initial regulatory flexibility analysis, and generally requires agencies promulgating final rules with such significant economic impact to respond, in a final regulatory flexibility analysis, to comments filed by the Chief Counsel for Advocacy of the Small Business Administration.

My Administration is firmly committed to eliminating excessive and unjustified burdens on small businesses, and to ensuring that regulations are designed with careful consideration of their effects, including their cumulative effects, on small businesses. Executive Order 12866 of September 30, 1993, as amended, states, "Each agency shall tailor its regulations to impose the least burden on society, including individuals, businesses of differing sizes, and other entities (including small communities and governmental entities), consistent with obtaining the regulatory objectives, taking into account, among other things, and to the extent practicable, the costs of cumulative regulations."

In the current economic environment, it is especially important for agencies to design regulations in a cost-effective manner consistent with the goals of promoting economic growth, innovation, competitiveness, and job creation.

Accordingly, I hereby direct executive departments and agencies and request independent agencies, when initiating rulemaking that will have a significant economic impact on a substantial number of small entities, to give serious consideration to whether and how it is appropriate, consistent with law and regulatory objectives, to reduce regulatory burdens on small businesses, through increased flexibility. As the RFA recognizes, such flexibility may take many forms, including:

- extended compliance dates that take into account the resources available to small entities;
- performance standards rather than design standards;
- simplification of reporting and compliance requirements (as, for example, through streamlined forms and electronic filing options);
- different requirements for large and small firms; and
- partial or total exemptions.

I further direct that whenever an executive agency chooses, for reasons other than legal limitations, not to provide such flexibility in a proposed or final rule that is likely to have a significant economic impact on a substantial number of small entities, it should explicitly justify its decision not to do so in the explanation that accompanies that proposed or final rule. Adherence to these requirements is designed to ensure that regulatory actions do not place unjustified economic burdens on small business owners and other small entities. If regulations are preceded by careful analysis, and subjected to public comment, they are less likely to be based on intuition and guesswork and more likely to be justified in light of a clear understanding of the likely consequences of alternative courses of action. With that understanding, agencies will be in a better position to protect the public while avoiding excessive costs and paperwork. This memorandum is not intended to, and does not, create any right or benefit, substantive or procedural, enforceable at law or in equity by any party against the United States, its departments, agencies, or entities, its officers, employees, or agents, or any other person. Nothing in this memorandum shall be construed to impair or otherwise affect the functions of the Director of the Office of Management and Budget relating to budgetary, administrative, or legislative proposals. among other things, and to the extent practicable, the costs of cumulative regulations."

The Director of the Office of Management and Budget is authorized and directed to publish this memorandum in the *Federal Register*.

APPENDIX H: PRESIDENTIAL MEMORANDUM: ADMINISTRATIVE FLEXIBILITY

MEMORANDUM FOR THE HEADS OF EXECUTIVE DEPARTMENTS AND AGENCIES

SUBJECT: Administrative Flexibility, Lower Costs, and Better Results for State, Local, and Tribal Governments

Over the last 2 years, my Administration has worked with State, local, and tribal governments through the Recovery Act and other means to create jobs, build infrastructure, and protect critical programs and services in the face of declining revenues. But through smarter government we can do even more to improve outcomes and lower costs for the American taxpayer.

Federal program requirements over the past several decades have sometimes been onerous, and they have not always contributed to better outcomes. With input from our State, local, and tribal partners, we can, consistent with law, reduce unnecessary regulatory and administrative burdens and redirect resources to services that are essential to achieving better outcomes at lower cost. This is especially urgent at a time when State, local, and tribal governments face large budget shortfalls and American taxpayers deserve to know that their funds are being spent wisely.

On January 18, 2011, I signed Executive Order 13563, which, among other things, calls for careful analysis of regulations by executive departments and agencies (agencies), including consideration of costs and benefits. Executive Order 13563 also requires retrospective analysis of existing significant rules and greater coordination across agencies to simplify and harmonize redundant, inconsistent, or overlapping requirements, thus reducing costs.

Executive Order 13563 applies to regulations involving and affecting State, local, and tribal governments. In particular, my Administration has heard from these governments that the array of rules and requirements imposed by various Federal programs and agencies may at times undermine their efforts to modernize and integrate program delivery. While appropriate data collection requirements are important to program accountability, some of these requirements are unduly burdensome, may not properly align compliance requirements with outcomes, are not synchronized across programs, and fail to give governments and taxpayers meaningful information about what works and what needs to be improved or be stopped. I believe that working together, State, local, and tribal governments and Federal agencies can distinguish between rules and requirements that support important goals -- such as promoting public health and welfare; protecting the rights of individuals, organizations, and private businesses; and assuring that programs produce intended outcomes -- from rules and requirements that are excessively burdensome or may not serve their intended purpose.

Through this memorandum, I am instructing agencies to work closely with State, local, and tribal governments to identify administrative, regulatory, and legislative barriers in Federally funded programs that currently prevent States, localities, and tribes, from efficiently using tax dollars to achieve the best results for their constituents.

Section 1. Coordination and Collaboration. To facilitate coordination across Federal agencies and State, local, and tribal governments, I direct the Director of the Office of Management and Budget (OMB) to lead a process, in consultation with State, local, and tribal governments, and agencies, to: (1) provide input to multiple agencies on State-specific, regional, or multistate strategies for eliminating unnecessary administrative, regulatory, and legislative burdens; (2) enable State, local, and tribal governments to request increased flexibility, as appropriate, from multiple agencies simultaneously and receive expeditious and judicious consideration of those requests; (3) establish consistent criteria, where appropriate, for evaluating the potential benefits, costs, and programmatic effects of relaxing, simplifying, or eliminating administrative, regulatory, and legislative requirements; and (4) facilitate consensus among State, local, and tribal governments and agencies on matters that require coordinated action.

The Director of the OMB shall also take the following actions:

- Review and where appropriate revise guidance concerning cost principles, burden minimizations, and audits for State, local, and tribal governments in order to eliminate, to the extent permitted by law, unnecessary, unduly burdensome, duplicative, or low- priority recordkeeping requirements and effectively tie such requirements to achievement of outcomes.
- With agencies that administer overlapping programs, collaborate with State, local, and tribal governments to standardize, streamline, and reduce reporting and planning requirements in accordance with the Paperwork Reduction Act. The OMB should play a lead role, with appropriate agencies, in helping to develop efficient, low-cost mechanisms for collecting and reporting data that can support multiple programs and agencies.
- Facilitate cost-efficient modernization of State, local, and tribal information systems, drawing upon the collaboration of the Chief Information Officer in the OMB and the Chief Technology Officer in the Office of Science and Technology Policy.
- Provide written guidance to agencies on implementation of this memorandum within 60 days of the date of this memorandum.

Sec. 2. Streamlining Agency Requirements. Within 180 days of the date of this memorandum, agencies shall take the following actions to identify regulatory and administrative requirements that can be streamlined, reduced, or eliminated, and to specify where and how increased flexibility could be provided to produce the same or better program outcomes at lower cost.

- Work with State, local, and tribal governments to identify the best opportunities to realize efficiency, promote program integrity, and improve program outcomes, including opportunities, consistent with law, that reduce or streamline duplicative paperwork, reporting, and regulatory burdens and those that more effectively use Federal resources across multiple programs or States. Agencies should invite State, local, and tribal governments to identify not only administrative impediments, but also significant statutory barriers, to efficiency and effectiveness in program implementation.

- Establish preliminary plans to (1) consolidate or streamline processes that State, local, and tribal governments must use to obtain increased flexibility to promote the same or better outcomes at lower cost; (2) establish transparent criteria or principles for granting such increased flexibility, including those that are generally available and those that may be granted conditionally; and (3) ensure continued achievement of program results while allowing for such increased flexibility.
- Identify areas where cross-agency collaboration would further reduce administrative and regulatory barriers and improve outcomes. This should include identifying requirements for State planning documents that are prerequisites for awards from individual Federal programs that could be consolidated into one plan serving a number of agencies and programs.
- Report the results of these actions to the Director of the OMB.

Sec. 3. General Provisions.

(a) This memorandum shall be implemented consistent with applicable law and subject to the availability of any necessary appropriations.
(b) Nothing in this memorandum shall be construed to impair or otherwise affect the functions of the Director of the OMB relating to budgetary, administrative, or legislative proposals.
(c) This memorandum is not intended to, and does not, create any right or benefit, substantive or procedural, enforceable at law or in equity by any party against the United States, its departments, agencies, or entities, its officers, employees, or agents, or any other person.

APPENDIX I: AGENCY CHECKLIST: REGULATORY IMPACT ANALYSIS

With this document, the Office of Information and Regulatory Affairs is providing a checklist to assist agencies in producing regulatory impact analyses (RIAs), as required for economically significant rules by Executive Order 12866 and OMB Circular A-4.

Nothing herein alters, adds to, or reformulates existing requirements in any way. Moreover, this checklist is limited to the requirements of Executive Order 12866 (available at: http://www.reginfo.gov/public/jsp/Utilities/EO_ 12866.pdf) and Circular A-4 (available at: http://www.whitehouse.gov/ OMB/circulars/a004/a-4.pdf); it does not address requirements imposed by other authorities, such as the National Environmental Policy Act, the Regulatory Flexibility Act, the Unfunded Mandates Reform Act, the Paperwork Reduction Act, and various Executive Orders that require analysis. Executive Order 12866 and Circular A-4, as well as those other authorities, should be consulted for further information.

Checklist for Regulatory Impact Analysis:

- Does the RIA include a reasonably detailed description of the ***need for the regulatory action***? [229,230]
- Does the RIA include an explanation of how the regulatory action will ***meet that need***? [231]

- Does the RIA use an appropriate *baseline* (i.e., best assessment of how the world would look in the absence of the proposed action)?[232]
- Is the information in the RIA based on *the best reasonably obtainable scientific, technical, and economic information and is it presented in an accurate, clear, complete, and unbiased manner*?[233]
- Are the data, sources, and methods used in the RIA provided to the public *on the Internet* so that a qualified person can reproduce the analysis?[234]
- To the extent feasible, does the RIA quantify and monetize the anticipated *benefits* from the regulatory action?[235],[236]
- To the extent feasible, does the RIA quantify and monetize the anticipated **costs**?[237]
- Does the RIA explain and support *a reasoned determination that the benefits of the intended regulation justify its costs* (recognizing that some benefits and costs are difficult to quantify)?[238]
- Does the RIA assess the *potentially effective and reasonably feasible alternatives*?[239]
    - Does the RIA assess the benefits and costs of different regulatory provisions separately if the rule includes a number of distinct provisions?[240]
    - Does the RIA assess at least one alternative that is less stringent and at least one alternative that is more stringent?[241]
    - Does the RIA consider setting different requirements for large and small firms?[242]
- Does the preferred option have the highest *net benefits* (including potential economic, environmental, public health and safety, and other advantages; distributive impacts; and equity), unless a statute requires a different approach?[243]
- Does the RIA include an explanation of why the planned regulatory action is *preferable* to the identified potential alternatives?[244]
- Does the RIA use appropriate *discount rates* for benefits and costs that are expected to occur in the future?[245]
- Does the RIA include, if and where relevant, an appropriate *uncertainty analysis*?[246]
- Does the RIA include, if and where relevant, a separate description of *distributive impacts* and *equity*?[247]
    - Does the RIA provide a description/accounting of transfer payments?[248]
    - Does the RIA analyze relevant effects on disadvantaged or vulnerable populations (e.g., disabled or poor)?[249]
- Does the analysis include a clear, plain-language *executive summary*, including an *accounting statement* that summarizes the benefit and cost estimates for the regulatory action under consideration, including the qualitative and non-monetized benefits and costs?[250]
- Does the analysis include a clear and transparent *table* presenting (to the extent feasible) anticipated benefits and costs (quantitative and qualitative)?[251]

APPENDIX J: INFORMATION QUALITY AND PEER REVIEW

A. Links for Agency Information Quality Correspondence

Links to Agencies that Received Correction Requests in FY 2010:

Department of Agriculture:
http://www.ocio.usda.gov/qi_guide
Department of Commerce:
http://ocio.os.doc.gov/ITPolicyandPrograms/Information_Quality/index.htm
Department of Health and Human Services:
http://aspe.hhs.gov/infoquality/requests.shtml
Department of the Interior, Fish and Wildlife Service:
http://www.fws.gov/informationquality
Department of the Interior, US Geological Survey:
http://www.usgs.gov/info_qual
National Aeronautics and Space Administration:
http://www.sti.nasa.gov/qualinfo.html
Department of Housing and Urban Development:
http://www.hud.gov/offices/adm/grants/qualityinfo/qualityinfo.cfm
Department of Labor:
http://www.dol.gov/cio/programs/InfoGuidelines/IQCR.htm
Environmental Protection Agency:
http://epa.gov/quality/informationguidelines/iqg-list.html
Federal Communications Commission:
http://www.fcc.gov/omd/dataquality/welcome.html
Federal Reserve Board:
http://www.federalreserve.gov/iq_correction.htm

Links to All Agencies' IQ Correspondence Web Pages:
Access Board:
http://www.access-board.gov/about/policies/infoquality.htm
Chemical Safety and Hazard Investigation Board:
http://www.csb.gov/UserFiles/file/legal/FinalDataQualityGuidelines.pdf
Commodity Futures Trading Commission:
http://www.cftc.gov/About/CFTCReports/bulletinpeerreview.html
Consumer Product Safety Commission:
http://www.cpsc.gov/library/correction/correction.html
Corporation for National and Community Service:
http://www.nationalservice.gov/home/site_information/quality.asp
Defense Nuclear Facilities Safety Board:
http://www.dnfsb.gov/about/information_quality.php
Department of Agriculture:
http://www.ocio.usda.gov/qi_guide

Department of Agriculture, Forest Service:
http://www.fs.fed.us/qoi

Department of Commerce:
http:/ocio.os.doc.gov/ITPolicyandPrograms/Information_Quality/index. htm

Department of Defense:
http://www.defenselink.mil/pubs/dodiqguidelines.html

Department of Defense, Army Corps of Engineers:
http://www.usace.army.mil/ceci/iqa/pages/mission.aspx

Department of Education:
http://www.ed.gov/policy/gen/guid/infoqualguide.html

Department of Energy:
http://www.cio.energy.gov/infoquality.htm

Department of Health and Human Services:
http://aspe.hhs.gov/infoquality/requests.shtml

Department of Housing and Urban Development:
http://www.hud.gov/offices/adm/grants/qualityinfo/qualityinfo. cfm

Department of Homeland Security:
http://www.dhs.gov/xabout/compliance/

Department of Justice:
http://www.usdoj.gov/iqpr/iqpr_disclaimer.html

Department of Labor:
http://www.dol.gov/cio/programs/InfoGuidelines/IQCR.htm

Department of State:
http://www.state.gov/misc/49492.htm

Department of the Interior:
http://www.doi.gov/ocio/iq

Department of the Interior, Bureau of Land Management:
http://www.blm.gov/wo/st/en/National_Page/Notices_used_in_Footer/data_quality.html

Department of the Interior, Fish and Wildlife Service:
http://www.fws.gov/informationquality

Department of the Interior, National Park Service:
http://www.nps.gov/policy/infoqualcorrect.htm

Department of Transportation, Surface Transportation Board:
http://www.stb.dot.gov/stb/InformationQualityGuidelines.htm

Department of Transportation:
http://docketsinfo.dot.gov/Dataquality.cfm

Department of Veteran Affairs:
http://www.rms.oit.va.gov/Information_Quality.asp

Environmental Protection Agency:
http://epa.gov/quality/informationguidelines/iqg-list.html

Equal Employment Opportunity Commission:
http://www.eeoc.gov/eeoc/plan/informationquality/index.cfm

Farm Credit Administration:
http://www.fca.gov/FCA-eb/fca%20new%20site/home/info_quality.html

Federal Communications Commission:

http://www.fcc.gov/omd/dataquality/welcome.html
Federal Deposit Insurance Corporation:
http://www.fdic.gov/about/policies/#information
Federal Energy Regulatory Commission:
http://www.ferc.gov/help/filing-guide/file-correct.asp
Federal Maritime Commission:
http://www.fmc.gov/about/information_quality_guideline_details.aspx
Federal Reserve Board:
http://www.federalreserve.gov/iq_correction.htm
Federal Trade Commission:
http://www.ftc.gov/ogc/sec515/index.htm
General Services Administration:
http://www.gsa.gov/portal/content/104725
Institute of Museum and Library Services:
http://www.imls.gov/about/guidelines.shtm
Internal Revenue Service:
http://www.irs.gov/irs/article/0,,id=131585,00.html
Merit Systems Protection Board:
http://www.mspb.gov/netsearch/viewdocs.aspx?docnumber=251846&version=252119&application=ACROBAT
National Aeronautics and Space Administration:
http://www.sti.nasa.gov/qualinfo.html
National Archives:
http://www.archives.gov/about/info-qual/requests/index.html
National Credit Union Administration:
http://www.ncua.gov/resources/RegulationsOpinionsLaws/ProposedRegulations.aspx
National Endowment for the Arts:
http://www.arts.gov/about/infoquality.html
National Endowment for the Humanities:
http://www.neh.gov/whoweare/dissemination.html
National Labor Relations Board:
http://www.nlrb.gov/about_us/public_notices/information_on_quality_guidelines.aspx
National Science Foundation:
http://www.nsf.gov/policies/infoqual.jsp
National Transportation Safety Board:
http://www.ntsb.gov/info/quality.htm
Nuclear Regulatory Commission:
http://www.nrc.gov/public-involve/info-quality.html
Nuclear Waste Technical Review Board:
http://www.nwtrb.gov/plans/plans.html
Occupational Safety & Health Review Commission:
http://www.oshrc.gov/infoquality/infoquality.html
Office of Federal Housing Enterprise Oversight:
http://www.fhfa.gov/Default.aspx?Page=56
Office of Government Ethics:
http://www.usoge.gov/management/info_quality.aspx

Office of Management and Budget:
http://www.whitehouse.gov/omb/inforeg/info_quality/information_quality.html
Office of Personnel Management:
http://www.opm.gov/policy/webpolicy/index.asp
Office of Special Counsel:
http://www.osc.gov/InfoQuality.htm
Overseas Private Investment Corporation:
http://www.opic.gov/publications/quality-guidelines
Peace Corps:
http://www.peacecorps.gov/index.cfm?shell=pchq.policies.docs
Pension Benefit Guaranty Corporation:
http://www.pbgc.gov/res/other-guidance/information-quality-guidelines.html
Small Business Administration:
http://www.sba.gov/information/index.html
Social Security Administration:
http://www.ssa.gov/515/requests.htm
Tennessee Valley Authority:
http://www.tva.gov/infoquality/
US International Trade Commission:
www.usitc.gov/documents/infoqualgdl.pdf
USAID:
http://www.usaid.gov/policy/info_quality/

B. Links for Agency Peer Review Agendas
Cabinet-Level Departments

Department of Agriculture:
http://www.ocio.usda.gov/qi_guide/qoi_officer_lst.html
    http://www.ocio.usda.gov/qi_guide/scientific_research.html
    Agricultural Research Service:
    http://www.ars.usda.gov//docs.htm?docid=19203&dropcache=true&mode=preview
    Animal and Plant Health Inspection Service:
    http://www.aphis.usda.gov/peer_review/peer_review_agenda.shtml
    Economic Research Service:
    http://www.ers.usda.gov/AboutERS/peerreview.htm
    Food Safety Inspection Service:
    http://www.fsis.usda.gov/Information_Quality/Peer_Review/index.asp
    Forest Service:
    http://www.fs.fed.us/qoi/peerreview.shtml
    Grain Inspection, Packers, and Stockyard Inspection Administration:
    http://www.gipsa.usda.gov/GIPSA/webapp?area=home&subject=iq&topic=pr
    Office of the Chief Economist:
    http://www.usda.gov/oce/peer_review

Department of Commerce:
http://ocio.os.doc.gov/ITPolicyandPrograms/Information_Quality/index.htm
- National Oceanic and Atmospheric Administration:
  http://www.cio.noaa.gov/Policy_Programs/prplans/PRsummaries.html

Department of Defense:
http://www.defenselink.mil/pubs/dodiqguidelines.html

Department of Education:
http://www.ed.gov/policy/gen/guid/iq/peerreview.html

Department of Energy:
http://cio.energy.gov/infoquality.htm

Department of Health and Human Services:
http://aspe.hhs.gov/infoquality/peer.shtml
- Center for Disease Control:
  http://www2a.cdc.gov/od/peer/peer.asp
- Food and Drug Administration:
  http://www.fda.gov/ScienceResearch/SpecialTopics/PeerReviewofScientificInformationandAssessments/default.htm
- National Toxicology Program:
  http://fmp-8.cit.nih.gov/sif/agenda.php
- Office of Public Health and Science:
  http://aspe.hhs.gov/infoquality/guidelines/ophspeer.html

Department of Homeland Security:
http://www.dhs.gov/xabout/compliance/editorial_0633.shtm

Department of Housing and Urban Development:
http://www.huduser.org/about/pdr_peer_review.html

Department of the Interior:
http://www.doi.gov/ocio/iq_1.html
- Bureau of Land Management:
  http://www.blm.gov/wo/st/en/National_Page/Notices_used_in_Footer/data_quality.html
- Bureau of Reclamation:
  http://www.usbr.gov/main/qoi/peeragenda.html
- Fish and Wildlife Service:
  http://www.fws.gov/informationquality/peer_review/index.html
- Bureau of Ocean Energy Management, Regulation and Enforcement:
  http://www.boemre.gov/qualityinfo/PeerReviewAgenda.htm
- National Park Service:
  http://www.nps.gov/policy/peerreview.htm
- Office of Surface Mining:
  http://www.osmre.gov/guidance/osm_info_quality.shtm
- US Geological Society:
  http://www.usgs.gov/peer_review

Department of Justice:
http://www.usdoj.gov/iqpr/iqpr_disclaimer.html

Department of Labor:
http://www.dol.gov/asp/peer-review/index.htm
  Employee Benefits Security Administration:
  http://www.dol.gov/ebsa/regs/peerreview.html
  Occupational Safety and Health Administration:
  http://www.osha.gov/dsg/peer_review/peer_agenda.html
  Mine Safety and Health Administration
  http://www.msha.gov/REGS/PEERReview/PEERreview.asp
Department of State:
http://www.state.gov/misc/49492.htm
Department of Transportation:
http://www.dot.gov/peerreview/
Department of Veterans Affairs:
http://www.rms.oit.va.gov/Peer_Review.asp

Other Agencies
Consumer Product Safety Commission:
http://www.cpsc.gov/library/peer.html
Environmental Protection Agency:
http://cfpub.epa.gov/si/si_public_pr_agenda.cfm
Federal Communications Commission:
http://www.fcc.gov/omd/dataquality/peer-agenda.html
Federal Energy Regulatory Commission:
http://www.ferc.gov/help/filing-guide/file-correct.asp
Federal Trade Commission:
http://www.ftc.gov/ogc/sec515/
National Aeronautics and Space Administration:
http://www.sti.nasa.gov/peer_review.html
Nuclear Regulatory Commission:
http://www.nrc.gov/public-involve/info-quality/peer-review.html
Office of Management and Budget:
http://www.whitehouse.gov/omb/inforeg/info_quality/information_quality.html
Small Business Administration:
http://www.sba.gov/content/sba-information-quality-peer-review-agenda
Tennessee Valley Authority:
http://www.tva.gov/infoquality

C. Agencies that Do Not Produce or Sponsor Information Subject to the Bulletin

See website links in section A of this Appendix.

Agency for International Development
Corporation for National and Community Service
Council on Environmental Quality
Defense Nuclear Facilities Safety Board
Department of the Treasury

Equal Employment Opportunity Commission
Farm Credit Association
Federal Maritime Commission
Federal Reserve
General Services Administration
Institute of Museum and Library Services
International Trade Commission
Merit Systems Protection Board
National Archives
National Credit Union Administration
National Endowment for the Arts
National Endowment for the Humanities
National Labor Relations Board
National Science Foundation
Nuclear Waste Technical Review Board
Office of Federal Housing Enterprise Oversight
Office of Government Ethics
Office of Personnel Management
Overseas Private Investment Corporation
Patent and Trade Office
Peace Corps
Pension Benefit Guaranty Corporation
Railroad Board
Securities and Exchange Commission
Selective Services System
Social Security Administration
Surface Transportation Board
US Occupational Safety and Health Review Commission

APPENDIX K: RESPONSE TO PEER REVIEWS AND PUBLIC COMMENTS

We would like to express our sincere thanks and appreciation for the extremely helpful peer review and public comments that we received on the draft 2011 report. In particular, we would like to thank our invited peer reviewers, Joseph Aldy (Harvard Kennedy School), Michael Greenstone (Massachusetts Institute of Technology), and Christine Jolls (Yale Law School). We are grateful for the time and effort they devoted to providing us with useful comments. We have made numerous changes in response to these comments.

We have read all comments carefully; we summarize here only a few of the major comments received and our responses. Full texts of the comments are available at OMB's website at http://whitehouse.gov/omb/inforeg_reports_ congress/.

Peer reviewer Aldy comments that it is important to remind readers that public policy is intended to make society better off and that benefit-cost analysis can help to promote that goal. We have provided this reminder. Specifically, we emphasize that "careful consideration of costs and benefits is best understood as a way of ensuring that regulations will improve social welfare, above all by informing design and development of various options so as to identify opportunities for both minimizing the costs of achieving social goals (cost-effectiveness) and maximizing net social benefits (efficiency)."

Peer reviewers Aldy and Greenstone both support the use of retrospective analysis, with Aldy suggesting that such analyses address not only the "top line" benefits and costs, but also the net social benefits of specific components of the rules. Greenstone proposes a number of measures designed to implement retrospective analysis in a way that produces credible results. These include systematic reporting of ex post benefits and costs; advance announcements of retrospective review and the date the results will be published; the funding of contractors or academics to conduct retrospective analysis; and the public posting of data. Greenstone also suggests designing the implementation of new regulations to allow for credible evaluations, including the use of randomized control trials or quasi-experimental approaches. Jolls similarly encourages agency experimentation to examine the effects of regulation and suggests that agencies can play a valuable role in experimentally implementing alternatives, to the extent permitted by law, and then studying their consequences.

We believe that these comments are extremely useful. To create a process of retrospective analysis, and a continuing culture of evaluation, OMB recommends that agencies use the best available techniques to assess the consequences of regulation, both as part of retrospective review and in the initial design of rules. As Greenstone and Jolls suggest and as we have noted, an especially promising approach involves randomized controlled trials, in which regulatory initiatives are used in some domains but not in similarly situated others, thus allowing a careful analysis of their effects.[252] Of course there are constraints – involving law, resources, and feasibility – in using randomized controlled trials in the regulatory context, but in some cases, they may be both appropriate and highly useful.

OIRA is now working closely with agencies to improve evaluation and to create a culture of retrospective analysis. The preliminary plans for retrospective review, released under Executive Order 13563, demonstrate that these improvements are well under way. The preliminary plans offer relevant discussion. For example, DHS states that it will "build in retrospective review at the earliest stages of regulatory development."[253] Its plan calls for the Department's component agencies to "incorporate a discussion of retrospective analysis goals into their rulemaking project planning" in order "to ensure that the component considers retrospective analysis through the lifespan of the regulation."[254] The Department of Labor states that it "is contemplating how to incorporate the use of experimental designs to determine the impact of various regulations."[255] The Department of Interior states that it "will consider" the use of "experimental or quasi-experimental designs, including randomized controlled trials."[256] Similarly, the Department of Treasury states that it will work to "develop and incorporate experimental designs into retrospective analysis, when appropriate."[257]

Such experimentation might, where feasible and consistent with law, also take the form of advance testing of regulatory alternatives, perhaps through pilot projects or randomized controlled trials, followed by study of their consequences.[258] Pilot projects and randomized experiments – such as DOT's National Highway Traffic Safety Administration's distracted driving demonstration programs discussed in the report – are likely to provide valuable information about what interventions are likely to be most useful.

With regard to retrospective analysis, Jolls also points out that, in some circumstances, altering an existing rule may be inefficient even if a retrospective analysis provides evidence that the rule should not have been adopted in the first place. Once private-sector actors have made long-term investments and adjustments in response to a rule, the disruption and uncertainty associated with a change may simply be too large. OMB agrees with this point and has noted it in chapter 1.

Both Aldy and Greenstone support the involvement of external experts to undertake ex post analysis of the benefits and costs of Federal regulations, with Greenstone suggesting a "Regulatory Review Board" that would have the power to request evaluations of existing regulations, to judge the quality of evidence with respect to a regulation, and possibly to fund an evaluation from its own resources. OMB appreciates these suggestions and acknowledges the importance of objective evaluation; it will take the suggestions into consideration in the future.

Aldy asks why 2001 dollars were used for all tables and figures. Circular A-4 currently states: "Please report all monetized effects in 2001 dollars. You should convert dollars expressed in different years to 2001 dollars using the GDP deflator." In the alternative, Aldy suggested providing a deflator in a footnote to allow the reader to convert to 2010 dollars. We have done so (footnote 2).

Aldy suggests making explicit that the definition of the value of a statistical life is a population-based measure. We have accepted his suggestion and included a footnote that reads "the average person in a population of 50,000 may value a reduction of mortality risk of 1/50,000 at $150. The value for reducing the risk of 1 *statistical* (as opposed to known or identified) fatality in this population would be $7.5 million, representing the aggregation of the willingness to pay values held by everyone in the population."

Aldy also points out that given the lumpy timing of investments to comply with regulations, benefit-cost analysis should present not simply a future year's benefits and costs (e.g., in 2020) but also the stream of annual benefits and costs. While OMB acknowledges the value of this suggestion, this report generally relies on agency estimates in monetizing benefits and costs and is limited by the data provided; OMB continues to encourage agencies to provide the stream of annual benefits and costs in their RIAs.

Jolls points out that the statement that "U.S competition law prohibits collusion among employers but allows collective bargaining by workers" appears misplaced given that it seems somewhat unnatural to suggest a tension between prohibiting companies from price-fixing, on the one hand, and permitting individuals to engage in collective action through unions, on the other. She also suggests revising the statement that "economic regulation . . . results in higher prices in the product market" given that economists often assume that economic regulation will lower product prices below what they would be in the absence of economic regulation. The report has been edited to reflect both concerns.

Jolls also suggests that Figure 2-1 would be more illuminating if it contained a second bar for each administration showing the number of major rules promulgated during the Administration. OMB notes that the number of major rules is stated on page 20 of this report.

Greenstone recommends that OIRA develop a checklist to determine the credibility of evidence in regulatory impact analyses in order to make clearer the quality of evidence that underlies the case for the regulation. He also suggests the importance of clearly distinguishing between private and social benefits. He urges that agencies and OIRA undertake a systematic study and offer resulting judgments about when consumer biases are likely to be a problem that requires regulation (e.g., in the context of energy efficiency).

OIRA appreciates these suggestions, and will consider them going forward. Several revisions have been made in this report, including a new discussion of social and private benefits in chapter 2, to reflect Greenstone's points. We recommend continued exploration of these issues, with particular attention to the circumstances in which a lack of information and potential biases on the part of consumers are likely to support regulatory interventions and to justify counting private savings as benefits. We also recommend that agencies should clearly separate social and private savings in their Regulatory Impact Analyses, and that when private savings are included, agencies should give careful attention to the conceptual and empirical issues.

Greenstone states that a complete analysis of the benefits of air pollution regulations requires an estimate of the loss of life expectancy associated with premature deaths. He suggests that the resulting information should be reported as a regular matter in estimating the benefit of reductions in air pollution. While this report generally relies on agency estimates in monetizing benefits and costs, OMB continues to encourage agencies (consistent with Circular A-4) to report results with multiple measures of effectiveness.

Aldy suggests that cost-effectiveness should be evaluated across agencies and that the report could present estimates for all rules with a primary or significant mortality risk reduction benefit. We agree that such an evaluation would be valuable and we will consider the suggestion in the future. Jolls notes that Table 2-5 presents the net cost per life saved for twelve recent health and safety rules for which calculation is possible; she suggests also including a description of whether monetizing morbidity costs is significantly less controversial or difficult than monetizing mortality costs. We acknowledge the point but in light of existing information, the only consistent metric that we are able to use across health and safety rules is "lives saved."

In line with the report's emphasis on transparency and disclosure, OMB continues to support Circular A-4's statement that "agencies should use their web site to provide OMB and the public with the underlying data, including mortality and morbidity data, the age distribution of the affected populations, and the severity and duration of disease conditions and trauma, so that OMB and the public can construct apples-to-apples comparisons between rulemakings that employ different measures." Increasing transparency would allow the public to draw meaningful comparisons between rulemakings that employ different effectiveness measures.

The Mercatus Center at George Mason University submitted comments supporting OMB's suggestion that agencies undertake retrospective analysis and encourages independent organizations to perform the analyses. OMB agrees and has made edits to further emphasize these points. The Mercatus Center also states that the research on "happiness" should be approached with a great deal of caution and suggests that growth and employment may be much better indicators of human well-being. OMB agrees – as stated in the report – that the precise relationship between GDP growth and subjective well-being has yet to be settled, and presents the literature as nascent and exploratory.

In response to OMB's request last year for suggestions about regulatory changes that might increase employment, innovation, and competitiveness, the HR Policy Association has resubmitted its comments focusing on FLSA regulations to the Department of Labor, and has copied OMB. OMB appreciates the time and thought put into this proposal and will continue to consider the recommended reforms.

APPENDIX L: REFERENCES

[1] Acemoglu, Daron & Angrist, Joshua D. "Consequences of Employment Protection? The Case of the Americans with Disabilities Act." *Journal of Political Economy*, 2001, *109*(5), 915-957.

[2] Adler, Matthew & Posner, Eric A. "Happiness Research and Cost-Benefit Analysis." *Journal of Legal Studies*, 2008, *37*(S2), S253-S292.

[3] Balleisen, Edward & Moss, David. *Government and Markets: Toward a New Theory of Regulation*, 2009, Cambridge, U.K.: The Tobin Project.

[4] Banerjee, Abhijit V. & Esther Duflo. "The Experimental Approach to Development Economics." *Annual Review of Economics*, 2009, *1*,151–178.

[5] Baum, Charles L. "The Effect of State Maternity Leave Legislation and the 1993 Family and Medical Leave Act on Employment and Wages." *Labour Economics*, 2003, *10*(5), 573-596.

[6] Becker, Randy & Henderson, Vernon. "Effects of Air Quality Regulation on Polluting Industries." *Journal of Political Economy*, 2000, *108*(2), 379-421.

[7] Berman, Eli & Bui, Linda TM. "Environmental Regulation and Labor Demand: Evidence from the South Coast Air Basin." *Journal of Public Economics*, 2001, *79*, 265-295.

[8] Berman, Eli & Bui, Linda TM. "Environmental Regulation and Productivity: Evidence from Oil Refineries." *The Review of Economics and Statistics*, 2001, *83*(3), 498-510.

[9] Bertrand, Marianne & Kramarz, Francis. "Does Entry Regulation Hinder Job Creation? Evidence from the French Retail Industry." *The Quarterly Journal of Economics*, 2002, *117*(4), 1369-1413.

[10] Biswas-Diener, R; Vitterso, J & Diener, E. (2010). The Danish effect: Beginning to explore high well-being in Denmark. *Social Indicators Research*, *97*, 229-246

[11] Blanchard, Olivier & Giavazzi, Francesco. "Macroeconomic Effects of Regulation and Deregulation in Goods and Labor Markets." *The Quarterly Journal of Economics*, 2003, *118*(3), 879-907.

[12] Blanchflower, David G & Oswald, Andrew J. *"Well-Being Over Time in Britain and the USA."* Hypertension and Happiness Across Nations. NBER Working Paper No. 12935. Cambridge, Mass.: National Bureau of Economic Research, 2007.

[13] Blanchflower, David G & Oswald, Andrew J. *"International Happiness,"* 2010. National Bureau of Economic Research Working Paper Series, available at http://www.nber.org/papers/w16668.pdf

[14] Bloom, David; Canning, David & Sevilla, Jaypee. "The Effect of Health on Economic Growth: A Production Function Approach," *World Development*, 2004, *32*,1: 1-13.

[15] Brunnermeier, Smita, B, & Levinson, Arik. "Examining the Evidence on Environmental Regulations & Industry Location." *The Journal of Environment and Development*, 2004, *13*,1, 6-41.

[16] Carpenter, Dan. "Confidence Games: How Does Regulation Constitute Markets?" in Edward Balleisen and David Moss, eds., *Government and Markets: Toward a New Theory of Regulation*, (New York: Cambridge University Press, 2009).

[17] Carpenter, Dan. "Protection without Capture: Dynamic Product Approval by a Politically Responsive, Learning Regulator," *American Political Science Review*, 2004, *98*, 4, 613-631

[18] Carpenter, Dan & Ting, MM. "Regulatory Errors with Endogenous Agendas," *American Journal of Political Science 51*, 4 (2007), pp. 835-853.

[19] Chay, Kenneth & Greenstone, Michael. "Does Air Quality Matter? Evidence from the Housing Market," *Journal of Political Economy*, 2005, *113*(2), 376-424.

[20] Clark, Andrew E; Frijters, Paul. & Shields, Michael A. "Relative Income, Happiness and Utility: An Explanation for the Easterlin Paradox and Other Puzzles." *Journal of Economic Literature*, 2008, *46*(1), 95-114.

[21] Cohen, Daniel & Soto, Marcelo. "Growth and Human Capital: Good Data, Good Results," *Journal of Economic Growth*, 2007, *12*, 51-76.

[22] Cole, Matthew A & Elliot, Rob J. "Do Environmental Regulations Cost Jobs? An Industry- Level Analysis of the UK." *The B.E. Journal of Economic Analysis & Policy*, 2007, *7*(1).

[23] Copeland, Curtis W. *How Agencies Monetize "Statistical Lives" Expected to Be Saved By Regulations*, CRS Report for Congress, Congressional Research Service, March 24, 2010.

[24] Dale, Larry; Antinori, Camille; McNeil, Michael & James McMahon. 2002. *Retrospective evaluation of declining prices for energy efficient appliances*. Proceedings of the ACEEE 2002 Summer Study on Energy Efficiency in Buildings. August 18-23, Pacific Grove, CA. Available at http://eec.ucdavis.edu/ACEEE/2002/pdfs/panel09/05_311.pdf.

[25] Deaton, Angus. "Income, Health, & Well-Being Around the World: Evidence from the Gallup World Poll," *Journal of Economic Perspectives*, 2008, *22*(2), 53-72

[26] Dean, Thomas J; Brown, Robert L. & Stango, Victor. "Environmental Regulation as a Barrier to the Formation of Small Manufacturing Establishments: A Longitudinal Examination." *Journal of Environmental Economics and Management*, 2000, *40*, 56-75.

[27] Deaton, Angus; Fortson, Jane & Tortora, Robert. "*Life (Evaluation), HIV/AIDS, and Death in Africa*." In International Differences in Well-Being, eds. Ed Diener, John F. Helliwell, and Daniel Kahneman. New York and Oxford: Oxford University Press, 2010: 105-36.

[28] Diener, John F. Helliwell, & Kahneman, Daniel. New York and Oxford: Oxford University Press, 2010: 16-33.

[29] Diener, Ed; Lucas, Richard; Schimmack, Ulrich; & Helliwell, Oliver. *Well-Being for Public Policy*. Oxford University Press, 2009.

[30] Diener, Ed; Kahneman, Daniel; Tov, William & Arora, Raksha. "*Income's Association with Judgments of Life Versus Feelings.*" In International Differences in Well-Being, eds. Ed Diener, John F. Helliwell, and Daniel Kahneman. New York and Oxford: Oxford University Press, 2010: 3-15.

[31] Djankov, Simeon; La Porta, Rafael; Lopez-de-Silanes, Florencio & Shleifer, Andrei. "The Regulation of Entry," *Quarterly Journal of Economics*, 2002, *107*, 1: 1-37

[32] Dynan, Karen E. & Ravina, Enrichetta. "Increasing Income Inequality, External Habits, and Happiness." *American Economic Review*, 2007, *97*(2), 226-231.

[33] Easterlin, Richard. Does Economic Growth Improve the Human Lot? Some Empirical Evidence. In P. David and M. Reder, eds. Nations and Households in Economic Growth: Essays in Honour of Moses Abramovita. New York and London: Academic Press, 1974.

[34] _____ "The Economics of Happiness." *Daedalus*, 2004, *133*(2), 26-33.

[35] _____ "A Puzzle for Adaptive Theory." *Journal of Economic Behavior & Organization*, 2005, *56*, 513-521.

[36] Englebrecht, Hans-Jürgen. "Natural Capital, Subjective Well-Being, & the New Welfare Economics of Sustainability: Some Evidence from Cross-Country Regressions." *Ecological Economics*, 2009, *69*, 380-388.

[37] Environmental Protection Agency. "*Valuing Mortality Risk Reductions for Environmental Policy: A White Paper.*" Dec. 10, 2010. Available at: http://yosemite.epa.gov/ee/epa/eerm.nsf/vwAN/EE-0563-1.pdf/$file/EE-0563-1.pdf.

[38] Frey, Bruno S & Stutzer, Alois. "*Happiness and Economics: How the Economy and Institutions Affect Human Well-Being.*" Princeton, N.J.: Princeton University Press, 2002.

[39] Fullerton, Don. "*Six Distributional Effects of Environmental Policy.*" NBER Working Paper 16703. Cambridge, Mass.: National Bureau of Economic Research, 2011. Available at: http://www.nber.org/papers/ w16703 NBER Working Paper No. 12935.

[40] Gabaix, Xavier & David Laibson, "Shrouded Attributes, Consumer Myopia, and Information Suppression in Competitive Markets," *Quarterly Journal of Economics*, 2006, *121*, 505.

[41] Gilbert, Daniel. Stumbling on Happiness. New York: Alfred A. Knopf, 2006.

[42] Goodstein, EB. *Jobs and the Environment: the Myth of a National Trade-Off*, Economic Policy Institute, Washington, D.C., 1994.

[43] Gray, Wayne B & Shadbegian, Ronald. "Environmental Regulation, Investment Timing, and Technology Choice." *The Journal of Industrial Economics*, 1998, *46*(2), 235-256.

[44] Greenstone, Michael. "The Impacts of Environmental Regulations on Industrial Activity: Evidence from the 1970 and 1977 Clean Air Act Amendments and the Census of Manufacturers." *Journal of Political Economy*, 2002, *110*(6), 1175-1219.

[45] Greenstone, Michael. "Toward a Culture of Persistent Regulatory Experimentation and Evaluation." In *New Perspectives on Regulation*, David Moss and John Cisternino (Eds.). Cambridge, MA: The Tobin Project, Inc., 2009.

[46] Greenstone, Michael; List, John A & Chad Syverson. "*The Effects of Environmental Regulation on the Competitiveness of U.S. Manufacturing.*" U.S. Census Bureau Center for Economic Studies Discussion Paper (February 2011).

[47] Gruber, Jonathan. "The Incidence of Mandated Maternity Benefits." *American Economic Review,* 1994, *84*(3); 622-641.

[48] Hagerty, M & Veenhoven, R. "Wealth and Happiness Revisited – Growing National Income Does Go with Greater Happiness." *Social Indicators Research*, 2003, *64*, 1-27.

[49] Hahn, Robert & John Hird, "The Costs and Benefits of Regulation: Review and Synthesis," *Yale Journal on Regulation 8* (1991), pp. 233-278.

[50] Hanna, Rema. "US Environmental Regulation and FDI: Evidence from a Panel of US-Based Multinational Firms, *American Economic Journal: Applied Economics,* 2010, *2*(3), 158-189.

[51] Harrington, Winston. *Grading Estimates of the Benefits and Costs of Federal Regulation: A Review of Reviews 33 tbl.*7 (Res.For the Future, Discussion Paper No. RFF DP 06-39, Sept. 2006), available at http://ssrn.com/abstract=937357.

[52] Harrington, Winston. *Grading Estimates of the Benefits andCosts of Federal Regulation: A Review of Reviews 33 tbl.*7 (Res.For the Future, Discussion Paper No. RFF DP 06-39, Sept. 2006), available at http://ssrn.com/abstract=937357.

[53] Harrington, Winston; Richard D. Morgenstern, & Peter Nelson. "*On the Accuracy of Regulatory Cost Estimates.*" Available at: http://www.rff. org/documents/RFF-DP-99-18.pdf

[54] Harter, James K. & Raksha Arora. "*The Impact of Time Spent Working & Job fit on Well- Being Around the World.*" In International Differences in Well-Being, eds. Ed Diener, John F. Helliwell, & Daniel Kahneman. New York and Oxford: Oxford University Press, 2010: 398430.

[55] Ifcher, John & Homa Zarghamee, "Happiness and Time Preference: The Effect of Positive Affect in a Random-Assignment Experiment," *American Economic Review*, 2011 (forthcoming). Available at http://papers.ssrn.com/sol3/papers.cfm?abstract_ id= 1491247.

[56] Inglehart, R; Foa, R: Peterson, C & Welzel, C. "Development, Freedom, and Rising Happiness: A Global Perspective (1981-2007)." *Perspectives on Psychological Science*, 2008, *3*, 264-285.

[57] Isen, AM. "Positive Affect, Cognitive Processes, and Social Behavior." In Berkowitz (Ed.), *Advances in Experimental Social Pscyhology*. New York: Russell Sage foundation, 1987.

[58] Jaffe, Adam B, et al. "Environmental Regulation and the Competitiveness of U.S. Manufacturing: What Does the Evidence Tell Us?" *Journal of Economic Literature*, 1995, *33*(1), 132-163.

[59] Jaffe, Adam & Karen Plumer, "Environmental Regulation and Innovation: A Panel Data Study," *Review of Economics and Statistics,* 1997, 610-9.

[60] Adam B. Jaffe & Robert N Stavins, "The Energy Paradox and the Diffusion of Conservation Technology," *Resource and Energy Economics*, 1994, *16*, 91, 92–94.

[61] Jolls, Christine. "Accommodation Mandates." *Stanford Law Review*, 2000, *53*, 223-306.

[62] Jorgenson, Dale W & Wilcoxen, Peter J. "Environmental Regulation and U.S. Economic Growth." *RAND Journal of Economics*, 1990, *21*(2), 3 14-340.

[63] Kahn, Matthew E. "The Beneficiaries of Clean Air Act Regulation." *Regulation Magazine*, 2001 *24*(1).

[64] Kahn, Matthew E. "Particulate Pollution Trends in the United States." *Journal of Regional Science and Urban Economics*, 1997, *27*, 87-107.

[65] Kahneman, Daniel. "*Objective Happiness.*" In D. Kahneman, E. Diener, & N. Schwarz (Eds.). Well-being: the foundations of hedonic psychology. New York: Russell Sage Foundation, 1999.

[66] Kahneman, Daniel & Angus Deaton. "High Income Improves Evaluation of Life But Not Emotional Well-Being." *Proceedings of the National Academy of Sciences*, 2010, *107*(38) (2010).

[67] Kahneman, Daniel; Krueger; Alan B; Schkade, David; Schwarz, Norbert & Stone, Arthur. "Toward National Well-Being Accounts." *American Economic Review*, 2004, *94*(2), 429-434.

[68] Kahneman, Daniel; David A. Sckade; Claude Fischler; Alan B. Krueger & Amy Krilla. "The Structure of Well-Being in Two Cities: Life Satisfaction and Experienced Happiness in Columbus, Ohio; and Rennes, France." In International Differences in Well-Being, eds. Ed Diener, John F. Helliwell, & Daniel Kahneman. New York and Oxford: Oxford University Press, 2010, 398-430.

[69] Kamenica, Emir, Sendhil Mullainathan, & Richard Thaler. "Helping Consumers Know Themselves." *American Economic Review: Papers & Proceedings*, 2011, *101*, 417-422.

[70] Kaplow, Louis & Steven Shavell. Fairness vs. Welfare. Cambridge: Harvard University Press, 2002.

[71] Keller, Wolfgang, & Levinson, Arik. "Pollution Abatement Costs and Foreign Direct Investment Inflows to U.S. States." *The Review of Economics and Statistics*, 2002, *84*(4), 691703.

[72] Krueger, Alan B, ed. *Measuring the Subjective Well-Being of Nations: National Accounts of Time Use and Well-Being.* The University of Chicago Press, 2009.

[73] Krueger, Alan B, et al. "National Time Accounting: The Currency of Life." *Measuring the Subjective Well-Being of Nations: National Accounts of Time Use and Well-being,* Alan B. Krueger, ed. Chicago: The University of Chicago Press, 2009, 9-86.

[74] Krueger, Alan B & Schkade, David A. "The Reliability of Subjective Well-Being Measures." *Journal of Public Economics,* 2008, *92*(8-9), 1833-1845.

[75] La Porta; Rafael, Rafael; Florencio Lopez-de-Silanes, & Andrei Shleifer, "Corporate Ownership around the World," *Journal of Finance*, *54* (1999), pp. 471–517.

[76] Lane, Robert E. *The Loss of Happiness in Market Democracies.* New Haven: Yale University Press, 2001.

[77] Lanoie, Paul; Michel Patry & Richard Lajeunesse, "Environmental Regulation and Productivity: Testing the Porter Hypothesis," *Journal of Productivity Analysis*, 2008, *30*, 121-8.

[78] Levinson, Arik, & Taylor, M Scott. "Unmasking the Pollution Haven Effect." *International Economic Review*, 2008, *49*,1, 223-254.

[79] List, John A; Millimet, Daniel L; Fredriksson, Per G & McHone, W. Warren. "Effects of Environmental Regulations on Manufacturing Plant Births: Evidence from a Propensity Score Matching Estimator." *The Review of Economics and Statistics*, 2003, *85*(4), 944-952.

[80] Luttmer, Erzo FP. "Neighbors as Negatives: Relative Earnings and Well Being." *The Quarterly Journal of Economics,* 2005, *120*(3), 963-1002.

[81] Miller, Wilhelmine; Robinson, Lisa A & Lawrence, Robert S, eds. *Valuing Health for Regulatory Cost-Effectiveness Analysis.* National Academies Press, 2006.

[82] Morgenstern, Richard D; Pizer, William A & Jhih-Shyang Shih. "Jobs Versus the Environment: An Industry-Level Perspective." *Journal of Environmental Economics and Management*, 2002, *43*, 412-436.

[83] Moss, David & John Cisternino, eds., *New Perspectives on Regulation*, 2009. Cambridge, U.K.: The Tobin Project.

[84] National Research Council. *Estimating the Public Health Benefits of Proposed Air Pollution Regulations*. National Academies Press, 2002.

[85] National Research Council. *Estimating Mortality Risk Reduction and Economic Benefits from Controlling Ozone Air Pollution.* National Academies Press, 2008.

[86] Neumark, David & William L Wascher. Minimum Wages. Cambridge: The MIT Press, 2008.

[87] Nordhaus, William D. "*Principles of National Accounting For Non-Market Accounts.*" National Bureau of Economic Research Paper (Feburary 6, 2004). Available at http://www.nber.org/CRIW/CRIWs04/ nordhaus.pdf.

[88] Nordhaus, William D. & Edward C. Kokkelenberg. *Nature's Numbers: Expanding the National Economic Accounts to Include the Environment.* National Academies Press, 1999.

[89] Oswald, Andrew J & Stephen Wu. "Measures of Human Well-Being: Evidence from the U.S.A." *Science*, 2010, *327*, 576-579.

[90] Peoples, James. "Deregulation and the Labor Market." *Journal of Economic Perspectives,* 1998, *12*(3), 111-130.

[91] Ruhm, Christopher. "The Economic Consequences of Parental Leave Mandates: Lessons From Europe." *The Quarterly Journal of Economics*, 1998, *113*(1), 285-317.

[92] Sen, Amartya. *Development as Freedom*, Oxford University Press, 1999. Sen, Amartya. *Commodities and Capabilities*, Oxford University Press, 1999.

[93] Stiglitz, Joseph; Sen, Amartya & Fitoussi, Jean-Paul. *Mismeasuring Our Lives: Why GDP Doesn't Add Up*, The New Press, 2010.

[94] Stevenson, Betsey & Wolfers, Justin. "Economic Growth and Happiness: Reassessing the Easterlin Paradox." Brookings Papers on Economic Activity, Spring 2008a, 1-87.

[95] Stevenson, Betsey & Wolfers, Justin. "Happiness Inequality in the United States." *Journal of Legal Studies*, 2008b, *37*(S2), S3 3-S80.

[96] Stiglitz, Joseph; Sen, Amartya & Fitoussi, Jean-Paul. *Mismeasuring Our Lives: Why GDP Doesn't Add Up*, The New Press, 2010.

[97] Stone, AA, Schiffman, S, Schwartz, JE, Broderick, JE & Hufford, MR. "Patient Non-Compliance with Paper Diaries." *British Medical Journal*, 2002, *324*, 1193-94.

[98] Summers, Lawrence. "Some Simple Economics of Mandated Benefits," *The American Economic Review*, 1989, *79*(2), 177-183.

[99] Temple, Jonathan, "The New Growth Evidence," *Journal of Economic Literature*, 1999, *37*, 1, 112-156.

[100] van Stel, Andre; David Storey and A. Roy Thurik, "The Effect of Business Regulations on Nascent and Young Business Entrepreneurship," *Small Business Economics, 28,* (2007), pp. 171-186.

[101] Vitarelli, Anthony. "Behavioral Economics in Federal Regulation", 27 *Yale Journal on Regulation*, 2010, *27*(1).

[102] Waldfogel, Jane. "The Impact of the Family & Medical Leave Act." *Journal of Policy Analysis and Management,* 1999, *18*(2), 281-302.

[103] Walker, W Reed. "Environmental Regulation and Labor Reallocation: Evidence from the Clean Air Act." *American Economic Review: Papers & Proceedings*, 2011, *101*, 442-447.

[104] Warr, P. "*Well-Being and the Workplace.*" In D. Kahneman, E. Diener, and N. Schwarz (Eds.). Well-Being: The Foundations of Hedonic Psychology. New York: Russell Sage Foundation, 2003.

[105] Xing, Yuquing, & Kolstad, Charles D. "Do Lax Environmental Regulations Attract Foreign Investment?" *Environment and Resource Economics*, 2002, *21*, 1-22.

End Notes

[1] Section 624 of the Treasury and General Government Appropriations Act of 2001, Pub. L. No. 106-554, 31 U.S.C. § 1105 note.

[2] These estimates do not include the joint EPA/DOT CAFE rule as an "EPA" rule.

[3] A major rule is defined in Subtitle E of the Small Business Regulatory Enforcement Fairness Act of 1996 as a rule that is likely to result in: "(A) an annual effect on the economy of $100,000,000 or more; (B) a major increase in costs or prices for consumers, individual industries, Federal, State, or local government agencies, or geographic regions; or (C) significant adverse effects on competition, employment, investment, productivity, innovation, or on the ability of United States-based enterprises to compete with foreign-based enterprises in domestic and export markets." P.L. 104-121 Sec. 804, 5 U.S.C. § 804(2).

[4] A written statement containing a qualitative and quantitative assessment of the anticipated benefits and costs of the Federal mandate is required under the Section 202(a) of the Unfunded Mandates Reform Act of 1995 for all rules that may result in: "the expenditure by State, local, and tribal governments, in the aggregate, or by the private sector, of $100,000,000 or more (adjusted annually for inflation) in any one year." 2 U.S.C. § 1532(a).

[5] A regulatory action is considered "economically significant" under Executive Order 12866 § 3(f)(1) if it is likely to result in a rule that may have: "an annual effect on the economy of $100 million or more or adversely affect in a material way the economy, a sector of the economy, productivity, competition, jobs, the environment, public health or safety, or State, local, or tribal governments or communities."

[6] All previous Reports are available at: http://www.whitehouse.gov/omb/inforeg_regpol_reports_congress/.

[7] OMB used agency estimates where available. The benefit and cost ranges represent lowest and highest agency estimates using both 3 and 7 percent discount rates. If an agency quantified but did not monetize estimates, we used standard assumptions to monetize them, as explained in Appendix A. We adjusted estimates to 2001 dollars, the requested format in OMB Circular A-4, using the latest available Gross Domestic Product (GDP) deflator (e.g., estimates in 2010 dollars are deflated by a factor of 0.819). All amortizations are performed using a discount rate of 7 percent, unless the agency has already presented annualized, monetized results using a different explicit discount rate. OMB did not independently estimate benefits or costs when agencies did not provide quantified estimates.

[8] Section 3(b) of Executive Order 12866 excludes "independent regulatory agencies as defined in 44 U.S.C. 3502(10)" from OMB's regulatory review purview.

[9] See Greenstone (2009). In its 2009 Report, OMB recommended greater use of retrospective analysis; we continue to support that recommendation.

[10] See, e.g., Kahn (2001).

[11] This count includes all final and interim final rules from all Federal agencies (including independent agencies).

[12] Counts of OMB reviewed rules are available through the "review counts" and "search" tools on OIRA's regulatory information website (www.reginfo.gov). In addition, the underlying data for these counts are available for download in XML format on the website.

[13] OMB discusses, in this Report and in previous Reports, the difficulty of estimating and aggregating the benefits and costs of different regulations over long time periods and across many agencies using different methodologies. Any aggregation involves the assemblage of benefit and cost estimates that are not strictly comparable. In part to address this issue, the 2003 Report included OMB's new regulatory analysis guidance, OMB Circular A-4, that took effect on January 1, 2004, for proposed rules and January 1, 2005, for final rules. The guidance recommends what OMB defines as "best practices" in regulatory analysis, with a goal of strengthening the role of science, engineering, and economics in rulemaking. The overall goal of this guidance is a more transparent, accountable and credible regulatory process and a more consistent regulatory environment. OMB expects that as more agencies adopt our recommended best practices, the benefits and costs we present in future reports will become more comparable across agencies and programs. OMB continues to work with the agencies to ensure that their impact analyses follow the guidance.

[14] In many instances, agencies were unable to quantify all benefits and costs. We have conveyed the essence of these unquantified effects on a rule-by-rule basis in the columns titled "Other Information" in Appendix A of this and previous Reports. The monetized estimates we present necessarily exclude these unquantified effects.

[15] The 2006 Report is available at http://www.whitehouse.gov/omb/inforeg_regpol_reports_congress/. We note that there are ongoing discussions with respect to the scientific assumptions underlying the benefits per ton numbers that we use to monetize benefits that were not monetized. If, for instance, assumptions similar to those described at http://www.epa.gov/air/benmap/bpt.html were used, these estimates would be higher.

[16] This total includes the impacts of EPA's 2005 Clean Air Interstate Rule. On July 11, 2008, the DC Circuit Court vacated the rule; however, in response to EPA's petition, the court on December 23, 2008, remanded the rule without vacatur, which keeps this rule in effect while EPA conducts further proceedings consistent with the court's July 11 opinion. On August 2, 2010, EPA published in the Federal Register the proposed rule titled "Federal Implementation Plans to Reduce Interstate Transport of Fine Particulate Matter and Ozone." This rule, once finalized, will replace the Clean Air Interstate Rule. This total also includes the impacts of EPA's 2006 PM NAAQS which was inadvertently dropped from last year's aggregates.

This total excludes the impacts of two rulemakings we inadvertently neglected to remove from the 10-year aggregates in previous reports. The first rule is EPA's 2005 "Clean Air Mercury Rule--Electric Utility Steam Generating Units," On February 8, 2008, the D.C. Circuit vacated a precursor EPA rule removing power plants from the Clean Air Act list of sources of hazardous air pollutants, and at the same time vacated the Clean Air Mercury Rule. The second rule is EPA's 2004 -National Emission Standards for Hazardous Air Pollutants: Industrial/Commercial/Institutional Boilers and Process Heaters." On June 19, 2007, the United States Court of Appeals for the District of Columbia Circuit vacated and remanded this rule to EPA.

We also note that this report does not include an estimate of the costs and benefits of the final 2008 revisions to the National Ambient Air Quality Standards for Ozone. The reason is that those revisions remain in litigation and on January 19, 2010, EPA published a proposed reconsideration and tightening of the primary and secondary ozone standards. As a result, for the purposes of this particular Report, we did not consider the latest round of ozone rulemakings to be finalized. Of course it remains true that the ozone rule was finalized and for some purposes, it would be reasonable to treat its costs and benefits as part of the total catalogue of rulemaking impacts in FY 2008.

[17] The approach of adding ranges likely overstates the uncertainty in the total benefits and costs for each agency. The actual ranges are probably somewhat tighter than our estimates.

[18] These estimates do not include the joint EPA/DOT CAFE rule as an "EPA" rule.

[19] For example, a committee of the National Research Council/National Academy of Sciences released the study *Estimating the Public Health Benefits of Proposed Air Pollution Regulations* (2002), which recommends improvements to EPA benefits estimates. In addition, we continue to work with EPA to incorporate recommendations from recent NRC reports such as Miller, et al (2006) and National Research Council (2008). See also Environmental Protection Agency (2010).

The wide range of benefits estimates for particle control does not capture the full extent of the scientific uncertainty in measuring the health effects associated with exposure to fine particulate matter and its constituent elements. Six of the key assumptions in the benefits estimates are as follows:

1. Inhalation of fine particles is causally associated with premature death at concentrations near those experienced by most Americans on a daily basis. The weight of available epidemiological evidence supports a determination of causality. Biological mechanisms for this effect, while not completely understood, are supportive of this determination.

2. All fine particles, regardless of their chemical composition, are equally potent in causing premature mortality. This is an important assumption, because particulate matter (PM) produced via transported precursors emitted from electrical generating utilities (EGUs) may differ significantly from direct PM released from diesel engines and other industrial sources, but the scientific evidence is not yet sufficient to allow differentiation of effect estimates by particle type.

3. The impact function for fine particles is approximately linear within the range of ambient concentrations under consideration. Thus, the estimates include health benefits from reducing fine particles in areas with varied concentrations of PM, including both regions that are in attainment with fine particle standard and those that do not meet the standard.

4. The forecasts for future emissions and associated air quality modeling are valid. Although recognizing the difficulties, assumptions, and inherent uncertainties in the overall enterprise, these analyses are based on peer-reviewed scientific literature and up-to-date assessment tools, and we believe the results are highly useful in assessing benefits of air quality regulations..

5. Some rules apply a national dollar benefit-per-ton estimate of the benefits of reducing directly emitted fine particulates from specific source categories. Because they are based on national-level analysis, the benefitper-ton estimates used here do not reflect local variability in population density, meteorology, exposure, baseline health incidence rates, or other local factors that might lead to an over-estimate or under-estimate of the actual benefits of controlling directly emitted fine particulates.

6. The value of mortality risk reduction is taken largely from studies of the willingness-to-accept risk in the labor market.

[20] Agencies often design health and safety regulation to reduce risks to life, and valuation of the resulting benefits can be an important part of the analysis. What is sometimes called the "value of a statistical life" (VSL) is best understood not as the "valuation of life," but as the valuation of *statistical mortality risks*. For example, the average person in a population of 50,000 may value a reduction in mortality risk of 1/50,000 at $150. The value of reducing the risk of 1 *statistical* (as opposed to known or identified) fatality in this population would be $7.5 million, representing the aggregation of the willingness to pay values held by everyone in the

population. Building on an extensive and growing literature, OMB Circular A-4 provides background and discussion of the theory and practice of calculating VSL. It concludes that a substantial majority of the studies of VSL indicate a value that varies "from roughly $1 million to $10 million per statistical life." Circular A-4 generally reports values in 2001 dollars; if we update these values to 2010 dollars the range would be $1.2-$12.2 million. In practice, agencies have tended to use a value above the mid-point of this range (i.e., greater than $6.7 million in 2010 dollars).

Two agencies, EPA and DOT, have developed official guidance on VSL. In its 2009 update, DOT adopts a value of $6.0 million ($2009), and requires all the components of the Department to use that value in their RIAs. EPA recently changed its VSL to an older value of $6.3 million ($2000) and adjusts this value for real income growth post-2000. In its final rule setting a new primary standard for nitrogen dioxide, for example, EPA adjusted this VSL to account for a different currency year ($2006) and for income growth to 2020, which yields a VSL of $8.9 million. EPA stated in this RIA, however, that it is continuing its efforts to update this guidance, and that it anticipated presenting results from this effort to its Science Advisory Board, with draft guidance following soon thereafter. EPA has also recently published a white paper "to highlight some key topics related to the valuation of mortality risks, and to describe several possible approaches for synthesizing the empirical estimates for mortality risk reductions from existing hedonic wage and stated preference studies for the purpose of valuing mortality risk reductions associated with future EPA policies." Some of these issues include the possibilities of reporting value estimates in terms of risk changes, rather than "statistical lives"; adding a "cancer differential" to the standard estimates of mortality risk reduction values for policies expected to reduce carcinogenic pollutants; examining the role of altruism in valuing risk reductions; and, finally, incorporating alternative approaches to benefit transfer techniques. See Environmental Protection Agency (2010).

For the agencies that have not developed binding internal guidelines, we have done a brief review of RIAs and other materials to understand how VSLs have been used in practice. Although the Department of Homeland Security has no official policy on VSL, it sponsored a report through its U.S. Customs and Border Protection, and has used the recommendations of this report to inform VSL values for several recent rulemakings. This report recommends $6.3 million ($2008) and also recommends that DHS adjust this value upward over time for real income growth (in a manner similar to EPA's adjustment approach).

Other regulatory agencies that have used a VSL in individual rulemakings include DOL's Occupational Safety and Health Administration (OSHA) and HHS' Food and Drug Administration (FDA). In OSHA's rulemaking setting a Permissible Exposure Limit for Hexavalent Chromium, OSHA specifically referred to EPA guidance to justify a VSL of $7.0 million ($2003), as the types of air exposure risks regulated in this rulemaking were similar to those in EPA rulemakings. The FDA has consistently used values of $5.0 and $6.5 million ($2002) in several of its rulemakings to monetize mortality risks, but it also uses a monetary value of the remaining life-years saved by alternative policies. This is sometimes referred to as a "Value of a Statistical Life Year" or VSLY. (See Circular A4 for discussion.)

Our review suggests that, in recent years, actual agency practice has generally avoided significant inconsistencies. In current dollars, we have not found recent values below $6 million or above $9.5 million, and hence agency practice suggests a narrower band than that found in the literature review in Circular A-4. For a recent overview by the Congressional Research Service, see Copeland (2010).

[21] This table includes all rules reported in Table 1-1. The ranges will not necessarily match previously reported estimates for a fiscal year in past reports as rules have been dropped over time as described in this and past reports. See Appendix A for a complete list of rules included in these totals.

[22] This total excludes the impacts of EPA's 2004 "National Emission Standards for Hazardous Air Pollutants: Industrial/Commercial/Institutional Boilers and Process Heaters," previously included in our 10-year aggregate. On June 19, 2007, the United States Court of Appeals for the District of Columbia Circuit vacated and remanded the national emission standards for hazardous air pollutants for industrial/commercial/institutional boilers and process heaters. We inadvertently omitted removing this rule from the 10-year aggregates in previous reports.

[23] This total excludes the impacts of EPA's 2005 "Clean Air Mercury Rule--Electric Utility Steam Generating Units," previously included in our 10-year aggregate. On February 8, 2008, the D.C. Circuit vacated EPA's rule removing power plants from the Clean Air Act list of sources of hazardous air pollutants. At the same time, the Court vacated the Clean Air Mercury Rule. We inadvertently omitted removing this rule from the 10-year aggregates in previous reports.

[24] This total includes the impacts of EPA's 2006 PM NAAQS which was inadvertently dropped from last year's aggregates.

[25] This chart includes the impacts of EPA's 2005 Clean Air Interstate Rule, which (as explained in a previous footnote) was vacated and subsequently remanded without vacatur and likely will be replaced by a new rule, "Federal Implementation Plans to Reduce Interstate Transport of Fine Particulate Matter and Ozone." This rule, once finalized, will replace the Clean Air Interstate Rule.

[26] This is particularly true for EPA's air pollution regulations. Caution should be used in comparing benefits and costs over time in light of several factors, including new scientific evidence regarding the relationship between

pollutants and health endpoints; changes in the EPA's choice of assumptions when uncertainty remains (e.g., regarding the shape of the concentration – response function as low levels); and differences in techniques for monetizing benefits (including changes to the value assigned to a statistical life). Aggregate estimates in the report reflect differences in approaches and assumptions over time. Summing across time does not reflect how EPA would calculate the benefits of prior rules today.

[27] For example, FDA's trans fat rule was proposed by the Clinton administration and issued by the Bush Administration, while the groundwork for EPA's 2004 non-road diesel engine rule was set by the NAAQS rules issued in 1997.

[28] This count excludes rules that were withdrawn from OMB review or rules that were rescinded, stayed, or vacated after publication. It also counts joint rules as a single rule, even if they were submitted to OMB separately for review.

[29] Counts of OMB-reviewed rules are available through the "review counts" and "search" tools on OIRA's regulatory information web site (www.reginfo.gov).

[30] We discussed the relative contribution of major rules to the total impact of Federal regulation in detail in the "response-to-comments" section on pages 26-27 of the 2004 Report. In summary, our evaluation of a few representative agencies found that major rules represented the vast majority of the benefits and costs of all rules promulgated by these agencies and reviewed by OMB.

[31] EPA's Construction and Development Effluent Limitation Guideline published on December 1, 2009, contained estimates of benefits and costs. However, effective January 4, 2011, EPA has stayed the numeric limitation of 280 nephelometric turbidity units (NTU) in the Guideline and will propose a revised limit in a future rulemaking. Therefore, the rule is not included in these estimates.

[32] DOT's primary estimates for benefits and costs of Positive Train Control would yield negative net benefits of $711 million while ADS-B would also yield negative net benefits of $51 million. DOT's primary estimates of benefits and costs for Distribution Integrity Management were nearly equal, essentially resulting in neither net benefits nor net costs.

[33] Six of the nine are joint-rulemaking with Department of Labor and Treasury to implement health insurance reforms.

[34] In 2010, OMB issued a memorandum on "Increasing Openness in the Rulemaking Process – Use of the Regulation Identifier Number (RIN)," available at: http://www.whitehouse.gov/ sites/default/files/omb/assets/ inforeg/IncreasingOpenness_04072010.pdf. The memorandum provides that agencies should use the RIN on all relevant documents throughout the entire "lifecycle" of a rule. We expect that this requirement will help members of the public to find regulatory information at each stage of the process and will promote informed participation.

[35] The agency provided benefit and cost estimates for 2020. In order to annualize, as with previous NAAQS rulemakings, OMB assumed that the benefits and costs would be zero in the first year after the rule is finalized, the benefits and costs would increase linearly until year 2020, and the benefit and cost estimates would equal the 2020 estimates thereafter.

[36] DOT and EPA estimates differ somewhat due to programmatic differences between the two rules and differences in estimation modeling. The range of cost and benefit are based the total cost and benefits estimates for model years 2012-2016 in DOT's RIA, annualized over the life of those vehicles. The primary estimates are based on the total cost and benefits estimates for model years 2012-2016 in EPA's RIA annualized at 7% over the life of those vehicles.

[37] The rule quantifies but does not monetize potential benefits and costs. However, it provides monetized estimates of the private sector transfers (see Table A-1).

[38] This rule reinstates a 1 996 final rule (as required by statute), and points to the original RIA. It does not provide an incremental analysis of the impacts of the rule compared to a baseline that takes into account current levels of compliance with the rule. Thus, the 1996 RIA may well overstate both costs and benefits.

[39] The agency provides a discussion of the rule's potential impact on the use of preventative services and the associated benefits (health improvements), costs (medical costs), and transfers (health insurance premiums).

[40] The agency presents estimated benefits and costs for the entire coordinated strategy, both national and international levels, to control emissions from ocean-going vessels. It includes (1) the engine and fuel controls finalizing under the Clean Air Act; (2) the proposal submitted by the United States Government to the International Maritime Organization to amend MARPOL Annex VI to designate U.S. coasts as an Emission Control Area in which all vessels, regardless of flag, would be required to meet the engine and marine fuel sulfur requirements in Annex VI; and (3) the new engine emission and fuel sulfur limits contained in the amendments to Annex VI that are applicable to all vessels regardless of flag under the Act to Prevent Pollution from Ships. The estimates, although informative and illustrative, do not fully reflect the benefits and costs of the rule.

[41] Emphasizing the conceptual and empirical challenges in presenting an analysis of benefits and costs, EPA uses a case study approach to assess the consequences of an expansion of renewable fuel use, whether caused by the RFS2 program or by market forces. The analytical approach taken by EPA is to predict what the world would be like, in terms of a range of economic and environmental factors, if renewable fuel use increases to the level

required by the RFS2 standards. EPA then compares this prediction to two reference cases without the RFS2 program. The estimates, although informative and illustrative, do not reflect the benefits and costs of the rule. In addition, EPA has the statutory authority annually to review and lower the requirements for cellulosic ethanol, based on market supply. For both 2010 and 2011, EPA used this authority to lower the requirements significantly. Therefore, the original case study of the gallon mandates no longer represents the current RFS2 requirements.

[42] EPA noted that the Greenhouse Gas Tailoring rule would provide significant regulatory relief to state permitting agencies, because without the rule, the number of permits required (as many as 6 million) would overwhelm the resources of permitting authorities and severely impair the functioning of the programs. EPA estimated illustrative savings of $22.5 billion for permitting authorities and $55 billion for sources. These savings estimates are not included in this report because it is not straightforward to identify the baseline from which to decide whether the rule creates benefits or imposes costs, though to be sure the rule does significantly reduce costs as compared with a situation in which permits were required more generally.

[43] Pub. L. No. 104-121.

[44] Footnote 3, above, states the criteria for including rules in the report. In practice, a rule was considered "major" for the purposes of the report if (a) it was estimated to have either annual costs or benefits of $100 million or more or (b) it was likely to have a significant impact on the economy.

[45] Memorandum for the Heads of Executive Departments and Agencies, and of Independent Regulatory Agencies, M-11-10, "Executive Order 13563, 'Improving Regulation and Regulatory Review,'" p. 6, available at http://www.whitehouse.gov/sites/default/files/omb/ memoranda/2011/m11-10.pdf

[46] OMB did not finalize a Report in 1999; OMB reconstructed the estimates for this period based on GAO reports. Prior to the 2003 Report, OMB did not report on independent agency major rules on a fiscal year basis, but rather on an April-March cycle. Similar to last year, OMB is reporting all of the rules from 2000 through 2010 on a fiscal year basis (see Table C-1). The number of rules presented in earlier Reports may therefore not match the number of rules presented here.

[47] We note that EPA's rules setting air quality standards for ozone and particulate matter may ultimately lead to expenditures by State, local, or tribal governments of $100 million or more. However, Title II of the Unfunded Mandates Reform Act provides that agency statements of compliance with Section 202 must be conducted "unless otherwise prohibited by law." 2 U.S.C. § 1532 (a). The conference report to this legislation indicates that this language means that the section "does not require the preparation of any estimate or analysis if the agency is prohibited by law from considering the estimate or analysis in adopting the rule." H.R. Conf. Rep. No. 104-76 at 39 (1995). EPA has stated, and the courts have affirmed, that under the Clean Air Act, the criteria air pollutant ambient air quality standards are health-based and EPA is not to consider costs in setting the standards.

[48] Benefits were estimated to be constant across time and so annualized benefits are equal at 3 and 7 percent discount rates.

[49] While causal links have not been definitively established, a growing body of evidence has found associations between exposure to DBPs and various forms of cancer, as well as several adverse reproductive endpoints (e.g., spontaneous abortion).

[50] Section 202(2) of Pub. L. No. 104-121.

[51] 5 U.S.C. §§ 601-612.

[52] Dean, et al. (2000).

[53] Becker (2005).

[54] *Id.*, p. 163.

[55] *Id.*, p. 165.

[56] Neumark & Wascher (2008).

[57] Summers (1989).

[58] Jolls (2000).

[59] Acemoglu and Angrist (2001).

[60] Gruber (1994).

[61] Waldfogel (1999) and Baum (2003). Ruhm (1998) examines parental leave mandates in Europe and finds that they are associated with increases in women's relative employment levels and reductions in their relative wages.

[62] Berman and Bui (2001b).

[63] Data include information from 1979, 1980, 1981, 1985, 1988 and 1991.

[64] Berman and Bui (2001).

[65] See, e.g., Greenstone (2002); Kahn (1997). See also Walker (2011), for a recent finding of negative effects on employment as a result of environmental regulation.

[66] Jaffe et al, pp. 157-8.

[67] Keller and Levinson (2002), p. 691.

[68] Xing and Kolstad (2002), p. 1.

[69] Hanna (2010), p. 160.

[70] Brunnermeier and Levinson (2004), p. 6.
[71] Levinson and Taylor (2008).
[72] Peoples (1998).
[73] Blanchard and Giavazzi (2003).
[74] Bertrand and Kramarz (2002).
[75] See Sen (1999a, 1999b), Krueger (2009), Kahneman, et al. (2004), and Stiglitz, et al. (2010).
[76] Nordhaus & Kokkelenberg (1999); Nordhaus (2004).
[77] See Krueger (2009) for a discussion of subjective well-being and its measurement. See also Stevenson and Wolfers (2008b) showing movements in happiness inequality that do not parallel movements in income inequality.
[78] See Deeton (2008); Hagerty & Veenhoven (2003); Stevenson & Wolfers (2008a); Inglehart, Foa, Peterson, & Welzel (2008). For a finding of "a clear positive link between average levels of subjective well-being and GDP per capita across countries," see Stevenson and Wolfers (2008a).
[79] Stevenson and Wolfers (2008a) characterize this conclusion as one that has garnered a "clear consensus in the literature."
[80] See Inglehart et al. (2008). Lane (2001) claims that once an individual rises above a basic "subsistence level," the major sources of well-being are not income but rather friends and family life.
[81] Diener et al. (2010); Kahneman (1999).
[82] Krueger & Schkade (2008); Diener et al. (2010).
[83] Krueger, et al (2009). Krueger and Schkade (2008) also have examined the reliability of subjective well-being measures. For a general account, see Diener, et al. (2009). See also Kahneman et al (2004), Kahneman & Krueger (2006), Krueger, ed. (2009).
[84] See, e.g., Vitarelli (2010); Adler and Posner (2008).
[85] Luttmer (2005).
[86] See Dynan & Ravina (2007).
[87] Kahneman & Deaton (2010).
[88] Biswas-Diener (2010).
[89] Kahneman (2010).
[90] See Branchflower & Oswald (2004).
[91] See Blanchflower & Oswald (2010).
[92] Oswald & Wu (2010). In more technical terms, their paper claims to "offer[] a crosscheck on the spatial compensating-differentials theory of economics and regional science."
[93] Deaton et al (2010).
[94] Harter and Arora (2010).
[95] Isen (1987); Warr (1999).
[96] Ifcher & Zarghamee (2011).
[97] Englebrecht (2009).
[98] See, e.g., Temple (1999)
[99] For a recent empirical analysis using new OECD data to find a strong positive impact of increased education on economic output, see Cohen & Soto (2007).
[100] See, e.g., Bloom et al (2004). Bloom et al. survey the existing literature on health and economic outcomes, and find in their own cross-country analysis that a one year increase in life expectancy generates a 4 percent increase in economic output, controlling for other variables.
[101] Djankov et al (2002).
[102] van Stel et al (2007). They also find that regulations improving access to credit have a positive impact on entrepreneurship.
[103] One of the few such studies is an analysis by Hahn and Hird (1991), which estimates the net costs of regulations on the economy to be $46 billion, with aggregate annual transfer payments between $172.1 and $209.5 billion. But the authors note that their estimates have a wide range of uncertainty due to difficulties in estimation methods and available data. Further, this study is likely to be outdated due to major policy and economic developments in the years since its publication.
[104] Berman and Bui (2001 a) provide a helpful summary of some of this literature. It should be recalled that many environmental regulations affect provision of non-market goods that are not explicitly reflected in standard measures of economic activity. Thus, in addition to the direct economic costs imposed by environmental regulations, these same regulations have social welfare and other non-market impacts that are not captured in these studies.
[105] Jorgensen & Wilcoxen (1990).
[106] *Id*, p. 509.
[107] *Id*, p. 499. SCAQMD is South Coast Air Quality Management District.
[108] Gray & Shadbegian (1998).
[109] *Id*, at 254-25 5.
[110] Becker & Henderson (2000).

[111] *Id.*, at 414-415.
[112] Greenstone (2002).
[113] *Id*, at 1213.
[114] List, et al. (2003).
[115] Hanna (2010).
[116] Jaffe and Plummer (1997).
[117] See Lanoie et al (2008).
[118] Jaffe & Plumer (1997), at 618.
[119] Chay & Greenstone (2005). Fullerton (2011) uses a carbon permit system – specifically, the cap-and-trade legislation that passed the U.S. House of Representatives in 2009 (which then stalled in the Senate) – to illustrate six different types of distributional effects: (1) the higher prices of carbon-intensive products, (2) changes in relative returns to factors like labor, capital, and resources, (3) allocation of scarcity rents from a restricted number of permits, (4) distribution of the benefits from improvements in environmental quality, (5) temporary effects during the transition, and (6) capitalization of all those effects into prices of land, corporate stock, or house values. He concludes that, in this particular case, many or all effects may be regressive – that is, the net burden as a fraction of income is higher for the poor than for the rich.
[120] Kahn (2001).
[121] Carpenter (2009). For more historical and formal modeling approaches to this same argument, see, e.g., Carpenter (2004) and Carpenter & Ting (2007).
[122] *Id.* See also La Porta et al (1999).
[123] On the possible social gains from using alternative regulatory approaches, see generally Moss & Cisternino (2009).
[124] *Id.* See also Balleisen and Moss, eds. (2009).
[125] For a detailed discussion of the relationship between cost-benefit analysis and social welfare, see Adler and Posner (2008).
[126] See Banerjee and Duflo (2011).
[127] For recent discussion, see Kamenica et al. (2011).
[128] See OMB, *2010 Report to Congress on the Benefits and Costs of Federal Regulations and Unfunded Mandates on State, Local, and Tribal Entities* (2010), pp. 40-47, available at http://www.whitehouse.gov/sites/default/files/omb/legislative/reports/2010_Benefit_Cost_Report.pdf.
[129] See USDA News Release, "First Lady, Agriculture Secretary Vilsack and Surgeon General Benjamin Launch MyPlate Icon as a New Reminder to Help Consumers to Make Healthier Food Choices," available at http://www.usda.gov/wps/portal/usda/usdahome?contentid=2011/06/0225.xml&navid=NEWS_RELEASE&navtype=RT&parentnav=LATEST_RELEASES&edeployment_action=retrievecontent.
[130] See Environmental Protection Agency and Department of Transportation, "Revisions and Additions to Motor Vehicle Fuel Economy Label," RIN 2060-AQ09; RIN 2127-AK73, available at http://www.epa.gov/fueleconomy/label/nprm-label2010.pdf
[131] For the purposes of showing general trends by Administration, figure 2-1 reports the total net benefits – benefits minus costs – based on primary agency estimates, or midpoints if only ranges are reported. See Appendix D for a list of rules included in the totals.
[132] Estimates are based on a range of values reported in previous Reports. See Appendix D and Table 1-5(a) for a list of rules included in the totals.
[133] Table 2-2 reports the top five rules with highest net benefits – benefits minus costs – based on the primary agency estimates, or midpoints if only ranges are reported.
[134] Table 2-3 reports the top five rules with highest benefits based on the primary agency estimates, or midpoints if only ranges are reported.
[135] Table 2-4 reports the top five rules with highest costs based on the primary agency estimates, or midpoints if only ranges are reported.
[136] Available at http://www.whitehouse.gov/sites/default/files/omb/inforeg/eo12866/eo13563_01182011.pdf.
[137] See, e.g., Kamenica, Mullainahtan & Thaler (2011).
[138] Greenstone (2009), at 13.
[139] *Id.*, at 118.
[140] See, e.g., Banerjee and Duflo (2011).
[141] U.S. Department of Transportation, "Traffic Safety Facts: Research Note, High Visibility Enforcement Demonstration Programs in Connecticut and New York Reduce Hand-Held Phone Use," available at http://www.distraction.gov/files/for-media/2010.09.17-7268-TSF-RN-HighEnforcementCT-NY.pdf
[142] NHTSA observes, however, that both States have had hand-held cell phone bans while driving for some time – 2001 for New York and 2005 for Connecticut. The laws alone may have served to keep these States at or below the national average, but the addition of high visibility enforcement and media emphasizing the enforcement drove the rates down even lower. High levels of national media and celebrity attention to distracted driving, such as by the Oprah Winfrey Show, may account for some of the high public awareness of

the issue and for the steady declines in observed hand-held cell phone use in the control sites and among women in three of the five sites overall.

[143] The preliminary plans can currently all be viewed at "Regulation Reform," available at http://www.whitehouse.gov/21stcenturygov/actions/21st-century-regulatory-system. Many agencies will also publish their preliminary plans online on their Open Government Webpages (www.agency.gov/open).

[144] Department of Labor, *Preliminary Plan for Retrospective Analysis of Exisiting Rules*, p. 8, available at http://www.whitehouse.gov/files/documents/2011-regulatory-actionplans/DepartmentofLaborPreliminaryRegulatoryReformPlan.pdf

[145] Environmental Protection Agency, *Improving Our Regulations: A Preliminary Plan for Periodic Retrospective Reviews of Existing Regulations*, pp. 13-14, available at http://www. whitehouse.gov/files/documents/2011-regulatory-action-plans/Environmental ProtectionAgencyPreliminaryRegulatoryReformPlan.pdf

[146] Department of Labor, *Preliminary Plan for Retrospective Analysis of Exisiting Rules*, pp. 8-9, available at http://www.whitehouse.gov/files/documents/2011-regulatory-actionplans/DepartmentofLaborPreliminaryRegulatoryReformPlan.pdf

[147] Department of Transportation, *Draft Preliminary Plan for Implementation of Executive Order 13563: Retrospective Review and Analysis of Exisiting Rules*, p. 20, available at http://www.whitehouse.gov/files/documents/2011-regulatory-actionplans/Departmentof TransportationPreliminaryRegulatoryReformPlan.pdf

[148] Environmental Protection Agency, *Improving Our Regulations: A Preliminary Plan for Periodic Retrospective Reviews of Existing Regulations*, pp. 9, 16, available at http://www.whitehouse.gov/files/documents/2011-regulatory-action-plans/Environmental ProtectionAgencyPreliminaryRegulatoryReformPlan.pdf.

[149] Department of Commerce, *Preliminary Plan for Retrospective Analysis of Exisiting Rules*, available at http://www.whitehouse.gov/files/documents/2011-regulatory-actionplans/DepartmentofCommercePreliminaryRegulatoryReformPlan.pdf

[150] Department of the Interior, *Preliminary Plan for Retrospective Regulatory Review*, pp. 10-114, available at http://www.whitehouse.gov/files/documents/2011-regulatory-action-plans/DepartmentoftheInteriorPreliminaryRegulatoryReformPlan.pdf

[151] Department of Health and Human Service, *Preliminary Plan for Retrospective Review of Exisiting Rules*, pp. 6-13, available at http://www.whitehouse.gov/files/documents/2011-regulatory-actionplans/HealthandHumanServicesPreliminaryRegulatoryReformPlan.pdf

[152] See Greenstone (2009) and, in other contexts, Banerjee and Duflo (2009).

[153] Department of Homeland Security, *Preliminary Plan for Retrospective Review of Existing Regulations*, p. 27, available at http://www.whitehouse.gov/files/documents/2011-regulatory-actionplans/DepartmentofHomeland SecurityPreliminaryRegulatoryReform Plan.pdf

[154] *Id.*

[155] Department of Labor, *Preliminary Plan for Retrospective Analysis of Existing Rules*, p., 20, available at http://www.whitehouse.gov/files/documents/2011-regulatory-actionplans/DepartmentofLaborPreliminaryRegulatoryReformPlan.pdf

[156] Department of the Interior, *Preliminary Plan for Retrospective Regulatory Review*, p. 19, available at http://www.whitehouse.gov/files/documents/2011-regulatory-actionplans/ Department of the Interior Preliminary RegulatoryReformPlan.pdf

[157] Department of the Treasury, *Preliminary Plan for Retrospective Analysis of Existing Rules*, p. 19, available at http://www.whitehouse.gov/files/documents/2011-regulatory-action-plans/DepartmentoftheTreasuryPreliminaryRegulatoryReformPlan.pdf.

[158] Harrington (2006).

[159] Specifically, Harrington argues that cost estimates are primarily focused on compliance expenditures, and thus exclude important cost categories such as employee training; management attention; discouraged innovation and investment; tax distortion effects, as well as the costs of rent-seeking (unproductive behavior undertaken by firms and individuals to influence regulatory decisions). Similarly, he contends that measurable benefits "tend to be concentrated types of public goods where the connections from the regulation to a physical effect that people value are clear, and where economists have been able to develop valuation methods that approximate individual willingness to pay for changes in those effects." As such, benefits that fail to meet these criteria often remain uncounted, such as the more-difficult-to-measure benefits of, say, ecological preservation. *Id.*, at 10. In addition to rules that fail to qualify for the 10-year look-back, Harrington also contends that "nearly 90 percent of the rules that [are] reviewed by OMB do not enter the benefit and cost estimate because they are nonmajor rules, which means primarily that each has an estimated cost and benefit that is less than $100 million per year."

[160] *Id.*, at 37.

[161] *Id.*, at 22 ("An ex ante estimate was considered accurate if [the benefit-cost ratio lay between 0.75 and 1.25.").

[162] *Id.*

[163] Dale et al. (2002).

[164] *Id.* (see Table 2, with OMB's calculations using the 25% accuracy range).

[165] Harrington, Morgenstern & Nelson (2010).

[166] Office of Technology Assessment (1995).

[167] See OMB, *Validating Regulatory Analysis: 2005 Report to Congress on the Costs and Benefits of Federal Regulations and Unfunded Mandates on State, Local, and Tribal Entities* (2005), pp. 46-47, available at http://www.whitehouse.gov/sites/default/files/omb/assets/omb/inforeg/2005_cb/final_2005_cb_report.pdf

[168] As in the Harrington (2006) study, OMB's 2005 report used the term "accurate" to mean "that the post-regulation estimate is within +/- 25 percent of the pre-regulation estimate." *Id.*, at p. 42.

[169] Available at http://www.whitehouse.gov/sites/default/files/omb/inforeg/for-agencies/POTUS-Memo-on-Regulatory-Flexibility-Small-Business-and-Job-Creation-01-18-2011.pdf.

[170] Available at http://www.whitehouse.gov/omb/circulars_a004_a-4/.

[171] Available at http://www.whitehouse.gov/sites/default/files/omb/inforeg/regpol/RIA_Checklist.pdf.

[172] Cf. Kaplow and Shavell (2002).

[173] See Office of Management and Budget, Office of Information and Regulatory Affairs, *2009 Report to Congress on the Benefits and Costs of Federal Regulations and Unfunded Mandates on State, Local, and Tribal Entities*, at p. 42, available at http://www.whitehouse.gov/omb/inforeg_regpol_reports_congress/

[174] OMB refers to the meta-analyses by Mrozek and Taylor (2002) and Viscusi and Aldy (2003) as sources of this range: Both examine only the hedonic wage literature.

[175] See note 20, supra.

[176] Viscusi and Aldy (2003)

[177] Kochi (2006) and Bellavance (2009)

[178] Including Peer Reviewer Christine Jolls, see Appendix G and her peer report, available at http://www.whitehouse.gov/omb/inforeg_regpol_reports_congress.

[179] Gabiax and Laibson (2006).

[180] For discussion, see, for example, Jaffe and Stavins (1994) (examining the factors that influence public adoption of energy-conserving technologies and the potential effects of regulation).

[181] Available at http://www.whitehouse.gov/sites/default/files/omb/assets/inforeg/Increasing_Openness_04072010.pdf. Executive Order 12866, Sec. 4(b) requires each regulatory action in the Unified Regulatory Agenda—a semiannual compendium of all regulations under development or review—to contain, among other things, a RIN.

[182] Available at http://www.whitehouse.gov/sites/default/files/omb/assets/inforeg/edocket_final_5-28-2010.pdf

[183] These strategic goals include 1) increasing the public's access to regulatory content; 2) building a common taxonomy and protocols for managing dockets and regulatory documents; and 3) compiling comprehensive electronic dockets and increasing agency efficiency. The document also details plans for system enhancements to FDMS and Regulations.gov, as well as new interfaces the RISC/OIRA Consolidated Information System (ROCIS) to reduce agency burdens in managing regulatory dockets by pre-populating electronic dockets in FDMS based on existing information in the Unified Agenda.

[184] Reginfo.gov site statistics for site visitors were measured by comparing March 1-December 31, 2010 data sets to March 1-December 31, 2009 data sets.

[185] In March 2010, the U.S. Department of Agriculture was the first Federal agency to use the homepage link to host an introductory video for the "Let's Move" Campaign, featuring First Lady Michelle Obama.

[186] Regulations.gov site statistics for site visitors were measured by comparing January 1-December 31, 2010 data sets to January 1-December 31, 2009 data sets.

[187] OMB and USTR, Memorandum for the Heads of Executive Departments and Agencies and Independent Regulatory Agencies, M-11-23, "Export and Trade Promotion, Public Participation, and Rulemaking," available at http://www.whitehouse.gov/sites/default/files/omb/memoranda/2011/m11-23.pdf

[188] This guidance is available at: http://www.whitehouse.gov/omb/circulars/a004/a-4.pdf.

[189] These guidelines are available at: http://www.whitehouse.gov/omb/fedreg/reproducible2.pdf.

[190] This Bulletin is available at: http://www.whitehouse.gov/omb/memoranda/fy2005/m05-03.pdf.

[191] Available at http://www.whitehouse.gov/the-press-office/memorandum-heads-executive-departments-and-agencies-3-9-09.

[192] Available at http://www.whitehouse.gov/sites/default/files/microsites/ostp/scientific-integrity-memo1217_2010.pdf.

[193] See OMB, *Memorandum for the President's Management Council (2004)* http://www.whitehouse.gov/omb/inforeg/info_quality_posting_083004.pdf.

[194] See OMB, *Validating Regulatory Analysis: 2005 Report to Congress on the Costs and Benefits of Federal Regulations and Unfunded Mandates on State, Local, and Tribal Entities* (2005), available at http://www.whitehouse.gov/omb/inforeg/2005_cb/final_2005_cb_report.pdf

[195] See OMB, *Information Quality, a Report to Congress FY 2003*, (2003), http://www.whitehouse.gov/omb/inforeg/fy03_info_quality_rpt.pdf, and OMB, *Validating Regulatory Analysis: 2005 Report to Congress on the Costs and Benefits of Federal Regulations and Unfunded Mandates on State, Local, and Tribal Entities* (2005), available at http://www.whitehouse.gov/omb/inforeg/2005 cb/final 2005 cb report.pdf.

[196] As mentioned, a listing of webpages for Agency IQ correspondence is available in Appendix I of this report.

[197] See OMB, Memorandum for the Heads of Departments and Agencies, M-05-03, "Issuance of OMB's 'Final Information Quality Bulletin for Peer Review,'" available at http://www.whitehouse.gov/omb/memoranda/fy2005/m05-03.pdf.

[198] The Bulletin notes that information dissemination can have a significant economic impact even if it is not part of a rulemaking. For instance, the economic viability of a technology can be influenced by the government's characterization of its attributes. Alternatively, the Federal Government's assessment of risk can directly or indirectly influence the response actions of state and local agencies or international bodies.

[199] These assessments include, but are not limited to, state-of-science reports; technology assessments; weight-of-evidence analyses; meta-analyses; health, safety, or ecological risk assessments; toxicological characterizations of substances; integrated assessment models; hazard determinations; or exposure assessments.

[200] The Animal and Plant Health Inspection Service and the Food Safety and Inspection Service have strong peer review programs, as do the Economic Research Service and the Agricultural Research Service. .

[201] The National Oceanographic and Atmospheric Administration is the only agency within Commerce that has identified documents subject to the Bulletin; NOAA's peer review process is strong.

[202] The Food and Drug Administration, the Center for Disease Control and Prevention, and the National Toxicology Program are compliant with the Bulletin.

[203] The Fish and Wildlife Service has an exemplary peer review process. The US Geological Survey and the National Park Service are also compliant with the Bulletin.

[204] An example is the Environmental Protection Agency's incorporation with its science inventory project.

[205] An example is the agenda for the Department of Transportation.

[206] An example is the agendas for the Department of Health and Human Services and the Department of the Interior.

[207] For instance, the agenda for the Department of Commerce.

[208] For instance, the agenda for the Department of Transportation.

[209] For instance, agendas for the Department of Agriculture's Animal and Plant Health Inspection Service, the Department of Health and Human Services' Center for Disease Control, and the Environmental Protection Agency (See Appendix for URLs for these agencies' agendas.).

[210] For instance, some National Oceanographic and Atmospheric Administration documents that are part of the Endangered Species Act process (e.g., http://www.fakr.noaa.gov/protected resources).

[211] Interim final rules were not included in this chapter since "Section 202 [of the Unfunded Mandates Reform Act] . . . does not apply to interim final rules or non-notice rules issued under the 'good cause' exemption in 5 U.S.C. 553(b)(B)." See OMB, Memorandum for the Heads of Executive Departments and Agencies, M-95-09, "Guidance for Implementing Title II of S.1," 1995, available at http://www.whitehouse.gov/sites/default/files/omb/memoranda/m95-09.pdf.

[212] The preamble to the final rule states, "This rule would not result in the net expenditure by State, local and tribal governments, in the aggregate, or by the private sector, of $141,300,000 or more in any one year, nor would it affect small governments. Therefore, no actions are deemed necessary under the provisions of the Unfunded Mandates Reform Act of 1995."

[213] See *National Income and Product Accounts*, http://www.bea.gov.

[214] See *National Income and Product Accounts*, http://www.bea.gov.

[215] Based on date of completion of OMB review.

[216] On January 22, 2001, DOE promulgated a regulation that would have raised the energy efficiency of new central air conditioners by 30 percent. On May 23, 2002, DOE withdrew the 2001 rule and issued this final rule raising the minimum energy efficiency levels by 20 percent. The latter action was the subject of a litigation that concluded in 2004, with the court holding that DOE must implement the regulation promulgated on January 22, 2001. On August 17, 2004, DOE published revisions to the Code of Federal Regulations that reflected the energy efficiency increase of 30 percent that will take effect in 2006 (69 FR 50997). Thus, in our current 10-year aggregate we have replaced the benefits and costs of the 2002 final rule (originally reported in the 2003 report) with the benefits and costs of the original 2001 final rule.

[217] As explained in the 2010 Report, the benefits and costs of this rule are not included in the benefit and cost totals for the 10-year aggregate. This interim final rule reestablished policies on the maximum time truck drivers were able to drive per day and per week, and the minimum period before which truck drivers could restart the count of their weekly driving time. These policies were put in place through previous rulemakings on the same subject, but were vacated in 2007 by the United States Court of Appeals for the DC Circuit, which held that the Agency had failed to provide an opportunity for public comment on certain aspects of their Regulatory Impact Analysis. Furthermore, the analysis accompanying this interim final rule analyzed the impact of maintaining these policies relative to the disruptive impact of their prompt removal, not relative to previous fully-implemented policies. Since OMB already reported and attributed the benefits and costs of the Hours of Service Regulations to other rulemakings, and those policies were maintained by this interim final rule, we felt that including the benefits and costs of this rulemaking in the ten-year totals would constitute double counting.

[218] Superseded by the 2005 final rule (RIN 2127-AJ23).

[219] On June 19, 2007, the United States Court of Appeals for the District of Columbia Circuit vacated and remanded the national emission standards for hazardous air pollutants for industrial/commercial/institutional boilers and process heaters. Thus, we exclude this rule from the 10-year aggregates in previous reports. (Benefits: $3,752-$38,714 million; Costs: $876 million)

[220] On February 8, 2008, the D.C. Circuit vacated EPA's rule removing power plants from the Clean Air Act list of sources of hazardous air pollutants. At the same time, the Court vacated the Clean Air Mercury Rule. Thus, we exclude this rule from the 10-year aggregates. (Benefits: $1-2 million; Costs: $500 million)

[221] On July 11, 2008, the DC Circuit Court vacated the rule; however, in response to EPA's petition, the Court on December 23, 2008, remanded the rule without vacatur, which keeps this rule in effect while EPA conducts further proceedings consistent with the Court's July 11 opinion. On August 2, 2010, EPA published in the Federal Register the proposed rule titled "Federal Implementation Plans to Reduce Interstate Transport of Fine Particulate Matter and Ozone." This rule, once finalized, will replace the Clean Air Interstate Rule.

[222] Even though this rule was finalized and has not been overturned by a court, on January 19, 2010, EPA published a proposed reconsideration and tightening of the primary and secondary ozone standards. Therefore, for the purposes of this Report, we did not consider the latest round of ozone rulemakings finalized. (Benefits: $1,581-$14,934 million; Costs: $6,676-$7,730 million)

[223] Table C-2 excludes all fee assessment rules promulgated by independent agencies. FCC promulgated six fee assessment rules from 1997 through 2002. NRC promulgated 13 statutorily mandated fee assessment rules from 1997 through 2010.

[224] Based on date of completion of OMB review.

[225] Based on date of completion of OMB review.

[226] On January 22, 2001, DOE promulgated a regulation that would have raised the energy efficiency of new central air conditioners by 30 percent. On May 23, 2002, DOE withdrew the 2001 rule and issued this final rule raising the minimum energy efficiency levels by 20 percent. The latter action was the subject of a litigation that concluded in 2004, with the court holding that DOE must implement the regulation promulgated on January 22, 2001. On August 17, 2004, DOE published revisions to the Code of Federal Regulations that reflected the energy efficiency increase of 30 percent that will take effect in 2006 (69 FR 50997). Thus, in our current 10-year aggregate we have replaced the benefits and costs of the 2002 final rule (originally reported in the 2003 report) with the benefits and costs of the original 2001 final rule.

[227] The original table included a typographical error; the low end of the benefits estimate was reported as $1,250 million.

[228] Based on date of completion of OMB review.

[229] Required under Executive Order 12866, Section 6(a)(3)(B)(i): "The text of the draft regulatory action, together with a reasonably detailed description of the need for the regulatory action and an explanation of how the regulatory action will meet that need."

[230] Circular A-4 states: "If the regulation is designed to correct a significant market failure, you should describe the failure both qualitatively and (where feasible) quantitatively." (P. 4)

[231] See note 1 above.

[232] Circular A-4 states: "You need to measure the benefits and costs of a rule against a baseline. This baseline should be the best assessment of the way the world would look absent the proposed action... In some cases, substantial portions of a rule may simply restate statutory requirements that would be self-implementing, even in the absence of the regulatory action. In these cases, you should use a pre-statute baseline." (P. 15-16)

[233] Circular A-4 states: "Because of its influential nature and its special role in the rulemaking process, it is appropriate to set minimum quality standards for regulatory analysis. You should provide documentation that the analysis is based on the best reasonably obtainable scientific, technical, and economic information available... you should assure compliance with the Information Quality Guidelines for your agency and OMB's Guidelines for Ensuring and Maximizing the Quality, Objectivity, Utility, and Integrity of Information Disseminated by Federal Agencies..." (P. 17). The IQ Guidelines (paragraph V.3.a) define objectivity to include "whether disseminated information is being presented in an accurate, clear, complete, and unbiased manner." http://www.whitehouse.gov/omb/assets

[234] Circular A-4 states: "A good analysis should be transparent and your results must be reproducible. You should clearly set out the basic assumptions, methods, and data underlying the analysis and discuss the uncertainties associated with the estimates. A qualified third party reading the analysis should be able to understand the basic elements of your analysis and the way in which you developed your estimates. To provide greater access to your analysis, you should generally post it, with all the supporting documents, on the internet so the public can review the findings." (P. 17). OMB IQ Guidelines (paragraph V.3.b.ii) further states: "If an agency is responsible for disseminating influential scientific, financial, or statistical information, agency guidelines shall include a high degree of transparency about data and methods to facilitate the reproducibility of such information by qualified third parties."

[235] Required under Executive Order 12866, Section 6(a)(3)(C)(i): "An assessment, including the underlying analysis, of benefits anticipated from the regulatory action (such as, but not limited to, the promotion of the efficient functioning of the economy and private markets, the enhancement of health and safety, the protection

of the natural environment, and the elimination or reduction of discrimination or bias) together with, to the extent feasible, a quantification of those benefits."

[236] Circular A-4 states: "You should monetize quantitative estimates whenever possible. Use sound and defensible values or procedures to monetize benefits and costs, and ensure that key analytical assumptions are defensible. If monetization is impossible, explain why and present all available quantitative information." (P. 19). Circular A-4 also offers a discussion of appropriate methods for monetizing benefits that might not easily be turned into monetary equivalents.

[237] Required under Executive Order 12866, Section 6(a)(3)(C)(ii): "An assessment, including the underlying analysis, of costs anticipated from the regulatory action (such as, but not limited to, the direct cost both to the government in administering the regulation and to businesses and others in complying with the regulation, and any adverse effects on the efficient functioning of the economy, private markets (including productivity, employment, and competitiveness), health, safety, and the natural environment), together with, to the extent feasible, a quantification of those costs;" See also note 6 above.

[238] Executive Order 12866, Section 1(b)(6) states that to the extent permitted by law, "[e]ach agency shall assess both the costs and the benefits of the intended regulation and, recognizing that some costs and benefits are difficult to quantify, propose or adopt a regulation only upon a reasoned determination that the benefits of the intended regulation justify its costs." As Executive Order 12866 recognizes, a statute may require an agency to proceed with a regulation even if the benefits do not justify the costs; in such a case, the agency's analysis may not show any such justification.

[239] Required under Executive Order 12866, Section 6(a)(3)(C)(iii): "An assessment, including the underlying analysis, of costs and benefits of potentially effective and reasonably feasible alternatives to the planned regulation, identified by the agencies or the public (including improving the current regulation and reasonably viable nonregulatory actions)..."

[240] Circular A-4 states: "You should analyze the benefits and costs of different regulatory provisions separately when a rule includes a number of distinct provisions." (P. 17)

[241] Circular A-4 states: "you generally should analyze at least three options: the preferred option; a more stringent option that achieves additional benefits (and presumably costs more) beyond those realized by the preferred option; and a less stringent option that costs less (and presumably generates fewer benefits) than the preferred option." (P. 16)

[242] Circular A-4 states: "You should consider setting different requirements for large and small firms, basing the requirements on estimated differences in the expected costs of compliance or in the expected benefits. The balance of benefits and costs can shift depending on the size of the firms being regulated. Small firms may find it more costly to comply with regulation, especially if there are large fixed costs required for regulatory compliance. On the other hand, it is not efficient to place a heavier burden on one segment of a regulated industry solely because it can better afford the higher cost. This has the potential to load costs on the most productive firms, costs that are disproportionate to the damages they create. You should also remember that a rule with a significant impact on a substantial number of small entities will trigger the requirements set forth in the Regulatory Flexibility Act. (5 U.S.C. 603(c), 604)." (P. 8)

[243] Executive Order 12866, Section 1(a) states: "agencies should select those approaches that maximize net benefits (including potential economic, environmental, public health and safety, and other advantages; distributive impacts; and equity) unless a statute requires another regulatory approach."

[244] Required under Executive Order 12866, Section 6(a)(3)(C)(iii): "An assessment, including the underlying analysis, of costs and benefits of potentially effective and reasonably feasible alternatives to the planned regulation, identified by the agencies or the public (including improving the current regulation and reasonably viable nonregulatory actions), and an explanation why the planned regulatory action is preferable to the identified potential alternatives."

[245] Circular A-4 contains a detailed discussion, generally calling for discount rates of 7 percent and 3 percent for both benefits and costs. It states: "Benefits and costs do not always take place in the same time period. When they do not, it is incorrect simply to add all of the expected net benefits or costs without taking account of when they actually occur. If benefits or costs are delayed or otherwise separated in time from each other, the difference in timing should be reflected in your analysis.... For regulatory analysis, you should provide estimates of net benefits using both 3 percent and 7 percent.... If your rule will have important intergenerational benefits or costs you might consider a further sensitivity analysis using a lower but positive discount rate in addition to calculating net benefits using discount rates of 3 and 7 percent." (PP. 31, 34, 36)

[246] Circular A-4 provides a detailed discussion. Among other things, it states: "Examples of quantitative analysis, broadly defined, would include formal estimates of the probabilities of environmental damage to soil or water, the possible loss of habitat, or risks to endangered species as well as probabilities of harm to human health and safety. There are also uncertainties associated with estimates of economic benefits and costs, such as the cost savings associated with increased energy efficiency. Thus, your analysis should include two fundamental components: a quantitative analysis characterizing the probabilities of the relevant outcomes and an assignment of economic value to the projected outcomes." (P. 40). Circular A-4 also states: "You should

clearly set out the basic assumptions, methods, and data underlying the analysis and discuss the uncertainties associated with the estimates." (P. 17)

[247] Executive Order 12866, Section 1(b)(5) states; "When an agency determines that a regulation is the best available method of achieving the regulatory objective, it shall design its regulations in the most cost-effective manner to achieve the regulatory objective. In doing so, each agency shall consider incentives for innovation, consistency, predictability, the costs of enforcement and compliance (to the government, regulated entities, and the public), flexibility, *distributive impacts*, and *equity*" (emphasis added).

Circular A-4 states: "The term 'distributional effect' refers to the impact of a regulatory action across the population and economy, divided up in various ways (e.g., income groups, race, sex, industrial sector, geography)... Your regulatory analysis should provide a separate description of distributional effects (i.e., how both benefits and costs are distributed among sub-populations of particular concern) so that decision makers can properly consider them along with the effects on economic efficiency... Where distributive effects are thought to be important, the effects of various regulatory alternatives should be described quantitatively to the extent possible, including the magnitude, likelihood, and severity of impacts on particular groups." (P. 14)

[248] Circular A-4 states: "Distinguishing between real costs and transfer payments is an important, but sometimes difficult, problem in cost estimation. . . . Transfer payments are monetary payments from one group to another that do not affect total resources available to society. . . . You should not include transfers in the estimates of the benefits and costs of a regulation. Instead, address them in a separate discussion of the regulation's distributional effects." (P. 14)

[249] Circular A-4 states: "Your regulatory analysis should provide a separate description of distributional effects (i.e., how both benefits and costs are distributed among sub-populations of particular concern) so that decision makers can properly consider them along with the effects on economic efficiency. Executive Order 12866 authorizes this approach. Where distributive effects are thought to be important, the effects of various regulatory alternatives should be described quantitatively to the extent possible, including the magnitude, likelihood, and severity of impacts on particular groups." (P. 14)

[250] Circular A-4 states: "Your analysis should also have an executive summary, including a standardized accounting statement." (P. 3). OMB recommends that: "Regulatory analysis should be made as transparent as possible by a prominent and accessible executive summary—written in a "plain language" manner designed to be understandable to the public—that outlines the central judgments that support regulations, including the key findings of the analysis (such as central assumptions and uncertainties)...If an agency has analyzed the costs and benefits of regulatory alternatives to the planned action (as is required for economically significant regulatory actions), the summary should include such information." See *2010 Report to Congress on the Benefits and Costs of Federal Regulations and Unfunded Mandates on State, Local, and Tribal Entities* (2010), p. 51, available at: http://www.whitehouse.gov/sites/default/files/omb/legislative/reports/2010 Benefit Cost Report.pdf

[251] Circular A-4 states: "You need to provide an accounting statement with tables reporting benefit and cost estimates for each major final rule for your agency." (P. 44). Circular A-4 includes an example of a format for agency consideration. OMB recommends "that agencies should clearly and prominently present, in the preamble and in the executive summary of the regulatory impact analysis, one or more tables summarizing the assessment of costs and benefits required under Executive Order 12866 Section 6(a)(3)(C)(i)-(iii). The tables should provide a transparent statement of both quantitative and qualitative benefits and costs of the proposed or planned action as well as of reasonable alternatives. The tables should include all relevant information that can be quantified and monetized, along with relevant information that can be described only in qualitative terms. It will often be useful to accompany a simple, clear table of aggregated costs and benefits with a separate table offering disaggregated figures, showing the components of the aggregate figures. To the extent feasible in light of the nature of the issue and the relevant data, all benefits and costs should be quantified and monetized. To communicate any uncertainties, we recommend that the table should offer a range of values, in addition to best estimates, and it should clearly indicate impacts that cannot be quantified or monetized. If nonquantifiable variables are involved, they should be clearly identified. Agencies should attempt, to the extent feasible, not merely to identify such variables but also to signify their importance." See *2010 Report to Congress on the Benefits and Costs of Federal Regulations and Unfunded Mandates on State, Local, and Tribal Entities*, p. 51, available at: http://www.whitehouse.gov/sites/ default/files/omb/legislative/reports/2010 Benefit Cost Report.pdf

[252] See Greenstone (2009) and, in other contexts, Banerjee and Duflo (2011).

[253] Department of Homeland Security, Preliminary Plan for Retrospective Review of Existing Regulations, p. 27, available at http://www.whitehouse.gov/files/documents/2011-regulatory-actionplans/DepartmentofHomeland SecurityPreliminaryRegulatoryReformPlan.pdf.

[254] *Id.*

[255] Department of Labor, Preliminary Plan for Retrospective Analysis of Existing Rules, p., 20, available at http://www.whitehouse.gov/files/documents/2011-regulatory-actionplans/DepartmentofLaborPreliminary RegulatoryReformPlan.pdf.

[256] Department of the Interior, Preliminary Plan for Retrospective Regulatory review, p. 19, available at http://www.whitehouse.gov/files/documents/2011-regulatory-actionplans/DepartmentoftheInteriorPreliminaryRegulatoryReformPlan.pdf

[257] Department of the Treasury, Preliminary Plan for Retrospective Analysis of Existing Rules, p. 19, available at http://www.whitehouse.gov/files/documents/2011-regulatory-actionplans/DepartmentoftheTreasuryPreliminary RegulatoryReformPlan.pdf.

[258] See, e.g., Banerjee and Duflo (2011).

In: Benefits and Costs of Federal Regulations ...
Editors: Travis F. Watson and Leroy Gibson

ISBN: 978-1- 61942-293-3
© 2012 Nova Science Publishers, Inc.

Chapter 2

PEER REVIEW OF DRAFT REPORT ON BENEFITS & COSTS[*]

Joe Aldy

MEMORANDUM FOR CASS SUNSTEIN

SUBJECT: *Review of the Draft 2011 Report to Congress on the Benefits and Costs of Federal Regulations and Unfunded Mandates on State, Local, and Tribal Entities*

The *Draft 2011 Report to Congress on the Benefits and Costs of Federal Regulations and Unfunded Mandates on State, Local, and Tribal Entities* presents in a transparent, concise, and understandable manner the benefits and costs of the U.S. Government's regulatory program. In the context of the recent heated but not always illuminating public discussion of the economic impacts of Federal regulations, this report will serve as a thoughtful resource. The decomposition of benefits and costs of regulations by agencies, and in some cases by major categories of benefits, are instructive. The 10-year look back is valuable to illustrate the longer-term trends in benefits and costs of government regulations. The recommendations for reform will improve the implementation and consideration of economic analysis in the design of government rules. The Office of Management and Budget should be commended for a job well done in synthesizing and summarizing the economic benefits and costs of government regulations. In the following I present a few major comments on the report and then some detailed comments on the text.

---

[*] This is an edited, reformatted and augmented version of a Office of Management and Budget Publication, dated 2011.

MAJOR COMMENTS

The Case for Efficient Government Regulation: An economic assessment of the Federal government's regulatory regime would benefit from an explicit statement of the public policy rationale for government intervention, for example in the executive summary. Well-designed regulations target market failures – such as negative externalities from production and consumption, market power, and asymmetric information. In doing so, the regulatory interventions make society better off, in some cases as measured by GDP (e.g., by mitigating the adverse impacts of asymmetric information on behavior in and outcomes of markets and in mitigating the adverse effects of market power on prices, quantities, and innovation) and in some cases by taking a full account of economic benefits including those that are not measured in market activities (e.g., improving the quality of and extending life through measures that mitigate morbidity and mortality risks). Benefit-cost analysis serves two important roles in this process. First, it can inform the design and consideration of various options so that decision-makers understand the opportunities for both minimizing the costs of achieving a social goal (cost-effectiveness) and maximizing net social benefits (efficiency). Second, such analysis can identify cases in which poorly defined policy risks substituting government failure for market failure and imposing net costs on society. This analysis can inform remedies by the executive branch, or when legislative mandate proscribes efficient regulation, inform proposals for legislative reform to deliver a more effective Federal regulatory program. In sum, it is important to remind the reader at the front of the report that public policy is intended to make society better off and benefit-cost analysis of the rules implementing public policy serve to identify how government actions can increase net economic benefits to the whole of society.

Distributional Impacts of Government Regulations: Implicit in several sections of the report, although not explicitly addressed, are issues of distribution. Benefit-cost analysis provides a transparent basis for evaluating the efficiency of a proposed policy – Does it increase net social benefits? – but it does not provide determinative guidance on whether such a proposed policy is "fair," recognizing that fairness can have a variety of meanings to different constituencies. Nonetheless, the economic analysis of Federal rules can present information on the distribution of benefits and costs without a normative conclusion about any given distribution. Some of the implicit discussions of distribution include: (1) large benefits and costs of air quality regulations (page 15; benefits to the entire population, with particular benefits to those with more respiratory conditions, and costs borne by pollution-intensive activities); small business (pages 33-35; with a curious focus on just the costs of regulations); labor compensation (pages 36-40; primary focus on costs); Greenstone study on employment, capital, and output effects of the Clean Air Act (page 46; are these just the adverse impacts in non-attainment areas, and if so, do attainment areas gain?); and the Kahn study on the distribution of benefits by income and ethnicity (page 48). An alternative way of structuring the presentation would be to frame these issues in terms of the distributional implications of regulatory interventions. It is important to note explicitly that paying particular attention to one category or population affected by a policy (e.g., small businesses, specific industries, income groups, etc.) and providing additional weight to their concerns in making policy decisions increases the risk that the final regulation does not maximize net social benefits. Such trade-offs may be valid when considering the entire suite of motivations for a policy, beyond just the efficiency criterion represented by benefit-cost analysis, but such consideration should be transparent and informed.

Using Benefit-Cost Analysis to Improve Policy Design: The reporting on the benefits and costs of Federal regulations could benefit by a discussion of how benefit-cost analysis has improved policy design. This is implicit in the discussion of the value of retrospective analyses of implemented regulations. Beyond that important task, the report could identify examples in which policy design evolved from the proposed to final rule-making stages that improved cost-effectiveness of implementation and/or increased net social benefits. This could illustrate the value of transparency and public participation as well as the insights that can be drawn from initial economic analyses of proposed rules. In addition, it could be instructive to identify examples of regulatory innovations that have delivered greater social benefits at lower costs. For example, a section of the report could be organized to draw from some of the existing discussion of information disclosure; report on the successes of market-based instruments in Federal regulation; and other lessons of importance.

Cost-Effectiveness Measures of Federal Regulations: I strongly concur with the recommendation for an evaluation of cost-effectiveness across Federal agencies. A significant number of Federal agencies promulgate rules that reduce mortality risk (e.g., DHS, FDA, DOT, EPA, OSHA, CPSC, and others). Estimating the net costs per life saved and the net costs per life-year saved would identify opportunities for improving the effectiveness of the Federal regulatory program. The annual report should present estimates for all rules with a primary or significant mortality risk reduction benefit. The report could also consider other cost-effectiveness metrics relevant to more than one agency, such as dollars per BTU saved for policies that impact energy consumption and dollars per ton of CO_2 avoided for policies that impact greenhouse gas emissions.

Retrospective Analyses: The retrospective analyses called for in EO 13563 are an excellent idea. For especially large and/or complicated rules, it would be valuable for such analyses to address not only the top line benefits and costs, but also the net social benefits of specific components of the rules. Some elements of a large rule may deliver greater social benefits at lower costs than other elements. This information would help inform regulatory review and identify opportunities for which regulations could be modified to increase net social benefits.

As a part of the effort to promote transparency by sharing more data online, the Administration could enable external experts to undertake ex post analyses of the benefits and costs of Federal regulations. For example, a number of regulatory agencies have external boards of technical experts. These boards could be tasked with providing guidance to the regulatory agencies on how they should collect, compile, and post online data that would enable non-governmental experts to estimate the realized benefits and costs of regulations. This information could be organized and presented in a manner to facilitate full benefit-cost analyses where feasible, and where not feasible, then focus on providing sufficient information to generate appropriate measures of cost-effectiveness.

Detailed Comments

Choice of dollars: Why 2001 dollars for all tables and figures? Why not a more recent year's dollars? At the very least, it would be useful for the report to provide a deflator in a footnote so the reader can convert to 2010 dollars.

Footnote 20: The definition of the value of a statistical life should be refined to make it explicit that this is a population-based measure. For example, the footnote could read: "...for example, the average person in a population of 50,000 may value a reduction in mortality risk of 1/50,000 at $150. The value for reducing the risk of 1 statistical (as opposed to known or identified) fatality in this population would be $7.5 million, representing the aggregation of the willingness to pay values held by everyone in the population."

Footnote 33: Given the lumpy timing of investments to comply with regulations, benefit-cost analyses should not simply present a future year's benefits and costs (e.g., in 2020) but the stream of annual benefits and costs.

Additional papers from the academic literature on regulation and firm relocation:

[1] Ederington, J., Levinson, A. and Minier, J. (2005). Footloose and Pollution Free. *Review of Economics and Statistics, 87(1),* 92-99.
[2] Levinson, A. (2010). Offshoring Pollution: Is the United States Increasingly Importing Polluting Goods? *Review of Environmental Economics and Policy, 4(1),* 63-83.
[3] Levinson and Taylor. (2008). Unmasking the Pollution Haven Effect. *International Economic Review, 49(1).*

In: Benefits and Costs of Federal Regulations ...
Editors: Travis F. Watson and Leroy Gibson

ISBN: 978-1-61942-293-3
© 2012 Nova Science Publishers, Inc.

Chapter 3

REVIEW OF DRAFT 2011 REPORT TO CONGRESS ON THE BENEFITS AND COSTS OF FEDERAL REGULATIONS AND UNFUNDED MANDATES ON STATE, LOCAL, AND TRIBAL ENTITIES[*]

Christine Jolls

I have reviewed the draft report and am pleased to offer the following comments:

1) Overall, the draft report is an outstanding document that not only advocates, but itself displays, regulatory sensibility, clarity, and transparency.
2) My main substantive recommendation is the addition of reference to agency *experimentation* to examine the effects of regulation. Studies of such experimentation would usefully complement the retrospective analysis emphasized by the draft report (and, in some cases, would reduce the need for such retrospective analysis).
   a) *Experimentation.*
      The draft report's discussion of Executive Order 13563 refers to the President's directive to "consider flexible approaches to regulatory problems, including warnings and disclosure requirements" (p. 55). The idea that strategies in this category may "reduce burdens and maintain flexibility and freedom of choice for the public" (p. 55) is an extremely important one. (For a recent survey of such flexible legal strategies in place of traditional "mandates and bans" (p. 55), see "Bias and the Law," forthcoming in *American Behavioral Scientist*; copy attached with this review.) However, it is important to appreciate that different types of warnings and disclosures may have very different effects; therefore, agencies can play an immensely valuable role in *experimentally* implementing alternatives (to the extent permitted by law) and then studying their consequences.

---

[*] These remarks were delivered as a review given by Christine Jolls, Yale Law School and NBER, on 2011.

For example, in recent years the SEC experimentally examined the effects of loosening restrictions on short sales of stock by exempting one-third of the stocks in the Russell 3000 from short sale restrictions and then studying outcomes for those stocks compared to the non-exempt stocks. (The SEC experiment is described in detail in a report from the agency's Office of Economic Analysis, available at http://www.sec.gov/news/ studies/2007 /regshopilot020607.pdf.) The exempted stocks were randomly selected by sorting the Russell 3000 first by listing market and then by average daily dollar volume and then selecting every third company. The SEC's experimental study was able to provide illumination of the effects of short sale restrictions on trading volume and liquidity – effects that had previously been hotly disputed among financial economists.

The SEC's short sale rules involve bans on certain trades rather than a warning or a mandated disclosure. Because the number of decision variables (words versus pictures, size of the material, specific words and/or pictures used, etc.) is often much greater with warnings and disclosures than with other forms of regulation, the value of experimentation is typically profound. To illustrate, the FDA is presently considering 36 different proposed cigarette warning labels (http://www.regulations documentDetail;D=FDA-20 1 0-N-0568-000 1). A data-driven approach would allow the use of different labels in different randomly selected localities and would then examine effects of the labels on the purchase and consumption of cigarettes in these localities. Such experimental approaches compare very favorably with studies based on hypothetical surveys and other conventional methodologies.

 b) *Retrospective analysis.*

 The draft report gives considerable emphasis to retrospective analysis of already implemented regulations. While such analysis is undoubtedly extremely valuable, the report should incorporate reference to the possibility that, in some circumstances, altering an existing rule may be inefficient even if a retrospective analysis provides evidence that the rule should not have been adopted in the first place. Once private-sector actors have made long-term investments and adjustments in response to a rule, the disruption and uncertainty associated with a change may simply be too large.

3) The draft report's sustained discussion of empirical studies on the effects of employment, environmental, and other regulation (Part II of the report) would benefit from more discriminating treatment of the empirical studies. Studies published in leading peer-reviewed economics journals (the three leading general-interest journals – the *American Economic Review*, the *Quarterly Journal of Economics*, and the *Journal of Political Economy* – together with leading field-specific journals such as the *Rand Journal of Economics* and the *Journal of Labor Economics*) should receive more attention and weight than other studies, which will at times suffer from weaker methodology, data sources, or empirical analysis.

4) The draft report refers to recent financial regulation by entities not required to monetize regulatory benefits and costs (the Federal Reserve System and the Federal Trade Commission) (p. 30). If appropriate, the report should suggest the desirability

of congressional legislation requiring the same benefit-cost procedures for independent agencies as are now operative in executive agencies.

5) The draft report's statement on p. 36 that "U.S. competition law prohibits collusion among employers but allows collective bargaining by workers" seems misplaced (at least outside the halls of the University of Chicago). In general, it seems somewhat unnatural to suggest a tension between prohibiting companies from price-fixing, on the one hand, and permitting individual workers to engage in collective action through unions, on the other.

6) Likewise, the draft report's statement on p. 40 that "economic regulation ... results in higher prices in the product market" was somewhat surprising. Presumably in many cases the justification for economic regulation of utilities and other natural monopolies is that in the absence of regulation, the regulated entity would charge a highly inflated monopoly price. Ordinarily, then, economists assume that economic regulation will lower product prices below what they would be in the absence of economic regulation – though of course economic regulation may both fail to lower prices to the competitive level and introduce a range of new inefficiencies.

7) Figure 2-1 on p. 51 of the draft report would be more illuminating if it contained a second bar for each administration showing the *number* of major rules enacted during the administration. (The additional bars could be measured against the right-hand vertical axis.)

8) Table 2-5 on pp. 59-60 provides net costs per life saved for a series of rules, many of which entail "morbidity costs." A brief discussion of whether monetizing *morbidity* costs is significantly less controversial or difficult than monetizing *mortality* costs would be helpful in interpreting and motivating Table 2-5.

In: Benefits and Costs of Federal Regulations ...
Editors: Travis F. Watson and Leroy Gibson

ISBN: 978-1- 61942-293-3
© 2012 Nova Science Publishers, Inc.

Chapter 4

PEER REVIEW OF DRAFT REPORT ON THE BENEFITS AND COSTS OF FEDERAL REGULATIONS AND UNFUNDED MANDATES ON STATE, LOCAL, AND TRIBAL ENTITIES [*]

Michael Greenstone

April 18, 2011

Via Email to: Jennifer_H._Nou@omb.eop.go

Jennifer Nou
Office of Regulation and Information Policy
Office of Management and Budget
725 17th Street, NW
Washington, DC 20503

Dear Jennifer:

I am writing in response to your request for a review of the Draft 2011 Report to Congress on the Benefits and Costs of Federal Regulations and Unfunded Mandates on State, Local, and Tribal Entities. Thank you for this opportunity to participate in this important process.

My overall assessment is that this is an excellent report. It is a model of clarity and it is evident that OIRA is unafraid to tackle the important issues that feed into designing regulations that provide maximum benefits to American citizens at a minimum cost. It also draws upon the latest academic research in a way that is very productive for formulating

---

[*] These remarks were delivered as review given by Michael Greenstone, 3M Professor of Economics, Massachusetts Institute of Technology, on April 18, 2011.

policy, not just for making debating points. All of this is evident in many of the innovative regulatory policies that the Obama Administration has introduced.

Stepping back, it is clear that President Obama and his appointee, Administrator Sunstein, have charted a new and revolutionary course for regulatory policy. Its hallmarks are transparency, regulations that are designed to work based on how people behave in the real world, identifying low cost regulatory solutions such as better provision of information, a devotion to letting data and evidence guide regulatory decisions, and working to ensure that risks are regulated identically across the government. These are a remarkable set of accomplishments in a little more than two years (or substantially less time if one accounts for Sunstein's lengthy confirmation process).

In the remainder of this document, I will outline some suggestions on areas where further reforms/improvements in regulatory policy would be beneficial and may be feasible in the years ahead.

1. MAKING RETROSPECTIVE ANALYSES EFFECTIVE

The Administration's efforts to undertake retrospective analysis is an important step forward in policy, and one that has great promise to improve the functioning of the economy and Americans' lives. The key is that this nearly unassailable goal be implemented in a way that produces credible results. In this section, I have listed some ideas on how to increase the effectiveness of this initiative at improving the regulatory system.

a. Publication of Ex Ante and Ex Post Costs and Benefits of Significant Regulations

The draft report provides an impressive summary of the ex ante estimates of the benefits and costs of regulations implemented over the last decade. It would be natural to add a column to these tables that highlights the ex post benefits and costs based on retrospective analyses. This table could help to focus efforts for retrospective analyses on the most important rules and the ones that have not undergone retrospective evaluation in a long time.

b. Transparent and Credible Retrospective Evaluations

It is now common for medical researchers to announce that they are undertaking an evaluation of a new drug. Indeed, many medical journals refuse to consider articles for publication when the trial has not been registered in advance in order to build trust in the credibility of the results.

The retrospective evaluation of regulations could undertake a similar exercise in increasing the transparency and credibility of these evaluations. This could involve several steps.

i. Agencies could announce that they are undertaking a retrospective evaluation in advance of conducting the review.
ii. The announcement could specify the date that the evaluation results will be published.
iii. The announcement could specify the measures of costs and benefits that will be used. It would be natural to use the measures from the original RIA as the default but in some instances new measures of costs or benefits may have been recognized in the interim.
iv. For reasons of credibility and agency workloads, it would be natural to fund retrospective analyses by contractors or academics and have them work at arm's length.
v. All data that underlie a retrospective evaluation could be posted on the regulating agency's website so that it could be analyzed by others.

c. Designing New Regulations to Facilitate Credible Evaluations

For new regulations, it is sensible to design their implementation to facilitate a credible evaluation. The following are some suggestions on how to allow for these evaluations in cases where it is feasible or appropriate.

i. One possibility (especially in cases where there is a great deal of uncertainty around the benefits and costs) is to implement the regulation on a trial basis using a randomized control trial. In the ideal, this could be done by randomly assigning some firms/locations/consumers to a new regulation and leaving others unaffected. This may sound far-fetched, but I am currently conducting an evaluation of several different forms of regulating polluters in India using a randomized control trial approach.
The U.S. government has recently implemented a series of new and promising rules to increase information in the marketplace. In these situations, it is, for example, difficult to know which form of an information intervention (e.g., stickers for tires or cars) would be most useful. This seems like an especially appealing setting for conducting a randomized control trial to find out which form of information dissemination has the greatest benefit. Indeed, this type of horse race between competing methods is sensible from a good government perspective.
ii. If randomized control trial experiments are infeasible, regulations could be designed to allow for quasi-experimental evaluations. This could be done by giving states waivers to implement alternative forms of the regulations or by using discrete rules to determine the regulation's coverage (e.g., it might only apply to firms with more than a certain number of employees).

d. Regulatory Review Board

Another reform that could increase the credibility of the regulatory review process is to create a Regulatory Review Board. It would have the power to request evaluations of existing regulations, judge the quality of evidence on a regulation, and possibly to fund from its own resources an evaluation. The Board would focus on the most significant regulations. The potential members of the board could include the OIRA Administrator and representatives from the Chief of Staff's Office, the agencies, CEA, etc. It would lend further credibility to the board if it also included experts from academia and industry.

2. Lost Life Expectancy, Instead of Increased Mortality Rates

The report notes that the majority of benefits and costs come from the EPA's regulation of air pollution, especially fine particulate matter. Footnote 19 lays out many of the scientific uncertainties associated with measuring the mortality impacts of airborne particulate matter. However, it misses what I consider to be an issue of crucial significance that is really the next frontier in the literature on the air pollution-health relationship. Specifically, the associated literature has largely satisfied itself with demonstrating elevated mortality rates over short periods of time (occasionally, days or weeks). In the worst case, these literatures have identified cases where people have died a few days or weeks earlier than they would have in the absence of air pollution.

A complete analysis of the benefits of air pollution regulations requires an estimate of the loss of life expectancy associated with premature deaths. The resulting information should be reported as a regular matter in estimating the benefits of reductions of air pollution. It would be natural to report the cost per life year saved in tables that summarize a regulation's costs and benefits. Although this type of analysis is complicated, there is little doubt that society would prefer a regulation that extended the lives of 1,000 people by 20 years each to a regulation that extended 1,000 lives by 1 week each.

3. Private Benefits versus Social Benefits and Welfare Losses

The traditional and best supported case for regulation of markets is because there is a social benefit from the regulation that cannot readily be achieved by private markets. A classic case comes from firms' failing to internalize the health damages caused by the pollution they emit. The case for regulation in these settings is very strong.

However, the EPA, DOT, and DOE have recently initiated a series of rules all of which appear to depart from the standard case in justifying energy efficiency standards for vehicles and appliances. In particular, they assume that consumers are unaware of the fuel or energy efficiency of various products. With this assumption, regulations that set energy efficiency standards count the fuel savings as benefits and indeed RIA's are increasingly relying on this type of calculation. The potential problem is that in the standard case the fuel savings are private benefits in that they entirely accrue to the person making the choice of car or appliance and thus there is no social or external benefit. Thus, regulations that require products to have increased levels of energy efficiency may cause consumers to purchase products that they have knowingly rejected. In this case, it is inappropriate to count fuel or energy savings as a benefit.

This departure from the standard case is appropriate when consumers have a demonstrated bias or inability to make judgments about energy efficiency. However, the academic literature on this topic is in its nascent stages and in my judgment has failed to provide consistent evidence that consumers are making these errors. My suggestion is that agencies and OIRA undertake a systematic study and resulting judgment about when consumer biases are likely to be a problem that requires regulation.

A closely related idea is that these regulations reduce consumer welfare by causing individuals to purchase products that they would otherwise reject. For example, the CAFE standards might cause individuals to choose smaller cars with excellent fuel economy although absent CAFE they would prefer larger ones with mediocre fuel economy (in the presence of the smaller cars in the marketplace). The analysis of potential regulations would be stronger if this welfare loss were explicitly accounted for. To be clear, many regulations may still have benefits that exceed costs, even when accounting for this issue, but the benefits would come from the reductions in pollution and other external benefits.

4. CREDIBILITY CHECK LIST

Evidence on costs and benefits comes from many sources: models, observational studies, quasi- experiments, and randomized control trials. The estimated costs and benefits from these approaches are not of equal validity. The most reliable evidence comes from randomized control trials, with quasi-experiments probably being the next most reliable, and models and observational studies providing the least reliable.

My recommendation is that OIRA develop a checklist to determine the credibility of the evidence in RIAs. It is not possible or wise to wait for gold standard evidence before regulating, but it would be beneficial to make clear the quality of the evidence that underlies the case for the regulation. These announcements could dovetail nicely with the new plan to promote retrospective analyses because it would help to identify the settings where new research or evidence would be most valuable.

5. OTHER COMMENTS

The report rightly notes that a large share of regulatory costs and benefits comes from the regulation of airborne particulate matter. The report also notes the several scientific steps to causally relate the regulation of airborne particulate matter to improvements in health. It would be powerful if the report made it clear that funding research to cement the scientific basis for this relationship has tremendous consequences for U.S. regulatory policy. This is especially so with the increasing raft of rules that regulate other air pollutants with the goal of reducing particulates as a co-pollutant.

This point is very "in the weeds" but a great deal of EPA analysis of the benefits of air pollution reductions comes from models of air pollution rather than actual pollution monitoring data. In some recent research, I am finding that the predictions of these models do not match real world data all of the time. For example, I have found that reductions in NOx emissions do not lead to reductions in ambient particulates concentrations. I am not aware of the extent of this problem, but I think it should be taken as a cautionary note about using models rather than real world pollution concentration data when the latter is available.

I will end where I began. U.S. regulatory policy is central to the quality of Americans' lives. It affects the air we breathe, the water we drink, the products we can buy, the terms of the loans we take, and many other areas of our lives. This is an excellent report that clearly details the Administration's revolutionary accomplishments in regulatory policy over the last two years. It is also forward-looking and identifies some important ways to continue to reform and improve U.S. regulatory policy. In my comments, I have tried to identify some other areas that may be worth pursuing in a revised version of the report and in the coming years.

The bottom line though is that President Obama and Administrator Sunstein are fundamentally changing U.S. regulatory policy in ways that are improving the lives of Americans. These accomplishments and the plans for the future deserve the highest praise.

Sincerely,

Michael Greenstone
cc: Cass Sunstein via email: cass_sunstein@omb.eop.gov

In: Benefits and Costs of Federal Regulations ...
Editors: Travis F. Watson and Leroy Gibson

ISBN: 978-1- 61942-293-3
© 2012 Nova Science Publishers, Inc.

Chapter 5

PUBLIC COMMENT ON DRAFT REPORT ON THE BENEFITS AND COSTS OF FEDERAL REGULATIONS AND UNFUNDED MANDATES ON STATE, LOCAL, AND TRIBAL ENTITIES [*]

Richard A. Williams

May 2, 2011

Mr. Cass Sunstein
Administrator, Office of Information and Regulatory Affairs
Office of Management and Budget
725 17th Street, NW
Washington, DC 20503

Dear Mr. Sunstein:

The Regulatory Studies Program of the Mercatus Center at George Mason University is dedicated to advancing knowledge of the impact of regulation on society. As part of its mission, the Regulatory Studies Program conducts careful and independent analyses employing contemporary economic scholarship to assess rulemaking proposals and reports from the perspective of the public interest.

We appreciate the invitation to comment on the Draft 2011 Report to Congress on the Benefits and Costs of Federal Regulations and Unfunded Mandates on State, Local and Tribal Entities,and hope that our comments will be useful to the Office of Management and Budget.

Sincerely,
Richard A. Williams, Ph.D.
Director for Policy Studies

---

[*] These remarks were delivered as a draft report given by Richard Williams, Director for Policy Studies, George Mason University, on May 2, 2011.

The Regulatory Studies Program (RSP) of the Mercatus Center at George Mason University is dedicated to advancing knowledge of the impact of regulation on society. As part of its mission, RSP conducts careful and independent analyses employing contemporary economic scholarship to assess rulemaking proposals from the perspective of the public interest. Thus, this comment on the Draft 2011 Report to Congress on the Benefits and Costs of Federal Regulations and Unfunded Mandates on State, Local, and Tribal Entities (The Report) does not represent the views of any particular affected party or special interest group, but is designed to assist the Office of Information and Regulatory Affairs (OIRA) in the Office of Management and Budget (OMB) as it seeks advice on this draft report.

OIRA is to be congratulated on an excellent report, although we have some minor disagreements with the findings. We agree with all of OIRA's recommendations found on page 5 of the Report[1]. The following are some additional observations/recommendations:

I. INDEPENDENT AGENCIES

OMB should be commended for its section on the independent agencies. The Report cites the Government Accountability Office (GAO) report that notes that, of the 17 rules performed by independent agencies, not one assessed benefits and costs of their rules.[2] OMB states, "The absence of such information is a continued obstacle to transparency, and it might also have adverse effects on public policy."[3] We agree strongly with this conclusion. The lack of analysis will become particularly acute as more rules implementing the Dodd- Frank Wall Street Reform and Consumer Protection Act, since independent agencies have substantial new rulemaking responsibilities under this act. This is particularly troublesome with respect to the new Consumer Financial Protection Bureau, which is able to write rules "autonomously" without oversight from, apparently, any executive branch agency or even the Federal Reserve, where it is housed.

II. RETROSPECTIVE REVIEW

OMB should also be commended on its section soliciting recommendations on retrospective analysis. The suggestion that agencies actually "undertake" retrospective analysis is a good one. That would be improvement on just asking the public which rules need to be taken off of the books. Most the interest in any existing rules will be by those who must directly comply with the rules and their incentives are usually to keep the rules. Many of the rules, or at least a portion of them, were put into place at the behest of the regulated industry in the first place,to raise the cost of rival firms.[4] Additionally, firms may worry that, if a rule is removed, it might be replaced by one that is more stringent. The group that will not comment on existing rules, but who might be viewed as the most severely impacted, are new entrants into industries in the future. These entities don't comment because they don't exist yet. In a sense, there is no *guardian ad litem* to represent their interests.

An analysis of existing rules could demonstrate the effects on both incumbent firms and consumers, as well as the potential to affect new entrants. However, just as there is very little incentive for incumbent firms to remove rules, the same might also be said with respect to the agencies that often labored for years to produce them. This probably means that there needs to be an independent organization performing such analysis. Agencies can do their part by explaining in their Regulatory Impact Analyses (RIAs) which agency strategic goals under the Government Performance and Results Act (GPRA) the regulation is intended to advance. Agencies can also establish goals and measures for individual regulations and identify data that could be used to evaluate the regulation's effects in the future.[5]

III. IMPROVEMENTS IN ANALYSIS AND CLAIMED NET BENEFITS

The report claims that "OMB and the regulatory agencies have taken a number of steps to improve the rigor and transparency of analysis supporting public policy decisions."[6] We agree that this is an excellent use of OIRA resources and believe that they should continue to do so. However, OMB claims that they have achieved superior performance for their regulations as compared to the two previous administrations. In Figure 2-1: "Annual Net Benefits of Major Rules through the Second Fiscal Year of an Administration," the claim is made that the current administration has generated much higher net benefits in its second year than the previous two administrations. The current administration claims to have about $35.5 billion in net benefits as opposed to $2.3 in the Bush Administration and $10.6 in the Clinton Administration.[7] However, this claim should be viewed skeptically for several reasons. First, as the Mercatus Regulatory Report Card shows, the regulatory analyses that this report draws from are simply not good enough overall to make any claim about the relative net benefits of these rules. The chart below adds the scores from the Report Card for those regulatory analyses that have been evaluated[8]:

Agency	RIN	Title	Budget Effects	Regulatory Report Card Score
USDA	0560-AH90	Supplemental Revenue Assistance Payments Program (SURE)	0.1	
USDA	0560-AI07	Dairy Economic Loss Assistance Payment Program	0.2	
USDA	0578-AA43	Conservation Stewardship Program	2.7-3.2	
USDA	0584-AD30	SNAP: Eligibility and Certification Provisions of the Farm Security and Rural Investment Act of 2002	2.2	
DOC	0660-ZA28	Broadband Technology Opportunities Program	2.1	
DOD	0720-AB17	TRICARE: Relationship Between the TRICARE Program and Employer-Sponsored Group Health Coverage	>(0.1)	
DOD	0790-AI59	Retroactive Stop Loss Special Pay Compensation	0.4	
HHS	0938-AP40	Revisions to Payment Policies Under the Physician Fee Schedule for CY 2010 (CMS-1413-FC)	(11.0)	23/60

(Continued)

Agency	RIN	Title	Budget Effects	Regulatory Report Card Score
HHS	0938-AP41	Changes to the Hospital Outpatient Prospective Payment System and Ambulatory Sugical Center Payment System for CY 2010 (CMS-1414-F)	0.4	24/60
HHS	0938-AP55	Home Health Prospective Payment System and Rate Update for CY 2010 (CMS-1560-F)	(0.1)	25/60
HHS	0938-AP57	End Stage Renal Disease Bundled Payment System (CMS-1418-F)	(0.2)	32/60
HHS	0938-AP72	State Flexibility for Medicaid Benefit Packages (CMS-2232-F4) Revisions to the Medicare Advantage and Medicare	(0.7)	
HHS	0938-AP77	Prescription Drug Benefit Programs for Contract Year 2011 (CMS-4085-F)	(0.3)	18/60
HHS	0938-AP78	Electronic Health Record (EHR) Incentive Program (CMS-0033-F) Medicare Program; Changes to the Hospital Inpatient Prospective Payment Systems for Acute Care Hospitals and the Long Term Care	1.0-2.5	25/60
HHS	0938-AP80	Hospital Prospective Payment System and Fiscal Year 2011 Rates	(0.2)	
HHS	0991-AB64	Early Retiree Reinsurance Program	1.0	
HHS	0991-AB71	Pre-Existing Condition Insurance Plan Program	1.0	
STATE	1400-AC58	Schedule of Fees for Consular Services, Department of State and Overseas Embassies and Consulates	0.3-0.4	
DHS	1615-AB80	U.S. Citizenship and Immigration Services Fee Schedule	0.2	
DHS	1651-AA83	Electronic System for Travel Authorization (ESTA): Fee for Use of the System	0.1-0.2	
DHS	1660-AA44	Special Community Disaster Loans Programs	0-1.0	20/60
ED	1810-AB04	State Fiscal Stabilization Fund Program--Notice of Proposed Requirements, Definitions, and Approval Criteria	9.5	23/60
ED	1810-AB06	School Improvement Grants--Notice of Proposed Requirements Under the American Recovery and Reinvestment Act of 2009; Title I of the Elementary and Secondary Education Act of 1965	2.9	31/60

Agency	RIN	Title	Budget Effects	Regulatory Report Card Score
ED	1810-AB07	Race to the Top Fund--Notice of Proposed Priorities, Requirements, Definitions, and Selection Criteria	3.2	23/60
ED	1810-AB08	Teacher Incentive Fund--Priorities, Requirements, Definitions, and Selection Criteria	0.4	
ED	1840-AC96	Student Assistance General Provisions; TEACH Grant, Federal Pell Grant, and Academic Competitiveness Grant, and National Science and Mathematics Access To Retain Talent Grant Programs	0.2	
ED	1840-AC99	General and Non-Loan Programmatic Issues	0.2	17/60
ED	1840-AD01	Federal TRIO Programs, Gaining Early Awareness and Readiness for Undergraduate Program, and High School Equivalency and College Assistance Migrant Programs	1.0	
ED	1855-AA06	Investing in Innovation--Priorities, Requirements, Definitions, and Selection Criteria	0.5	19/60
DOE	1901-AB27	Loan Guarantees for Projects That Employ Innovative Technologies	3.5-4.0	5/60
DOE	1904-AB97	Weatherization Assistance Program for Low-Income Persons - Multi-Unit Buildings	4.0	10/60
VA	2900-AN54	Diseases Associated With Exposure to Certain Herbicide Agents (Hairy Cell Leukemia and Other Chronic B Cell Leukemias, Parkinson's Disease, and Ischemic Heart Disease)	4.1-5.4	

For those that actually did analysis that were scored, the average score was 21 out of 60, which certainly would not be a passing grade in anyone's class and hardly sufficient to draw accurate comparisons with regulations from previous administrations.

OIRA could, to make their table more descriptive, show which rules were initiated in an earlier administration.

An additional problem is that there is at least one major benefit claimed that may not, in fact, be a true net benefit. The rule that claims the highest estimated benefits is the Passenger Car and Light Truck Corporate Average Fuel Economy Standards MYs 2012 to 2016.[9] But the benefits in this rule were largely the result of the federal government substituting its preferences for discounting for the actual preferences of consumers. The claim is that consumers will save "more than $3,000 due to fuel savings" while only paying out approximately $1100. In the NHTSA analysis, at a 3% discount rate the present value of the fuel savings is $158 billion and the present value of the CO_2 reduction is $16.4 billion. The fuel savings appears to represent over 90% of the benefits. But consumers choose cars for many different reasons, and fuel economy is only one reason. Any regulation that begins with the assumption that consumer purchases are irrational (and that the agency is in a better position to determine what is rational) should be suspect. In particular, if 90% of the benefits are from correcting this "irrationality," it may very well be that there are net costs from reduced consumer surplus, not net benefits.[10] At a minimum, EPA should note that any benefits accruing from cars that consumers have not chosen based on their demonstrated preferences do not result from a market failure. EPA's choice of a discount rate of 3% is apparently much lower than consumers choose when investing in an automobile.

IV. HAPPINESS RESEARCH

While the push towards using behavioral economics to fashion more effective and less onerous regulations are to be applauded, OMB should approach research on "happiness" with a great deal of caution, particularly with respect to federal regulation. For example, there may be considerable variance between owner/operators of small businesses and owners/managers of large businesses as to how "happy" they are with regulations. Some results that should be considered include:

1) Republicans are "happier" than Democrats. PEW research shows that 88% of Republicans are "pretty happy" or "very happy" as opposed to only 77% of Democrats.[11] Only 9% of Republicans are "not too happy" whereas 20% of Democrats are not too happy. The difference appears to persist over time.
2) People that do not have children appear to be "happier."[12]
3) Since 1972, women's happiness has dropped, despite labor force participation rates rising to record levels.[13]
4) Religious people appear to be "happier."[14]
5) Divorced people are less "happy."[15]

It would be interesting to see precisely what federal policy prescriptions would follow from the above results. In fact, "Freedom" appears to account for the most happiness around the world, as reported in "Development, Freedom and Rising Happiness,"[16] although this seems to have escaped OMB's literature review.

Two articles were cited by the OMB report on the implications for regulatory policy and uses of cost-benefit analysis (footnote 81, missing from draft report by supplied by OIRA).[17] The one that seems closest to suggestions for incorporation of happiness metrics was "Happiness Metrics in Federal Rulemaking" by Anthony Vitarelli.[18] Vitarelli suggests that agency's supplement traditional benefit-cost analysis with a "happiness inquiry." He produces some interesting conclusions such as, "Consumers... are resilient and adapt quickly to (the) negative income effect."[19] If so, he concludes that agencies could give on-going costs less weight. However, when examining the implications for discount rates, he states that happiness research should "counsel in favor of a far higher discount rate" because of "individuals' propensity to adapt to changed circumstances. However, unlike the unquestioning acceptance of de-weighting the effects of costs on consumers, here he suggests that to use the results on discount rates would be "unsettling-and even offensive" if these results were accepted.[20]

Despite these issues, he suggests that agencies may soon find their regulations will be "arbitrary and capricious" if they are found missing the additional information supplied by happiness research. To the best of our knowledge, there is not a single statute that governs any of the federal agencies that mandates that they ensure that consumers are made any "happier" because of their regulations.

Finally, there is a literature that casts doubt on the entire idea that some measure of "happiness" is an appropriate goal for policy.[21] None of this literature appears to be mentioned in the OMB report.

As Professor Tyler Cowen of George Mason University has pointed out, because of the massive ambiguity of happiness as an endpoint, growth and employment are much better indicators of human well being; and growth is a particularly better metric for comparing policies.[22] In fact, benefit-cost analysis corrects GDP to include things that people find valuable but do not show up as being counted in GDP, particularly when these items can be measured using market-based willingness-to-pay results.

SUMMARY

OMB has produced a thorough and useful report based on the instructions in the Regulatory-Right-to Know-Act. Requiring agencies to produce both more (particularly in the case of independent agencies) and better quality analysis is the right direction for OIRA. However, OIRA should be cautious about over claiming success, particularly based on our analysis of the quality of regulatory impact analyses to date. Of course, OIRA must rely on the agencies for this analysis. The focus on retrospective review, in particular, how best to accomplish retrospective review, is a welcome one. Finally, we urge caution when embracing behavioral economics in analyzing the benefits of market interventions. In particular, we note that the happiness research may not ever develop into useful metrics and, given its current state, is not ready for prime time use in RIA's.

Richard A. Williams, PhD.
Director for Policy Studies

End Notes

[1] See this publication for a review of regulations impact on jobs. Williams, Richard A. "The Impact of Regulation on Investment and the U.S. Economy." http://mercatus.org/publication/impact-regulation-investment
[2] Draft 2011 "Report to Congress on the Benefits and Costs of Federal Regulations and Unfunded Mandates on State, Local and Tribal Entities," p. 4.
[3] *IBID*, p. 30.
[4] Salop, SC, Raising Rivals' Costs, The American Economic Review, 73(2) May, 1983.
[5] See the testimony by Jerry Ellig to the House Judiciary, March 29, 2011 on this subject at http://mercatus. org/sites/default/files/publication/Ellig%20Written%20Testimony%20House%20Judiciary%20March%2029%20201 1 .pdf . Very few agencies do this now.
[6] IBID. The Report, p. 65.
[7] IBID., The Report, p. 51.
[8] Not all rules have been scored (highlighted rules). If no score appears it is because the rule was proposed prior to 2008 and we only began scoring in 2008, the rule was a budget rule in 2010 and we only scored budget rules

in 2008 and 2009 or the rule was an interim final rule, not a proposal. Two rules did not show up on reginfo.gov, Broadband Technology Opportunities Program (0660-ZA28) and Early Retiree Reinsurance Program (0991-AB64).

[9] http://www.nhtsa.gov/staticfiles/rulemaking/pdf/cafe/CAFE_2012-2016_FRIA_04012010.pdf

[10] In its Regulatory Impact Analysis of the proposed regulation, EPA notes this "conundrum," and the Mercatus Regulatory Report Card gave this regulation a high score on identifying the systemic problem in part because the agencies were forthright about this puzzle.

[11] http://pewresearch.org/pubs/1005/republicans-happier

[12] Simon, Robin, "The Joys of Parenthood, Reconsidered" Contexts, 7(2) April 2008, pp. 40-46.

[13] Stevenson, Betsey and Justin Wolfers," The Paradox of Declining Female Happiness," American Economic Journal: Economic Policy 1(2), 2009.

[14] See, for example, Robbins, Mandy and Leslie J. Francis, "Are religious people happier? A study among undergraduates in Research in religious education by Francis, Leslie, et. al. Smyth Y Helwys Publishing, Georgeia, U.S. 1996.

[15] Lucas, Richard e. al., "Time Does not Heal All Wounds: A Longitudinal Study of Reaction and Adaptation to Divorce 16 Psychol., Science, 945, 947 (2005).

[16] Inglehart, Ronald, et. al. "Development, Freedom, and Rising Happinesss: A Global Perspective (1981-2007)

[17] The missing citations were: Vitarelli (2010); and Adler and Posner (2008).

[18] Vitarelli, Anthony, "Happiness Metrics in Federal Rulemaking," Yale Journal on Regulation, 27(1), 2010.

[19] *IBID*, p. 137

[20] *IBID*, P. 141.

[21] A summation of this literature can be found in Wilkinson, Will, "In Pursuit of Happiness Research: Is it Reliable? What Does it Imply for Policy?" Policy Analysis, 590, April 11, 2007

[22] Cowen, Tyler, "How to Think About Policy," in The Growth Imperative: A New Approach to the Theory of Economic Policy.

In: Benefits and Costs of Federal Regulations ...
Editors: Travis F. Watson and Leroy Gibson

ISBN: 978-1- 61942-293-3
© 2012 Nova Science Publishers, Inc.

Chapter 6

DRAFT 2011 REPORT TO CONGRESS ON THE BENEFITS AND COSTS OF FEDERAL REGULATIONS[*]

Daniel V. Yager

The Honorable Hilda Solis
Secretary of Labor
U.S. Department of Labor
200 Constitution Ave., NW
Washington, DC 20210

Re: Draft 2011 Report to Congress on the Benefits and Costs of Federal Regulations, 76 Fed. Reg. 18260 (April 1, 2011)

Dear Madame Secretary:

We are writing in response to the notice and request for comments issued by the Office of Management and Budget (OMB) regarding its Draft 2011 Report to Congress on the Benefits and Costs of Federal Regulations.[1] Last year, in reply to OMB's request in its 2010 Draft Report for suggestions about regulatory changes that might increase employment, innovation, and competitiveness Draft Report for 2010, HR Policy Association submitted a proposal for reform of regulations and regulatory processes related to the Fair Labor Standards Act (FLSA).[2] The Association's comments were endorsed by 11 leading U.S. employers. The OMB, in its 2010 Final Report, vowed to "consider the recommended reforms."[3] As a courtesy, on September 23, 2010, the Association forwarded its OMB comments regarding the FLSA to you for your department's review.

To date, however, neither the OMB nor the Department of Labor has addressed the concerns raised in the Association's 2010 comment letter. Yet, the problems that plague the

---

[*] These remarks were delivered as a draft report by Daniel Yager, Chief Policy Officer & General Counsel, on May 2, 2011.

outdated wage and hour law have continued and increased in magnitude and consequence. Accordingly, HR Policy Association resubmits its comments focusing on FLSA regulations and regulatory processes for your consideration. However, as directed in the OMB's 2011 Draft Report these comments are being directly submitted to the Department of Labor who has jurisdiction over the FLSA.[4] We have copied OMB on this comment letter.

HR Policy Association represents the chief human resource officers of more than 325 large employers doing business in the United States and globally. The Association's member companies employ more than ten million Americans, nearly nine percent of the private sector workforce in the United States. In responding to the request for "suggestions about regulatory changes that might serve to promote economic growth, with particular reference to increasing employment, innovation, and competitiveness", we would like to accomplish two goals. First, we articulate a holistic approach towards employment regulation that could help achieve the administration's goals of economic recovery and growth.

Second, and more specifically, we wish to highlight a particular area of needed reform— the Fair Labor Standards Act— a statute which was written for a different era whose regulations have failed to keep pace with changes in the workplace. The Fair Labor Standards Act, or FLSA, sets the federal regulatory floor for minimum wage and overtime matters. Further, it defines which employees are subject to overtime requirements and which are not. The law was first written in 1938, and the regulations promulgated under it reflect a mid-Twentieth Century industrial workplace, not today's 21st Century Digital Age work environment knit together by technology. Because of its myriad anomalies, the FLSA impedes employers in achieving progress toward the kinds of flexible workplace policies the administration is seeking to promote.[5] These restrictions apply primarily to the 92.6 million wage and salary employees who are not exempt from the Act.[6] Moreover, the enforcement trend being promoted by the Labor Department is towards toughening rules that no longer fit today's workplace instead of seeking to make them more relevant to contemporary needs.

THE ECONOMIC RECOVERY AND FACTORS ASSOCIATED WITH JOB CREATION

Given the current economic situation, the OMB report comes at a critical point for employment policy because the ability of employers to compete on a global scale is unequivocally tied to the workplace and the laws and regulations that shape it. Although we are encouraged by indications that the Great Recession may be over, the number of payroll jobs is still 7.2 million below the level that preceded the downturn and there are more than four unemployed Americans for every job opening.[7] Attempts to jump-start the recovery have involved massive federal expenditures coupled with sweeping policy changes touching virtually all areas of the economy. However, we are deeply concerned that existing employment policy—and the direction it appears to be heading—is undermining these expenditures because of its impact on U.S. competitiveness, innovation, and employment growth.

The comprehensive structure of U.S. workplace laws, regulations, and taxes plays a role in virtually every decision by an employer with respect to hiring, promotions, terminations, scheduling, sharing of data, use and design of facilities, and changes in operations. All of these laws and policies have a cost, and with each additional mandate or tax, another cost is layered onto employment decisions.

At the same time, the ability of employers to add new jobs to the economy depends to a large extent on the costs associated with those jobs. This is not just a question of the dollar amounts involved in wages and benefits. It also includes numerous other factors that influence the decision by an employer as to whether it is economically feasible to even continue an existing position, let alone adding new ones. When it comes to workplace regulation, these factors include, among other things:

- the administrative costs associated with compliance with a law or regulation, including the tracking and recordkeeping associated with the data needed to demonstrate compliance;
- the time spent by human resource officers, supervisors, managers, and company leadership in planning and ensuring compliance with each workplace rule;
- the legal costs associated with establishing protocols to ensure compliance while maintaining continuous internal auditing to make certain that these protocols are being followed;
- the potential legal costs for addressing complaints and, ultimately, litigation or defending against enforcement actions brought by the government or private parties where allegations of noncompliance are involved (including the costs of settlement where the expense of defending such actions may exceed the potential liability); and
- the inability to achieve savings or competitive advantages as a result of restrictions that preclude the development of more efficient and productive workplace policies and procedures, even where they may be to the mutual benefit of both the employer and the employees.

As the administration continues to strive for a full economic recovery, it is essential that it consider the interplay between the goals of adding and restoring jobs and the costs of employment regulation associated with each job.

THE CURRENT REGULATORY CLIMATE

Employers are deeply concerned about the relationship between government and business and the extent to which it becomes highly adversarial in the employment policy context. The most significant driver of the American economy for the past two centuries has been the ability of the private sector to create economic opportunities and jobs. Yet, we see a disturbing trend in the recent regulatory climate that instead seems to view employers as a malevolent force that must constantly be placed under severe restraints. There appears to be a general belief among many policymakers that, absent a strong governmental enforcement scheme, employers will not treat employees fairly and will take advantage of them. There is no question that there have been many instances over the years of certain companies taking actions that harmed employees, and it can be said that to some extent, business has brought this trend on itself. However, the political system in the United States is such that public policy results in the sins of the bad actors being punished by foisting harsh regulatory schemes on all employers regardless of their past behavior.

Association members believe that instead of continuing the adversarial relationship between government and business, particularly at a time of high unemployment, the government should try to work with employers to help create both jobs and the conditions for their placement in the United States. This can be manifested in numerous policy areas, including education, training, tax, and trade policy. Yet, when it comes to employment regulation, this is not the message they receive from the repeated statements and threats by government officials that employers should expect far stiffer enforcement of existing employment laws coupled with even tougher measures and mandates. What is needed instead are statements pledging a partnership with business to create new markets and long term employment opportunities.

A REEXAMINATION OF EMPLOYMENT POLICY

With this in mind, we seek a broad re-examination of the impact of the nation's regulatory structure covering the workplace and the employment relationship. We need to ask whether the nation has reached a tipping point where the nation's labor, employment, and benefit laws have become so complex, burdensome, and difficult to administer that they have become both counterproductive and job killers. In addressing this issue, we must recognize that many of these laws, including the Fair Labor Standards Act discussed herein, were formulated in a period when the workplace was significantly different than today, and there was less concern about goods and services being performed outside our borders under different, and often more flexible, regulatory schemes.

We wish to emphasize that we are not suggesting a race to the bottom that abandons fundamental employment protections. Indeed, the vast majority of laws regulating the workplace address legitimate concerns and they rest upon a set of core principles that nearly all people believe should be part of the employer-employee relationship. For example, there is a broad consensus that:

- Employees should be treated with respect by employers.
- Employees should not be taken advantage of by employers.
- Employees should not be discriminated against in hiring, compensation, advancement, and termination using inappropriate factors or criteria.
- Employees should not have to fear or suffer from bodily harm in their workplace that is reasonably preventable.
- Employees should be able to form a union and engage in collective bargaining if they choose to do so in an atmosphere free of coercion by either the employer or union organizers.

Although there will always be a small minority of employers that will try to take advantage of their employees just as there will always be a small minority of employees who will try to take advantage of their employer, it is important to recognize that the vast majority of employers understand that running a workplace that lacks respect for employees, fair compensation, essential health and safety protections, and non-discriminatory treatment ultimately becomes a self-defeating practice that results in a *loss* of competitive edge.

The frustration employers have with the existing regulatory regime is that it often takes overly prescriptive approaches that, if not adhered to in a very careful manner, can result in "gotcha" penalties for employers who had no intent to either violate the law or take advantage of their employees. Indeed, "one size fits all" prescriptions can inhibit the employer's ability to accommodate both its employees' needs as well as its own in a mutually satisfactory manner. Thus, as is often the case under the FLSA, companies and their employees often find themselves having to force the workplace into a construct designed solely to comply with the law. Several examples of this are provided below.

The problems employers confront in complying with workplace regulations are further exacerbated by the potential for costly litigation. The United States is one of the few nations that provides for enforcement of many of its employment laws through private actions before juries, frequently resulting in significant monetary damages. For many employers, even where their practices are in compliance with the law and regulations, it is far more cost effective and predictable to simply settle claims of noncompliance with the government agency or private attorney, rather than spend years in litigation where even a victory will not secure reimbursement for huge legal expenses.

Even employers who are in compliance with the law spend a considerable amount of time and resources dealing with nuisance lawsuits driven by the plaintiffs' bar. These suits are filed with the objective of shaking the employer down for a settlement in return for withdrawing the case. And after the lawyers take their cut of the settlement for both fees and "expenses," plaintiffs are often left with the crumbs. In the case of class actions which are now available for most employment laws, the problem is compounded as lawyers often walk away with huge fees while individual plaintiffs may only receive a modest share of the recovery. It should come as no surprise that the United States, among all the industrialized nations, has the highest number of lawyers per capita.[8]

The Association recognizes and applauds President Obama's Executive Order 13563, which suggests that regulatory decisions (including past decisions) must be made or revisited in a way that promotes economic growth, innovation, job creation, and competitiveness. To this end and because of the concerns discussed above, we strongly urge the Administration before it launches new regulatory and enforcement initiatives to undertake a thorough review of what is already on the books and determine whether these regulations need to be revised or abandoned by asking the following questions--

- How does the law and its regulations impact the hiring and retention of employees in the United States as well as the expansion of business here?
- Are the regulations up-to-date and readily understandable by all those affected by them?
- Can the regulations be easily and consistently applied and enforced?
- Is there sufficient flexibility in the rules such that employers can accommodate the need for family friendly policies without running afoul of the law?
- Are the rules consistent with what today's employees genuinely want and need while providing sufficient protections for low-wage workers?
- Can the regulations account for and allow for changes in the use of technology, the workplace, and employee lifestyles?

- Can the requirements be applied consistently across the 50 states and in the counties and cities of those states?
- Do policymakers and regulators fully understand the consequences of the regulatory scheme they have designed before it has been implemented?
- Do the rules demand information that employers do not have or cannot easily obtain without incurring new costs?
- Do the regulations contain any elements or requirements that unnecessarily create ill will among employees?
- What is the objective of the regulatory requirement, and what is the best way to achieve that objective without causing undue disruptions to employers?
- Do regulations impose requirements that are not contained in the statute?

THE FAIR LABOR STANDARDS ACT GENERALLY

With these questions in mind, we would ask you to consider the Fair Labor Standards Act. On its face, the FLSA is a very simple and defensible attempt to protect employees against exploitation and "sweatshop" working conditions. The dual purpose of the law is to provide a minimum wage (currently $7.25 per hour) and ensure that workers who are not otherwise exempt are paid time-and-a-half overtime for hours worked in excess of forty in a given workweek. Most employees who are exempt are "white collar" employees who must be paid a salary. However, these simple concepts have been translated into countless vague and inconsistent rules and exceptions that are increasingly out of step with the times.

Examples of Problems. Employers regularly deal with following kinds of situations forced by the statute's inflexibilities:

- Work schedules are carefully designed to avoid excessive overtime. Thus, even if employees would prefer to work eight days in a row, with six days off in a row, the employer cannot afford such a schedule because it would involve at least two full days of overtime.
- Because employers fear that FLSA violations will occur because of employees engaging in work that is not being tracked, they impose restrictions on the use of social media outside of working hours. Thus, nonexempt employees are discouraged or prohibited from checking emails off-hours due to the risk of not reporting their time worked, even though they may prefer to do this. In occupations, such as off-site repairmen, where the use of Blackberries or other personal digital assistants (PDAs) is essential, some employers require the employee to keep these at one of the employer's locations, picking it up and dropping it off there, regardless of the locations of site visits.
- The law creates disincentives toward engaging nonexempt employees in trouble-shooting and decision-making:
  - When something goes wrong on a shift and the current shift needs to call someone on the prior shift, the administrative burden of reporting the "time

worked" for the prior-shift employee's six-minute phone call discourages the contact.
- Nonexempt employees may be routinely excluded from off-site meetings or trips which could be beneficial to them and the company because of the administrative difficulty of determining what time is compensable and the actual cost, once determined.
- In team situations where nonexempt employees are actively involved in deciding how the work is to be performed, the employer often has to discourage them—to the point of imposing discipline—from engaging in "after hours" discussions with their co-workers or engaging in any other work, such as writing a proposal for addressing a particular problem.

Such division of employees based on job classification is increasingly out of sync with corporate cultures which depend on team-work. Further, the inability to participate in off-hours or off-site events stunts the career growth of nonexempt employees who lose the benefit of these activities.

- Nonexempt employees are often at a disadvantage when their employers offer non-workrelated events during the workday for employees to participate in, such as Earth Day celebrations, diversity network events, corporate United Way campaign events, and so forth. In 24/7 operations, these events will always be taking place during the working hours of some segment of the workforce. Thus, in order to participate, those nonexempt employees must be compensated for that time and are thus less likely to get management support for participating as fully as exempt employees, including being able to serve as leaders or organizers.
- Employers are discouraged from paying bonuses and other forms of incentive pay to nonexempt employees because the law requires such amounts to be included in the employees' rate of pay for purposes of calculating overtime. For example, an employer may want to extend pay-for-performance incentives to nonexempt employees by offering annual incentive payments for achieving certain performance targets. However, payment of the incentive will require recalculation of overtime pay for the year. Moreover, when making the decision to provide such incentives, the employer often doesn't know how much overtime the employees will work, thus preventing an accurate projection of costs. To avoid this administrative complexity and potential legal exposure, some employers might simply conclude that they are not going to extend incentive pay programs to nonexempt employees.

The FLSA Workplace. In considering the FLSA, it is important to understand the state of the American workplace when the 1938 law was enacted. The Depression-era workplace was characterized by:

- a fixed beginning and end to both the workday and the workweek in most American workplaces;
- with the exception of certain occupations (*e.g.*, repairmen and truck drivers), the performance of the vast majority of work taking place in the workplace because of the lack of communications technology allowing the performance of jobs from remote locations;

- a far more stratified and predictable designation of occupations, as compared to today's workplaces where there is a greater blurring of distinctions and a more rapid evolution of job descriptions; and
- a greater preponderance of manual labor because of the relative absence of technology and mechanization that transformed the way work is performed today.

The FLSA was passed at a time when Ford Motor Company was making Model A's on its production line with manual labor and relatively very little automation. With technology and robotics, today's production workers use their minds and computers to an extent that was beyond the imagination of science fiction writers in the Depression. Today, the entire concept of work is changing as the United States moves from a manufacturing to a service economy that is highly dependent on technology and much more mobile.

Yet, the basic structure of the FLSA has never been fundamentally reexamined. The FLSA and its regulations simply have not kept pace with the changes in the workplace. The FLSA was enacted in 1938 and, though it has been amended in a noteworthy manner 17 times, those amendments have for the most part been limited to expanding coverage to specific categories of employees and increasing the minimum wage, while occasionally addressing very narrow aspects of the law.[9] Even though the minimum wage seems to generate far greater attention in public policy discussions, most of the difficulties with the FLSA arise under the overtime requirement. As a result, there is a tremendous amount of litigation brought by the plaintiffs' bar exploiting the differences between Depression-era regulations and 21st Century workplace practices.

A considerable share of the friction within the FLSA arises from the "white collar" regulations, discussed below, which have created numerous difficulties in figuring out which employees are subject to overtime requirements and which are exempt. In 2004, the Bush Administration updated the regulations defining the white collar exemptions.[10] However, the revised regulations continue to cause compliance difficulties and generate significant litigation because of the continuing evolution of the workplace. Meanwhile, despite predictions that the changes would result in six million Americans losing overtime,[11] no studies have been offered since to verify that this happened. Moreover, our own informal contacts with our members indicate that, if anything, most employees whose status changed in the wake of the regulations were shifted from exempt to nonexempt.

Explosion of Litigation. In considering the FLSA's regulatory framework, it must be recognized that the statute provides not only for enforcement by the Department of Labor, but also by private actions. As a result, the private bar has taken advantage of the law's lack of clarity in pursuing highly lucrative class actions against employers who struggle to ascertain what is required. Thus, the number of FLSA lawsuits has quadrupled from about 1,500 per year in the early 1990s to over 6,000 in 2009,[12] and this does not count the number of cases brought under state laws which often vary from the federal law. Faced with the uncertainties of the law, companies often settle these cases, with a median settlement cost of $7.4 million for federal cases and $10 million for state cases.[13]

Lack of Preemption. On top of all the problems created by the federal wage and hour laws, additional inflexibilities and complexities are created by state laws, which are not preempted as long as they are more "protective."[14] Thus, California has significantly narrower criteria for which employees are exempt from overtime. For example, in order to be considered an exempt computer employee in California, an individual must perform duties involving the exercise of discretion more than 50 percent of the time in each work week and earn at least $79,050 annually.[15] Under Federal law, there is no discretion requirement, the exemption is measured over a longer period of time, is not based on a hard-and-fast percentage test, and the employee needs to earn $23,660 annually. Thus, two different employees, one working in California and another working in another state for the same company, may be subject to entirely different scheduling and compensation schemes even though they are performing exactly the same kind of work.

In addition, states may provide varying definitions of the workweek or other factors determining when overtime must be paid. In California, most employees must be paid overtime for any hours worked in excess of eight in a single day, regardless of how many hours he or she works the rest of the week. In addition, an employer must provide a 30 minute meal break during which the employee is relieved of all duties, unless the job requires the employee to be on duty during meals, such as a security guard at a remote location.[16] Thus, a nonexempt employee must be forced by the employer to take a half-hour lunch break, even if the employee would prefer a working lunch that would enable him or her to leave work a half hour earlier. In situations where nonexempt employees work closely with exempt employees, this is yet another situation where the wage and hour law creates divisions in the workplace.

With this as a basic background on the law, the following is a brief discussion of some of the problems that have evolved as the 1930s law remains fixed while the workplace continues to change.

WORKPLACE FLEXIBILITY

The administration is strongly encouraging employers to adopt workplace flexibility policies to help employees address the competing demands of work and family. On March 31, 2010, the White House conducted a Forum on Workplace Flexibility at which President Obama encouraged employers to "embrac[e] telecommuting, flextime, compressed work weeks, job sharing, flexible start and end times, and helping your employees generally find quality childcare and eldercare."[17] Yet, the Fair Labor Standards Act, which was written for a traditional, mid- Twentieth Century workplace, repeatedly frustrates the ability of employers to embrace such policies for employees who are covered by the statute (often referred to as "nonexempt employees").

Except for those employees who are exempt, the employer is required to pay employees overtime for all "hours worked" in excess of forty in a specific workweek. This requirement, coupled with the very strict, but often murky, rules regarding tracking hours breaks down when employers try to implement flexible workplace policies. For example, employers often have to reject individual arrangements sought by employees. Thus, two employees may want to do a shift swap between weeks, which would benefit their individual work-life balance. Jim wants to swap Friday shift for Sue's Monday shift. Both are willing, but doing so would convert what would be straight time to overtime for both employees, working 32 hours of straight time in one week and 48 hours in the next. Thus, accommodating the employees' request imposes additional costs on the company.

Telecommuting. For obvious reasons, many employees desire telecommuting that enables them to work from home or other locations outside the workplace. The flexibility of a telecommuting arrangement can benefit both employees and employers. However, neither the FLSA nor the U.S. Department of Labor's interpretative regulations directly addresses nonexempt telecommuting employees; telecommuting was unknown when they were written. In fact, neither the words nor the concept of "telecommuting, flextime, compressed work weeks, job sharing, flexible start and end times, and helping your employees generally find quality childcare and eldercare" are found in the FLSA regulations.

Thus, where an employer is required to track the "hours worked" by an employee, telecommuting can raise serious litigation/enforcement risks that discourage employers from offering such arrangements. For example, even with computer or telephone tracking systems that generate time reports showing login and logout times, an employer must still ensure that it accurately records all other hours worked when the employee is not "logged on." Moreover, even if an employer attempts to control the hours worked by nonexempt telecommuters by requiring agreements that set specific work-hour requirements and requiring that any overtime be approved in advance, this will not protect an employer from litigation or enforcement actions.[18]

Another FLSA issue that arises with telecommuting arrangements has to do with whether or not commuting time is compensable. Generally, travel time to and from work does not constitute hours worked. If, however, travel occurs after an employee's first principal activity in the workday, say telecommuting from home in the morning and then driving into work in the afternoon for a meeting, the "continuous workday" rule could be interpreted to make such travel compensable. Designing and implementing a policy and practice that will exclude travel-time pay by telecommuters is very difficult and by no means certain.

Flexible Scheduling. The strictures of the Fair Labor Standards Act also impede the ability of employers to respond to the wishes of nonexempt employees for flexible scheduling. A flexible work schedule is an alternative to the traditional "9-to-5" 40-hour work week that allows employees to vary their arrival and/or departure times or the days that they work. Because employees must be paid overtime for every hour worked in excess of forty *in a given workweek*, there is a financial disincentive for an employer to honor a request by employees to work longer hours in some weeks in exchange for shorter hours or longer weekends in others.

The FLSA only allows flexible schedules that remain within the weekly 40-hour limit, *i.e.*, working four 10-hour days each week, working three 10-hour days and two 5-hour days each week, and varying one's start and end times each day around some core hours while working no more than 40 hours each workweek. Unlike the public sector, private-sector employees are not allowed to "bank" over-time hours worked as comp-time in order to take paid time off in future pay periods for family situations or extra vacation days. Private-sector employees have no choice; they must be paid cash for the overtime they work in a pay period.

Beyond the standard five-day, 40-hour workweek, the FLSA does allow one inflexible variation —the so-called 9/80 model that creates a fictitious beginning and end to the workweek. Using this model, employees work a full two-week, 80-hour schedule in nine days rather than 10 and take a day every other week off, usually Friday. To do this, the employer must first artificially redefine the work week by designating a particular day, usually a Friday, where the workweek begins at noon on that day. Using this definition, which splits one day a week into two, the employees never work more than 40 hours in a week. When employees take off every other Friday, they are reducing two work weeks by four hours each, and making up the difference by working 36 hours Monday through Thursday. Thus, in each artificially defined "workweek," they are working 40 hours, even though in one normally-defined workweek they would be working 36 hours and in the other 44.[19] However, any variation on this—such as extending the time frame to a three or four week period, with two or three extra days off—would not be permitted, even if requested by the employees.

Moreover, the 9/80 schedule requires employers to keep careful track of work hours daily. For example, if an employee requests a deviation from the schedule in order to meet a personal need, such as offering to work the Friday that is supposed to be "off" in order to take the following Friday, the employer would be deterred from granting the request by having to pay overtime for that Friday. The situation becomes even more complicated in California, which requires an employee vote to implement a 9/80 work schedule and then has even more restrictive requirements than Federal law.

Electronic Communications Devices. The proliferation of electronic communication devices has a powerful potential for not only improving productivity but also helping employees, both salaried and hourly, accommodate the competing demands of work and family. However, the requirement to pay employees for "hours worked," when interpreted literally, can strain the ability of employers to comply with the law. As a result, many employers are imposing severe restrictions on the use of these devices outside the workplace.

If a nonexempt employee has access to his or her email account away from work—either through a laptop or a personal digital assistant—he or she is very likely to access that account outside normal working hours. If he or she is performing a significant amount of work, the employer would be expected to compensate the employee for that work. However, the employee may be simply checking to see if something needs urgent attention or taking a quick look to get a preview of the coming workday. He or she may even be checking to see if a co-employee has responded on a non-work-related matter but, in doing so, also glance at one that is work-related. At present, it is not clear whether such "de minimis" activities have to be compensated. Employers are also uncertain as to when such activities trigger the commencement of the workday or extend it past normal working hours.

Because the employee is essentially on his or her time, it is virtually impossible for the employer to track such occurrences or try to minimize them. The absence of clarity in the law on this issue, coupled with the aforementioned proliferation of wage and hour lawsuits, tends to drive many employers' policies, rather than employee preferences. Indeed, many employers who would otherwise be willing to purchase such devices for their employees—and allow them to also be used for personal needs—are deterred from doing so by the inability to effectively control the amount of work the employee may try to perform with them. The safest course for employers is to ban the use of electronic communications devices outside the workplace, despite the wishes of the employee. These complications created by the extraordinary advances in communications technology were not at issue when the FLSA was formulated.

DETERMINING EXEMPT STATUS

These flexibility issues do not arise where employees are exempt from the FLSA. Yet, the most difficult problems in recent years under the FLSA have revolved around determining which employees are or are not exempt. Because the FLSA's original purpose was to focus the statute's protections upon the "unprotected, unorganized and lowest paid" manufacturing workers,[20] comprehensive coverage was not contemplated. As described by the Department of Labor:

> Exemptions were premised on the belief that the workers exempted typically earned salaries well above the minimum wage, and they were presumed to enjoy other compensatory privileges such as above average fringe benefits and better opportunities for advancement, setting them apart from the nonexempt workers entitled to overtime pay. Further, the type of work they performed was difficult to standardize to any time frame and could not be easily spread to other workers after 40 hours in a week, making compliance with the overtime provisions difficult and generally precluding the potential job expansion intended by the FLSA's time-and-a-half overtime premium.[21]

Minimal Impact of Exempt Status on Earnings. Implicit in the arguments of those who press for the narrowest possible definition of the exemptions is the assumption that, by being exempt, employees are being underpaid. However, apart from the minimum wage, the FLSA does not regulate the *amount* that employees are paid. Rather, it determines *how* they are paid. Thus, being covered by the FLSA does not necessarily guarantee that an employee will earn more. The rules are the same regardless of whether he or she is paid $10 an hour or $100 an hour. The only issue is determining whether and when the employee must be paid one and one half times this amount for every hour worked over 40. Thus, if the value of the work of an employee to an employer is $950 after working 45 hours per week, the economics for the employer and the employee are the same regardless of whether the employee is exempt and earns a salary of $950 per week, or if the employee is nonexempt and earns $20 per hour ($20 times 40 plus $30 times 5 equals $950).

The amount an employee is paid is determined by a variety of factors, including market rates, education, experience, performance and so forth. Employers will generally establish compensation for an employee based on these factors. If an employee is exempt, the employer will provide a salary that reflects these factors. That salary will also likely be shaped by the number of hours contemplated in the job. If the job involves significant amounts of time beyond a normal forty hour workweek, which many white collar jobs do, the salary will reflect that as part of the objective of attracting and retaining the talent needed to meet the company's needs.

If, on the other hand, the employee's duties fail to meet the test for any of the exemptions, the employer will have to determine an appropriate hourly wage, based on the same kinds of factors that will also meet its talent attraction and retention needs. In setting that wage, the employer will consider the amount of overtime the employee is likely to work.

The point is that in today's economy, an employee over a period of time is likely to earn roughly the same amount, regardless of whether he or she is exempt or nonexempt. In addition to greater scheduling flexibility, the advantage of being exempt is that it is, by requirement, a salaried position, so there is a great deal more certainty by the employee regarding the amount that will be earned, even if it may involve a certain number of overtime hours that do not receive premium pay.

White Collar Exemptions Generally. As described previously, the most common exemptions are the so-called white collar exemptions:

- the administrative exemption, for those whose primary duty involves "the performance of office or non-manual work directly related to management policies or general business operations of his employer or his employer's business" where the work includes "the exercise of independent judgment and discretion;"
- the professional exemption, for those who are either of "a learned or educational profession requiring the consistent exercise of discretion and judgment" or "perform work requiring invention, imagination, or talent in a recognized field of artistic endeavor;" and
- the executive exemption, for those whose primary duty is "managing the enterprise, or managing a customarily recognized department or subdivision of the enterprise."

For an employee to fall within any of the white collar exemptions, he or she must be paid "on a salary basis." This creates a financial advantage for exempt employees that is not shared by nonexempt employees, who must rely on the availability of work to gain a full week's earnings. Generally, the exempt employee must be paid the full predetermined salary amount "free and clear" for any week in which the employee performs any work without regard to the number of days or hours worked. Deductions may not be made from the employee's predetermined salary for absences occasioned by the employer or by the operating requirements of the business. If the employee is ready, willing, and able to work, deductions may not be made for time when work is not available. Except for certain limited situations, salary deductions result in loss of the white-collar exemption and the potential risk of having to pay three years of back wages for any overtime worked.[22]

Examples of Areas of Uncertainty. The rules governing the exemptions are riddled with ambiguities and imprecision that employers and even the Department of Labor struggle with in applying them to a real workplace:

- *Entry-level degreed engineers and accountants.* The FLSA regulations state that to be an exempt professional, an employee must perform "work requiring advanced knowledge in a field of science or learning" involving the "consistent exercise of discretion and judgment."[23] Often, as new graduates start their first jobs, they exercise very little discretion or judgment. Instead, they follow the highly complicated rules and principles of the profession and/or directions from those to whom they report, until they acquire sufficient experience on the job. The quandary faced by the employer is determining when new engineers and accountants who, by every other standard would clearly be considered a professional, cross the threshold into the blurry FLSA definition of a professional.
- *Computer employees.* The FLSA regulations include an exemption for so-called "computer employees,"[24] but the definition is rooted in the technology of 1992, a time before many people had Internet access or email. Thus, computer programming

or systems design are the type of work that is explicitly exempted under this exemption. Yet, other areas of computer related work that are complex, require specialized technical knowledge of computer hardware and software, and require independent judgment and discretion may be excluded simply because the work also involves using manual effort and tools for setup, accessing, and maintaining computer systems. At the same time, however, the type of work performed by a network or database administrator earning $80,000 a year are not. Keeping computer networks up and running, fixing bugs, and improving the system are not "programming" work under FLSA regulations even though the individuals are clearly highly skilled and well-paid. Even where other exemption tests may apply, guidance for applying the exemption tests to information technology jobs is inadequate (*e.g.*, determining whether the work is related to management or the general business operations). Thus, employees may have highly similar educational backgrounds may be classified differently because of the narrow definition of computer employee in the regulations. Even a network or database administrators may have to punch a time clock every day while programmers and system designers do not have to, even if on a monthly or yearly basis they are receiving the same compensation.

- *Credentials.* For professional employees to be exempt, the advanced knowledge required for the exemption must be "customarily acquired through a prolonged course of specialized intellectual instruction." It is not clear what "customarily" means. As currently interpreted by some courts, an employer could have employees performing complicated engineering duties but they would have to be paid and treated differently if they acquired their knowledge and expertise in different ways. For example, the Second Circuit Court of Appeals recently decided that an engineer with 20 years experience who was a member of the American Society of Mechanical Engineers and performed work that involved complicated technical expertise and responsibility was nevertheless a nonexempt employee.[25]
- *Administrative exemption.* Particularly nettlesome is determining what level of "discretion and independent judgment" employees must have to qualify for the administration exemption. Not even the Wage and Hour Division (WHD) can make up its mind about whether or not particular jobs qualify for the administrative exemption. For example, on September 8, 2006, the WHD determined that mortgage loan officers are *bona fide* administrative employees who are exempt under the FLSA.[26] Yet, on March 24, 2010, WHD reversed itself and determined that they do not qualify for the exemption.[27] If the WHD cannot consistently determine who is a *bona fide* administrative employee, how are employers supposed to figure it out?
- *Executive exemption.* Applying the FLSA executive exemption where a manager directs the work of two or more full-time employees or their full-time employee equivalents can be difficult if the establishment experiences fairly regular turnover and one or more of the positions is vacant for some period of time. The regulations should be updated to clarify that the executive exemption is not lost in these situations.

Irrelevance of Employee Preferences Creates Morale Issues. Adding to the problems employers encounter in deciphering the murky rules surrounding each exemption is the issue of employee morale, which frequently gets overlooked by policymakers. While there is an assumption by many that employees generally prefer to be paid overtime, that is not necessarily the case. Many employees view exempt salaried positions as a sign of status, as opposed to "having to punch a time clock." They enter their professions knowing that hours will fluctuate, often involving extra evening and weekend work with a corresponding ability to often take time off as needed without having to worry about lost wages. The guaranteed pay associated with a salary is viewed by many employees as far more desirable than the fluctuations of hourly pay, even where that may occasionally mean a slightly larger paycheck. In situations where nonexempt employees work closely with exempt employees, such as paralegals working with attorneys, the distinction between exempt and nonexempt can create cultural tensions and resentment where the nonexempt employees covet the flexibilities and status of being a salaried employee.

Many positions that in recent years have come into question over exempt status have historically been considered exempt by common industry practice and thus individuals enter those occupations with that expectation. Moreover, employees generally recognize that the amount they will be paid will be based on what the employer views the job to be worth, regardless of what the strictures are on precisely how that amount is to be calculated.

The explosion of wage and hour class actions and the enormous costs associated with contesting such actions have exacerbated the tensions in this area. Many employers who believe there is a strong argument for retaining exempt status of employees have decided to nevertheless reclassify those positions as nonexempt for fear of litigation being initiated or as a result of a settlement of litigation where the outcome was uncertain. In many instances, those employers have confronted serious morale problems among those employees who have lost the exemption and the flexibility and status that go with it. Those employers have found that the employees draw little comfort in knowing that they will now face the uncertainties and inflexibilities of being paid a wage rather than a salary. Yet, the FLSA does not allow for employee preference in dictating whether an employee must be paid hourly as opposed to salaried.

Pitfalls of Reclassification. In assessing the exempt status of their workforce, employers who decide that they should "play it safe" by reclassifying employees as nonexempt have to grapple with another problem in addition to the morale issues just described. For failure to pay overtime to nonexempt employees, the FLSA provides up to two years back pay, which can be doubled and extended to three years in some cases, depending on a court's conclusions about whether an employer acted in good faith or should have known overtime was owed. Meanwhile, there is no "safe harbor" for an employer who voluntarily reclassifies its employees. Thus, an employer who reclassifies a large number of employees may very well capture the interest of a plaintiffs' lawyer, thus triggering a lawsuit. The employer's ability to defend itself will be hampered by its own actions, which will be perceived as an acknowledgement by the employer that it was violating the law prior to the reclassification.

DOL Recordkeeping Initiative. The problems employers encounter in dealing with these and the numerous other areas of uncertainty will be exacerbated if the Department of Labor Wage and Hour Division proceeds with its announced intention to propose sweeping new recordkeeping requirements. According to the Department's Fall 2010 Regulatory Agenda:

> Any employers that seek to exclude workers from the FLSA's coverage will be required to perform a classification analysis, disclose that analysis to the worker, and retain that analysis to give to WHD enforcement personnel who might request it.[28]

This benign-sounding requirement seems to assume that employers in the United States will have very little difficulty in ascertaining the exempt or nonexempt status of nearly every employee in the United States in a manner that will brook little or no disagreement with either a Wage and Hour Division investigator or a plaintiff's attorney. In a perfect world, that would be the case but, as described in the above illustrations, it frequently is not. Rather than promoting clarity and transparency, the inherent uncertainties in these situations are likely to stimulate litigation to test the employer's conclusions. At that point, the employer will have to make a determination as to whether a court is likely to agree and whether it will be worth the legal expenses of associated with taking that chance. Even if the employer continues to believe that the employees meet the murky exemption requirements, it may try to contain its costs by settling.

Rather than going forward with this litigation-fomenting approach that will create serious morale issues in workplaces across the United States, we believe the Department should first seek to correct the lack of clarity in the existing rules in a manner that recognizes the needs of both employers and employees. The Department in the previous administration sought to accomplish this goal with mixed results. There was some progress which laid a groundwork for further clarification, but considerable confusion still remains. We would be willing to work closely with the Department to address this need. However, we would emphasize that such an approach will not work if it begins with the assumption that all employees wish to be paid an hourly wage. The end result should be a set of clearly defined rules that ensure that overtime is provided in those situations that meet the traditional characteristics of an hourly wage worker.

DETERRENTS TO FINANCIAL REWARDS FOR PERFORMANCE

The inflexible manner in which overtime pay must be calculated under the FLSA can undermine an employer's ability to reward employees. The law requires the employer to pay a nonexempt employee one and one half times his or her "regular rate of pay" for every hour worked over forty. In its simplest form, an employee's regular rate of pay is his or her base hourly pay rate. However, the FLSA broadly defines the regular rate to encompass "all remuneration for employment paid to, or on behalf of, the employee."[29] This means that other kinds of compensation, including most bonuses, are included in the calculation of the regular rate.

The FLSA excludes from the regular rate *ad hoc* bonuses that employers do not announce to employees ahead of time.[30] These are called "discretionary bonuses" because the employer maintains discretion over whether the bonus will be paid and how much the bonus will be when paid. Holiday bonuses are a good example. Unfortunately, such bonuses are of limited value to employers and employees because they are not driven by goals set in advance nor are they typically ongoing and thus lack the incentive potential of nondiscretionary bonuses.

In contrast to discretionary bonuses, if an employer announces a program that provides a bonus to employees if they meet certain goals stated in the program, the FLSA requires that the bonuses be included in the employees' regular rates of pay.[31] These bonuses are considered "nondiscretionary" bonuses because the employer has surrendered its discretion over whether to pay the bonus. If the employees meet the goals stated in the plan, then they will receive the full bonus. Because payment is automatic, the FLSA considers the bonus as part of the employee's base pay, and the employer must include the bonus in the employees' regular rates of pay when calculating overtime.

This requirement undermines the ability of employers to predict employment costs. The employer may know how much the bonus is, but it may not know how many overtime hours the employee will be working that will carry the additional costs added to the regular rate by the bonus.

The regular-rate requirement also undermines attempts to reinforce teamwork and minimize distinctions between hourly and salaried employees. Many times employers want to reward all employees equally to reinforce the notion of teamwork. When the overtime recalculation is added, however, the bonus amounts will differ with the amount of overtime worked by each employee. Unless none of the employees worked overtime, or they all worked exactly the same amount of overtime, each employee's bonus will be different.

Adding bonuses to the regular rate in calculating overtime may not be an insurmountable problem for employers but, as with so many other aspects of the FLSA, it creates a strong deterrent to an employee-friendly policy. In the end, the safest and most predictable course for the employer is to *not* provide bonuses to nonexempt employees.

CONCLUSION

The dual objectives of promoting employment growth and encouraging flexible workplace policies should compel the administration to re-examine the Fair Labor Standards Act in light of today's workplace, rather than moving forward with the aggressive enforcement policy that the Department of Labor has outlined. We certainly do not question the need for basic wage and hour protections to protect against the kinds of "sweatshop" conditions that prompted the Act. We also recognize that many of the issues that we raise could only be addressed through changes in the statute itself. We invite the administration to join with us and other stakeholders in a dialogue that seeks to address the many questions we have raised in an informed manner, with the goal of targeting enforcement resources where they are truly needed, while enabling the American workplace to evolve in a manner that best suits the needs of 21st Century employers and employees.

Sincerely,

Daniel V. Yager
Chief Policy Officer & General Counsel
cc: Cass R. Sunstein,
Administrator, Office of Information and Regulatory Affairs

End Notes

[1] 76 Fed. Reg. 18620-621 (April 1, 2011).
[2] Office of Management and Budget, Office of Information and Regulatory Affairs, 2010 Report to Congress on the Benefits and Costs of Federal Regulations and Unfunded Mandates on State, Local, and Tribal Entities, 121.

[3] *Id.*

[4] 76 Fed. Reg. 18621 (April 1, 2011) ("suggestions about particular rules that should be reevaluated, as well as studies of particular rules, should be directed to the agencies themselves").

[5] See "Workplace Flexibility at the White House," available at http://www.whitehouse.gov/blog/2010/04/01/workplace-flexibility-white-house

[6] Applied Economic Strategies, estimate based on the economic analysis in the 2004 final rule on 29 CFR Part 541.

[7] Applied Economic Strategies, estimate based on the latest available Bureau of Labor Statistics data.

[8] American Bar Association, Council of European Lawyers and other sources.

[9] See 54 Stat. 615 (1940), 61 Stat. 64 (1947), 63 Stat. 910 (1949), 69 Stat. 711 (1955), 70 Stat. 1118 (1956), P.L. 87-30 (1961), P.L. 88-38 (1963), P.L. 89-601 (1966), P.L. 93-259 (1974), P.L. 95-151 (1977), P.L. 99-150 (1985), P.L. 101-157 (1989), P.L. 104-26 (1995), P.L. 104-188 (1996), P.L. 105-334 (1998), P.L. 106-202 (2000), and P.L. 110-28 (2007).

[10] 69 Fed. Reg. 22122, (April 23, 2004).

[11] Ross Eisenbrey, "Longer Hours, Less Pay - Labor Department's new rules could strip overtime protection from millions of workers," Economic Policy Institute, Briefing Paper #152, July 14, 2004.

[12] U.S. Courts, Annual Report of the Director, Table C-2A, various years.

[13] Samuel Estreicher and Kristina Yost, "Measuring the Value of Class and Collective Action Employment Settlements: A Preliminary Assessment, New York University School of Law, Working Paper No. 08-03, January 2008.

[14] 29 U.S.C. 218.

[15] California Labor Code Section 515.5.

[16] Even in those instances, there must be a written agreement for an on-the-job paid meal period that is revocable by the employee at any time. California Code of Regulations, Title 8, § 11040.

[17] Remarks by the President at Workplace Flexibility Forum, March 31, 2010, available at http://www.whitehouse.gov/the-press-office/remarks-president

[18] Although more than 60 years ago the Supreme Court distinguished between employees who are "waiting to be engaged" and those who are "engaged to wait," that decision did not contemplate today's telecommuting employees. 323 U.S. 134 (1944).

[19] Thus, the following schedule would not include overtime:

Week one
- Friday –0 hours (entire day off); workweek begins at noon
- Monday – 9 hours
- Tuesday – 9 hours
- Wednesday – 9 hours
- Thursday – 9 hours
- Friday AM– 4 hours
- Workweek ends Friday at noon; employee worked 40 hours that "week"

Week two
- New workweek begins same Friday at noon – 4 hours
- Monday – 9 hours
- Tuesday – 9 hours
- Wednesday – 9 hours
- Thursday – 9 hours
- Friday – 0 hours (entire day off); employee worked 40 hours that "week"

[20] Letter from President Franklin D. Roosevelt to the U.S. Congress, May 24, 1937, reprinted in Report on S. 2475, The Fair Labor Standards Act, H.R. Rep. 1452, 5 (1937).

[21] 69 Fed. Reg. 22124, (April 23, 2004).

[22] There is no requirement that a salary be paid if an employee performs no work for an entire workweek, and full-day salary deductions are permissible only under certain limited circumstances. These include when:
- An employee is absent for personal reasons. For example, if a person is absent for 2 full days to handle personal affairs, the employer could deduct from the salary for 2 full-day absences. However, if the exempt employee is absent for one-and-a-half days for personal reasons, the employer can deduct only for the 1 full-day absence.
- An employee is absent for sickness or disability if the deduction is made in accordance with a bona fide plan, policy, or practice of providing compensation for loss of salary.
- Full day deductions may also be made for disciplinary suspensions related workplace conduct violations such as sexual harassment or violence; and
- Full day deductions may be made for penalties imposed in good faith for infractions of safety rules of major significance (for example, smoking in an explosives plant, oil refinery, or coal mine).

The only time partial-day salary deductions for exempt employees is permissible is when an employee takes intermittent leave under the Family and Medical Leave Act. In this case employers only have to pay a proportionate part of the full salary for the time actually worked.

[23] 29 C.F.R. 541.301(b).
[24] 29 C.F.R. 541.400.
[25] *Young v. Cooper Cameron Corporation*, 586 F.3d 201, (2d Cir. 2009).
[26] U.S. Department of Labor, Wage and Hour Division, Administrator Opinion Letter FLSA2006-3 1, September 8, 2006, available at: http://wayback.archive-it.org/1287/20090116135435/http://www.dol.gov/esa/ whd/opinion /FLSA 2006/2006_09_08_3 1_FLSA.pdf.
[27] U.S. Department of Labor, Wage and Hour Division, Administrator's Interpretation No. 2010-1, March 24, 2010.
[28] Available at http://www.dol.gov/regulations
[29] 29 U.S.C. 207(e).
[30] 29 U.S.C. 207(e)(1).
[31] 29 U.S.C. 207(e)(1).

INDEX

A

abatement, 22, 24, 25, 26, 31
abuse, 76, 83
accounting, 5, 7, 18, 27, 33, 43, 49, 70, 96, 97, 111, 140, 155
Administrative Procedure Act, 59
adverse effects, 18, 21, 22, 23, 26, 32, 128, 139, 144, 158
age, 28, 29, 74, 121, 144, 179, 183
Agricultural Research Service, 62, 115, 137
air pollutants, 155
air quality, 9, 11, 25, 29, 32, 129, 132, 144
altruism, 130
American Bar Association, 182
American Recovery and Reinvestment Act, 18, 72
Americans with Disabilities Act, 24, 122
Appropriations Act, 4, 5, 55, 128
assessment, vii, 4, 18, 22, 41, 49, 56, 57, 59, 111, 128, 129, 137, 138, 139, 140, 144, 151
assets, 26, 131, 136, 138
asymmetric information, 33, 144
atmosphere, 168
authorities, 21, 87, 102, 104, 110, 132
Automatic Dependent Surveillance – Broadcast (ADS-B), 14
automation, 25, 172

B

bargaining, 26
barriers, 22, 40, 108, 109, 110
beneficial effect, 23, 43
beneficiaries, 13, 77
benefits, vii, viii, 1, 2, 3, 4, 5, 6, 7, 8, 9, 10, 11, 13, 14, 16, 17, 18, 20, 22, 23, 24, 27, 33, 34, 35, 36, 38, 39, 41, 42, 43, 44, 45, 46, 47, 48, 49, 51, 52, 53, 59, 60, 63, 64, 68, 69, 70, 74, 76, 77, 79, 80, 81, 82, 83, 84, 85, 86, 87, 96, 97, 98, 102, 108, 111, 118, 119, 120, 121, 128, 129, 130, 131, 132, 134, 135, 137, 138, 139, 140, 143, 144, 145, 146, 148, 151, 152, 153, 154, 155, 158, 159, 161, 163, 167
Benefits and Costs of Federal Regulations, i, iii, v, vii, viii, 1, 5, 63, 134, 136, 140, 143, 147, 151, 157, 158, 163, 165, 181
bias, 41, 49, 139, 155
boilers, 130, 138
bonds, 21
bonuses, 171, 180, 181
Broadband, 17, 71BTU, 145
Bureau of Labor Statistics, 28, 182
Bureau of Land Management, 56, 113, 116
businesses, 21, 22, 30, 43, 52, 106, 108, 139, 162

C

Cabinet, 51, 61, 115
cancer, 20, 130, 132
capital accumulation, 30
capital expenditure, 22, 31
carbon, 31, 68, 134
case study, 42, 86, 131
ceteris paribus, 22
CFR, 89, 182
challenges, 2, 16, 27, 28, 34, 37, 45, 59, 106, 131
chemical, 21, 129
childcare, 28, 173, 174
childhood, 34
children, 7, 16, 35, 44, 80, 81, 162
classes, 22, 23, 66
classification, 171, 179
Clean Air Act, 26, 31, 32, 65, 67, 68, 86, 100, 124, 125, 127, 129, 130, 131, 132, 138, 144
climate, 35, 51, 84, 167
Clinton Administration, 159

CO2, 145, 161
coal, 182
Code of Federal Regulations, 137, 138
collective bargaining, 23, 120, 149, 168
collusion, 23, 120, 149
commercial, 66, 67, 73, 130, 138
commuter rail system, 67
compensation, 23, 24, 66, 85, 144, 168, 169, 173, 176, 178, 180, 182
competition, 23, 30, 120, 128, 149
competitive advantage, 167
competitiveness, viii, 3, 23, 30, 33, 36, 38, 102, 107, 121, 139, 165, 166, 169
competitors, 25, 105
complement, vii, 4, 147
compliance, 3, 4, 5, 10, 20, 21, 22, 23, 32, 40, 42, 50, 63, 64, 67, 74, 102, 104, 105, 106, 107, 108, 113, 116, 131, 132, 135, 138, 139, 140, 167, 169, 172, 176
complications, 175
computer, 173, 174, 177
computer systems, 178
Concentrated Animal Feeding Operations, 93
Congress, v, vii, viii, 1, 4, 5, 17, 21, 63, 96, 118, 123, 128, 134, 136, 140, 143, 147, 151, 157, 158, 163, 165, 181, 182
consensus, 30, 33, 109, 133, 168
Constitution, 102, 165
consumers, 25, 27, 33, 35, 49, 52, 82, 121, 128, 153, 154, 155, 158, 161, 162, 163
consumption, 25, 26, 33, 144, 145, 148
control measures, 42
controlled trials, 4, 39, 41, 119
controversial, 39, 60, 121, 149
coordination, 103, 105, 108, 109
COPD, 73
correlation, 9, 29, 32
cost, viii, 3, 4, 5, 6, 7, 9, 10, 11, 18, 20, 23, 25, 26, 28, 29, 31, 33, 34, 38, 39, 41, 42, 44, 45, 46, 47, 48, 49, 52, 64, 67, 68, 69, 70, 76, 77, 78, 79, 81, 82, 83, 84, 85, 86, 87, 88, 96, 97, 98, 107, 108, 109, 110, 111, 118, 120, 121, 128, 131, 134, 135, 137, 139, 140, 144, 145, 146, 149, 151, 152, 154, 158, 162, 163, 167, 169, 171, 172
costs of compliance, 139
Council of Europe, 182
Court of Appeals, 59, 129, 130, 137, 138, 178
cryptosporidium, 20
cultural norms, 29
culture, 4, 39, 41, 119
currency, 130
Customs and Border Protection, 130

D

damages, 46, 48, 139, 154, 169
decomposition, vii, 143
deflator, 69, 96, 120, 128, 146
demand curve, 23
democracy, 104
Department of Agriculture, 8, 9, 35, 56, 61, 62, 71, 88, 112, 113, 115, 137
Department of Commerce, 56, 61, 62, 69, 71, 96, 112, 113, 116, 135, 137
Department of Defense, 57, 71, 113, 116
Department of Education, 71, 113, 116
Department of Energy, 8, 9, 13, 61, 62, 64, 66, 72, 89, 113, 116
Department of Health and Human Services, 8, 9, 40, 56, 57, 61, 62, 64, 67, 73, 76, 89, 112, 113, 116, 137
Department of Homeland Security, 8, 82, 91, 113, 116, 130, 135, 140
Department of Justice, 8, 13, 14, 83, 91, 113, 116
Department of Labor (DOL), 8, 9, 13, 14, 15, 16, 41, 47, 56, 61, 63, 76, 83, 91, 99, 104, 112, 113, 117, 119, 121, 130, 131, 135, 140, 165, 172, 176, 177, 179, 181
Department of the Interior, 2, 40, 56, 61, 63, 83, 112, 113, 116, 135, 137, 141
Department of the Treasury, 76, 85, 117, 135, 141
Department of Transportation, 8, 9, 13, 14, 35, 37, 39, 40, 47, 48, 61, 63, 64, 66, 68, 84, 87, 92, 99, 101, 113, 117, 119, 128, 129, 134, 135, 137, 145, 154
Departments of Agriculture, 61
depression, 29
deprivation, 7
DHS, 17, 21, 41, 119, 130, 145, 160
diesel engines, 129
direct cost, 139
direct measure, 25
disability, 2, 182
disclosure, 2, 3, 32, 33, 34, 35, 38, 60, 103, 105, 121, 145, 147, 148
discrimination, 2, 23, 24, 44, 74, 139
diseases, 77
disinfection, 20
disorder, 76
disposition, 60
distortions, 13
distribution, 20, 76, 121, 134, 144
District of Columbia, 59, 129, 130, 138
diversity, 171
drinking water, 20

E

earnings, 29, 76, 177
economic activity, 30, 32, 33, 133
economic consequences, 44
economic development, 133
economic efficiency, 46, 140
economic growth, 3, 5, 20, 21, 22, 23, 27, 28, 30, 32, 33, 34, 36, 37, 38, 42, 51, 52, 102, 106, 107, 166, 169
economic incentives, 102
Economic Research Service, 62, 115, 137
economics, viii, 34, 69, 96, 128, 133, 148, 162, 163, 176
economies of scale, 52
education, 29, 133, 164, 168, 176
educational attainment, 30
educational background, 178
efficiency level, 137, 138
electricity, 27, 35
electronic communications, 175
emission, 42, 65, 86, 130, 131, 138
employees, 24, 33, 44, 104, 105, 107, 110, 153, 166, 167, 168, 169, 170, 171, 172, 173, 174, 175, 176, 177, 178, 179, 180, 181, 182
employers, viii, 23, 24, 40, 120, 149, 165, 166, 167, 168, 169, 170, 171, 172, 173, 174, 175, 177, 178, 179, 180, 181, 182
employment, viii, 21, 22, 23, 24, 25, 26, 27, 74, 121, 128, 132, 139, 144, 148, 163, 165, 166, 167, 168, 169, 180, 181
endangered species, 139
energy, 42, 46, 49, 66, 73, 113, 116, 120, 123, 136, 137, 138, 139, 154, 155
Energy Independence and Security Act, 65
Energy Policy and Conservation Act, 68
enforcement, 24, 39, 40, 83, 104, 105, 134, 140, 166, 167, 168, 169, 172, 174, 179, 181
engineering, 69, 96, 128, 178
entrepreneurship, 30, 51, 133
environment, 3, 23, 35, 38, 69, 96, 102, 107, 128, 139
environmental conditions, 32
environmental factors, 87, 131
environmental impact, 50, 57
environmental protection, 27
Environmental Protection Agency (EPA), 1, 8, 9, 13, 40, 55, 56, 61, 64, 65, 84, 85, 93, 104, 112, 113, 117, 124, 129, 130, 134, 135, 137138, 145, 154, 155, 162, 164
environmental quality, 13, 27, 134
environmental regulation(s), 22, 23, 26, 27, 31, 32, 132, 133

Equal Employment Opportunity Commission, 113, 118
equity, 6, 16, 43, 44, 45, 80, 82, 102, 104, 105, 107, 110, 111, 139, 140
ethanol, 132
ethnicity, 144
Europe, 127, 132
European Commission, 51
evidence, 3, 22, 23, 25, 26, 27, 30, 32, 33, 53, 119, 120, 129, 130, 132, 148, 152, 154, 155
evolution, 172
Executive Order, 2, 3, 4, 5, 6, 7, 10, 13, 17, 18, 21, 23, 30, 33, 35, 36, 37, 38, 39, 40, 41, 42, 43, 44, 45, 49, 50, 53, 102, 103, 104, 106, 108, 110, 119, 128, 132, 135, 136, 138, 139, 140, 147, 169
exercise, 29, 152, 173, 177
expenditures, 4, 20, 21, 25, 32, 63, 64, 76, 132, 135, 166
experimental design, 41, 119
explosives, 182
export market, 128
exports, 4, 40, 51, 52
exposure, 10, 32, 129, 130, 132, 137, 171
external benefits, 155

F

FAA, 67, 84
Fair Labor Standards Act, viii, 165, 166, 168, 170, 173, 174, 181, 182
fairness, 7, 32, 43, 44, 45, 102, 144
faith, 179, 182
families, 74
Family and Medical Leave Act (FMLA), 23
family life, 133
family members, 74
FDA, 37, 47, 68, 90, 130, 131, 145, 148
FDI, 124
fear, 168, 170, 179
Federal Communications Commission, 56, 57, 61, 98, 112, 113, 117
Federal Government, 7, 10, 60, 63, 76, 137, 161
Federal Highway Administration, 63
federal law, 172
Federal Register, 7, 71, 105, 107, 129, 138
Federal Reserve, 2, 18, 19, 55, 56, 98, 112, 114, 148
Federal Reserve Board, 55, 56, 112, 114
Federal Reserve System, 2, 18, 19, 98, 148
Federal Student Aid, 34
Federal Trade Commission, 2, 18, 19, 62, 98, 114, 117, 148
federalism, 21

financial, 2, 16, 18, 27, 60, 62, 76, 80, 138, 148, 174, 177
financial markets, 27
financial regulation, 148
financial sector, 2, 18
firm size, 22
fiscal year 2009, 5
fish, 43
Fish and Wildlife Service, 56, 57, 63, 112, 113, 116, 137
fixed costs, 21, 139
flexibility, 20, 22, 33, 38, 40, 42, 62, 103, 106, 107, 109, 110, 140, 147, 169, 173, 174, 176, 179, 182
FLSA, viii, 121, 165, 166, 169, 170, 171, 172, 174, 175, 176, 177, 178, 179, 180, 181, 183
fluctuations, 179
food, 35
Food and Drug Administration, 9, 32, 57, 116, 130, 137
force, 86, 167, 169
Ford, 172
foreign affairs, 51, 52
foreign assets, 26
foreign direct investment, 26, 32
foreign investment, 32
foundations, 106, 125
framing, 33
France, 27, 29, 122, 126
freedom, 33, 35, 38, 103, 147
freedom of choice, 33, 38, 103, 147
friction, 172
fringe benefits, 176
funding, 28, 119, 155
funds, 76, 108

G

GAO, 2, 6, 17, 18, 19, 132, 158
GDP, 27, 28, 33, 69, 96, 120, 121, 127, 128, 133, 144, 163
General Services Administration, 114, 118
global scale, 166
government failure, 34, 144
government intervention, 144
governments, 4, 5, 20, 21, 28, 52, 63, 64, 65, 66, 67, 68, 108, 109, 110, 128, 132, 137
GPRA, 159
grants, 28, 60, 63, 112, 113
Great Recession, 166
greenhouse, 68, 87, 145
Gross Domestic Product, 27, 69, 96, 128
guidelines, 55, 59, 64, 114, 115, 116, 130, 136, 138

H

habitat, 139
happiness, viii, 28, 29, 121, 133, 162, 163
harmonization, 38, 83, 103
hazardous air pollutants, 65, 129, 130, 138
health, 7, 10, 13, 16, 24, 29, 44, 46, 52, 60, 74, 76, 77, 78, 79, 80, 81, 121, 129, 131, 132, 133, 137, 138, 139, 154, 155, 169
Health and Human Services, 61
health care, 77, 78, 80, 81
health care costs, 77, 80, 81
health care system, 77
health condition, 78
health effects, 129
health expenditure, 76
health insurance, 7, 16, 24, 44, 74, 78, 79, 131
health problems, 80
health promotion, 80
HHS, 15, 16, 17, 37, 47, 57, 59, 97, 101, 130, 159, 160
hiring, 23, 24, 166, 168, 169
Hispanic population, 32
HIV, 7, 15, 74, 123
homeland security, 2
host, 26, 62, 136
hourly wage, 176, 180
House of Representatives, 134
housing, 32, 66
Housing and Urban Development, 8, 55, 56, 61, 91, 99, 112, 113, 116
human capital, 30
human dignity, 7, 43, 44, 102
human health, 139

I

imagination, 172, 177
immigrants, 74
immunization, 77
impact assessment, 21
impact energy, 145
improvements, 3, 10, 13, 27, 32, 34, 51, 83, 119, 129, 131, 134, 152, 155
incidence, 7, 33, 44, 129
income, 13, 16, 27, 28, 29, 30, 43, 44, 46, 85, 130, 133, 134, 140, 144, 162
independence, 44
industries, 10, 24, 25, 26, 31, 32, 103, 128, 144, 158, 179
inflation, 4, 21, 63, 64, 69, 96, 128
information exchange, 52
information technology, 178

infrastructure, 30, 108
injuries, 8, 47, 48, 69, 70
integrity, 3, 38, 54, 109, 136
internal processes, 54
Internal Revenue Service, 114
International Maritime Organization, 86, 131
investment(s), 21, 30, 31, 32, 120, 128, 135, 146, 148, 163

J

job creation, 3, 4, 22, 23, 30, 33, 36, 38, 51, 52, 102, 106, 107, 169
job mobility, 78
jurisdiction, 59, 166
justification, 44, 45, 139, 149

L

labor force, 162
labor market, 22, 23, 24, 26, 129
law enforcement, 63, 105
laws, 23, 64, 102, 134, 166, 168, 169, 172
lead, 26, 32, 52, 56, 67, 76, 80, 81, 82, 105, 109, 129, 132, 156
leadership, 167
legislation, 132, 134, 149
legislative proposals, 104, 105, 107, 110
life expectancy, 30, 46, 74, 121, 133, 154
life satisfaction, 28, 29, 30
liquidity, 148
litigation, 56, 59, 129, 137, 138, 167, 169, 172, 174, 179, 180
loans, 21, 63, 156
local government, 51, 63, 67, 128
loneliness, 29
lower prices, 149

M

management, 57, 62, 114, 135, 171, 177, 178
manufacturing, 26, 27, 31, 32, 172, 176
market failure, 23, 33, 34, 138, 144, 162
media, 134, 170
Medicaid, 9, 17, 73, 75, 79, 160
medical care, 16
Medicare, 9, 17, 73, 75, 160
medication, 80
mental health, 76
Mercury, 65, 94, 129, 130, 138
meta-analysis, 46
minimum wage, 23, 166, 170, 172, 176

models, 24, 32, 54, 59, 155
monetized benefits, vii, 1, 2, 6, 8, 9, 13, 14, 20, 45, 96, 111
monopoly, 33, 149
Montreal Protocol, 67
morale, 179, 180
morbidity, 11, 46, 47, 48, 77, 121, 144, 149
mortality, 3, 6, 10, 45, 46, 77, 120, 121, 129, 130, 144, 145, 146, 149, 154
multinational companies, 26
multinational firms, 32
myopia, 33

N

National Academy of Sciences, 28, 60, 125, 129
National Aeronautics and Space Administration, 56, 62, 112, 114, 117
National Ambient Air Quality Standards, 14, 37, 48, 86, 94, 95, 129
national income, 27
National Park Service, 63, 113, 116, 137
National Research Council, 126, 127, 129, 138
national security, 60
negative effects, 25, 26, 132
net exports, 26
net social benefit, 3, 34, 119, 144, 145
nitrogen, 56, 65, 130
NOAA, 56, 137
Nuclear Regulatory Commission, 2, 18, 19, 62, 98, 114, 117

O

Obama, viii, 36, 37, 53, 136, 152
obesity, 34
objectivity, 41, 103, 138
Occupational Safety and Health Act (OSHA), 23, 40, 42, 47, 130, 145
OECD, 133
oil, 40, 182
Office of Management and Budget (OMB), vii, viii, 1, 2, 3, 4, 5, 6, 7, 11, 13, 16, 17, 18, 19, 20, 22, 23, 24, 26, 30, 33, 34, 36, 41, 42, 43, 44, 46, 47, 50, 51, 53, 54, 55, 57, 59, 61, 62, 63, 64, 68, 69, 70, 71, 86, 96, 97, 98, 99, 100, 101, 105, 107, 109, 110, 115, 117, 118, 119, 120, 121, 128, 130, 131, 132, 134, 135, 136, 137, 138, 140, 143, 151, 157, 158, 159, 162, 163, 165, 166, 168
OPA, 85
openness, 3, 50, 52
operations, 25, 67, 166, 171, 177, 178
opportunities, 3, 34, 42, 109, 119, 144, 145, 167, 176

Overseas Private Investment Corporation, 115, 118
oversight, 62, 85, 158
overtime, 166, 170, 171, 172, 173, 174, 175, 176, 177, 179, 180, 181, 182
ozone, 22, 31, 129, 132, 138

P

payroll, 166
peer review, 4, 53, 54, 59, 60, 61, 62, 63, 118, 137
penalties, 169, 182
Pension Benefit Guaranty Corporation, 98, 115, 118
permit, 11, 60, 74, 78, 134
petroleum, 25, 31, 95
planned action, 3, 44, 140
plants, 22, 25, 26, 31, 32
policy, viii, 6, 28, 30, 34, 38, 52, 53, 54, 62, 113, 115, 116, 130, 133, 144, 145, 152, 155, 156, 162, 163, 166, 167, 168, 174, 181, 182
policymakers, 54, 167, 170, 179
political system, 167
pollutants, 130, 131
polluters, 153
polluting industries, 26, 31, 32
pollution, 1, 10, 22, 25, 26, 31, 32, 33, 35, 40, 45, 46, 121, 130, 144, 154, 155
population, 24, 28, 77, 78, 120, 129, 140, 144, 146
population density, 129
positive relationship, 27
potential benefits, 109, 131
power plants, 129, 130, 138
predictability, 38, 39, 102, 140
premature death, 10, 121, 129, 154
present value, 31, 47, 161
preservation, 135
prevention, 2, 47, 77
price elasticity, 77
principles, 18, 21, 34, 38, 43, 55, 64, 102, 109, 110, 168, 177
private benefits, 49, 121, 154
private sector, 4, 13, 16, 20, 21, 52, 59, 60, 63, 64, 65, 66, 67, 68, 103, 106, 128, 131, 137, 166, 167
product market, 26, 27, 120, 149
production costs, 25
program outcomes, 109
programming, 177
project, 41, 119, 137
proliferation, 175
promote innovation, 103
protection, 3, 32, 44, 76, 138, 182
psychology, 125
public awareness, 39, 134
public education, 63

public goods, 135
public health, 3, 23, 38, 44, 45, 102, 108, 111, 128, 139
public interest, 51, 60, 157, 158
public officials, 50
public policy, 18, 28, 54, 118, 144, 158, 159, 168, 172
public safety, 105
public sector, 20, 174
public service, 56, 63
purchasing power, 27

Q

qualifications, 33
quality standards, 132, 138
quantification, 2, 3, 6, 16, 43, 44, 45, 139

R

race, 140, 153, 168
rape, 2, 7, 44
real income, 130
real wage, 27
recession, 106
recommendations, vii, 3, 5, 34, 35, 38, 129, 130, 143, 158
recovery, 2, 18, 37, 40, 166, 167, 169
recreational, 16
redundancy, 38
Reform(s), 3, 4, 5, 16, 19, 20, 33, 34, 39, 40, 63, 64, 79, 90, 97, 110, 121, 128, 131, 132, 135, 137, 143, 144, 152, 153, 156, 158, 165, 166,
regulations, vii, viii, 1, 2, 3, 5, 6, 7, 10, 11, 12, 13, 16, 21, 22, 23, 24, 25, 26, 27, 30, 31, 32, 33, 34, 39, 40, 41, 42, 44, 45, 46, 49, 52, 53, 64, 68, 69, 70, 77, 78, 79, 81, 82, 84, 85, 88, 96, 97, 98, 102, 103, 104, 106, 107, 108, 118, 119, 120, 121, 128, 129, 130, 133, 136, 140, 143, 144, 145, 146, 148, 151, 152, 153, 154, 155, 159, 161, 162, 163, 165, 166, 169, 170, 172, 174, 177, 178, 183
regulatory agencies, vii, 1, 2, 6, 17, 18, 42, 53, 128, 130, 145, 159
regulatory impact analyses, viii, 6, 110, 120, 163
regulatory program., vii, 143, 144, 145
regulatory requirements, 35, 38, 39, 40, 85, 102, 103
Regulatory-Right-to-Know Act, vii, 1
relevance, 7, 29, 59
reliability, 133
relief, 22, 87, 132
renewable fuel, 65, 86, 87, 131
rent, 135

requirements, 2, 10, 18, 20, 22, 31, 32, 35, 38, 40, 41, 43, 52, 60, 64, 65, 66, 67, 77, 86, 103, 106, 107, 108, 109, 110, 111, 131, 132, 138, 139, 147, 166, 170, 172, 174, 175, 177, 179, 180
resentment, 179
resources, 10, 41, 63, 82, 87, 104, 106, 107, 108, 109, 114, 119, 120, 132, 134, 137, 140, 154, 159, 169, 181
response, vii, viii, 23, 26, 31, 40, 42, 56, 57, 63, 77, 118, 120, 121, 129, 131, 137, 138, 148, 151, 165
restrictions, 26, 27, 52, 148, 166, 167, 170, 175
retirement, 34
revenue, 21
risk(s), 7, 16, 20, 21, 26, 33, 35, 43, 46, 52, 64, 78, 80, 81, 105, 120, 129, 130, 137, 139, 144, 145, 146, 152, 170, 174, 177
robotics, 172
rules, vii, 1, 2, 3, 4, 5, 6, 7, 8, 9, 10, 11, 13, 14, 16, 17, 18, 19, 20, 21, 22, 23, 32, 33, 34, 35, 36, 38, 39, 40, 41, 42, 44, 45, 46, 49, 50, 51, 53, 54, 60, 63, 64, 67, 69, 70, 83, 84, 87, 96, 98, 103, 106, 108, 110, 119, 120, 121, 128, 129, 130, 131, 132, 134, 135, 137, 138, 143, 144, 145, 148, 149, 152, 153, 154, 155, 158, 159, 161, 163, 166, 169, 170, 173, 176, 177, 178, 180, 182

S

safety, 3, 13, 23, 32, 38, 42, 44, 45, 46, 52, 60, 66, 84, 102, 111, 121, 128, 129, 137, 138, 139, 169, 182
Salmonella, 37, 47, 90, 101
savings, 10, 18, 34, 35, 40, 49, 77, 85, 87, 88, 121, 132, 154, 161, 167
scarce resources, 46
scarcity, 134
scholarship, 157, 158
science, 3, 34, 38, 59, 60, 62, 69, 96, 102, 128, 133, 137, 172, 177
Science Advisory Board, 130
scope, 59, 60, 64
security, 21, 44, 173
service provider, 83
sewage, 63
sex, 140
sexual harassment, 44, 182
sexual orientation, 44
sexual violence, 44
shape, 131, 166
shareholders, 32
skin cancer, 20
small businesses, 21, 22, 42, 106, 107, 144, 162
small communities, 106

small firms, 22, 107, 111, 139
smog, 35
smoking, 29, 57, 182
SNAP, 17, 71, 159
social benefits, 33, 46, 120, 145
social costs, 13, 26
Social Security Administration, 115, 118
social welfare, 3, 82, 119, 133, 134
society, 13, 21, 33, 34, 46, 50, 74, 102, 106, 118, 140, 144, 154, 157, 158
software, 178
species, 43, 57
spending, 24, 25, 79, 81
spontaneous abortion, 132
stakeholders, 4, 38, 52, 103, 181
state, viii, 25, 26, 29, 32, 44, 51, 87, 113, 117, 132, 137, 163, 171, 172, 177
state laws, 172
statistics, 136
statutes, 6, 21
statutory authority, 132
statutory mandate, 2, 14
steel, 25
stock, 31, 148
structure, 29, 166, 168, 172
subjective experience, 30
subjective well-being, 27, 28, 29, 30, 33, 121, 133
subsistence, 133
substance abuse, 76
sulfur, 31, 65, 86, 131
supply curve, 23
Supreme Court, 182
sustainable development, 30

T

target, 24, 144
taxes, 29, 166
taxonomy, 50, 136
taxpayers, 13, 108
techniques, 6, 18, 20, 35, 38, 41, 43, 45, 102, 119, 130, 131
technological advances, 51
technology, 25, 32, 43, 49, 50, 105, 136, 137, 166, 169, 171, 172, 175, 177
Tennessee Valley Authority, 62, 115, 117
tension, 120, 149
terrorist attack, 43
testing, 34, 39, 119
therapy, 73, 74
threats, 168
threshold level, 28
time frame, 175, 176

time periods, 11, 69, 96, 128
time use, viii, 28, 163
Title I, 4, 18, 63, 64, 72, 100, 132, 137, 160
Title II, 4, 63, 64, 132, 137
Title IV, 100
Title V, 16, 87
total costs, 8, 42
total factor productivity, 31
trade, 4, 20, 26, 51, 52, 134, 145, 168
trading partners, 4, 40, 51
training, 65, 135, 168
transfer payments, 111, 133, 140
transparency, 4, 18, 34, 38, 42, 44, 45, 49, 51, 53, 54, 55, 60, 97, 106, 121, 138, 145, 147, 152, 158, 159, 180
Treasury, 4, 5, 16, 41, 55, 119, 128, 131
treatment, 20, 23, 24, 34, 63, 77, 148, 169
trial, 4, 152, 153
tribal officials, 4, 64, 103
truck drivers, 137, 171
turnover, 30, 54, 178

U

U.S. Department of Agriculture, 35, 136
U.S. Department of Agriculture XE "Department of Agriculture" (USDA), 35
U.S. Department of Labor, 165, 174, 183
U.S. economy, 24
U.S. Geological Survey, 56
U.S. Geological Survey (USGS), 56
Unfunded Mandates on State, Local, and Tribal Entities., 151

uniform, 7, 69, 70, 76, 81, 96
uninsured, 78, 79
unions, 26, 120, 149
USA, 122
USDA, 17, 35, 57, 134, 159
USGS, 57

V

valuation, 8, 32, 69, 70, 129, 130, 135
variables, 2, 3, 26, 27, 29, 34, 43, 44, 45, 133, 140, 148
vehicles, 40, 67, 68, 84, 131, 154
Visa Waiver Program, 91
vote, 175

W

wages, 5, 20, 21, 22, 23, 24, 26, 132, 167, 177, 179
water, 20, 44, 45, 46, 63, 66, 105, 139, 156
wealth, 27, 30, 79, 80, 81
web, 51, 55, 57, 60, 62, 121, 131, 136
welfare, 3, 16, 23, 27, 29, 49, 81, 102, 105, 108, 119, 155
well-being, 27, 28, 29, 121, 122, 133
workers, 7, 23, 24, 26, 27, 33, 120, 149, 169, 170, 171, 172, 176, 179, 182
workforce, 166, 171, 179
working conditions, 23, 105, 170
working hours, 170, 171, 175
workplace, 23, 166, 167, 168, 169, 171, 172, 173, 174, 175, 177, 181, 182